THE DYNAMICS OF NOW

Issues in Art and Education

THE DYNAMICS OF NOW

Papers submitted at conferences held at the Tate Gallery
in 1995, 1996, 1997 and 1998, organised by the Wimbledon School of Art
in collaboration with the Tate Gallery

Edited by William Furlong,
Polly Gould and Paul Hetherington

WIMBLEDON SCHOOL OF ART

IN ASSOCIATION WITH

TATE PUBLISHING

This is the third volume in this series of conference publications.
The first volume, *Artists in the 1990s: Their Education and Values*
was published in 1994. The second volume, *Aspects of the Fine Art
Curriculum* was published in 1996.

Cover:
detail from *The Knife Edge Academy*
a prospectus in six screenprints with original collage and hand work
by Bruce McLean and Mel Gooding 1995

ISBN 1 85437 270 X
A catalogue record for this publication is available from the British Library
Published in 2000 by Tate Gallery Publishing Limited, Millbank, London SW1P 4RG
© Wimbledon School of Art and contributors 2000 All rights reserved
Designed and typeset by Caroline Johnston
Printed in Great Britain by B.A.S. Printers Limited,
Over Wallop, Hampshire

Contents

Introduction

This publication of four recent conferences organised by Wimbledon School of Art in collaboration with the Tate Gallery demonstrates the School's continuing commitment to research. The conferences represent a unique contribution to the discourses of fine art education, practice and theory in the late 1990s. The agendas and themes of each conference arose out of discussion and debate among the research staff at Wimbledon and, as a consequence, address the actual preoccupations, concerns and contexts of the artist as practitioner and teacher.

Acknowledgement and thanks are due to: Colin Painter, Principal of Wimbledon School of Art between 1980 and 1997, who originally conceived this series of Tate conferences; Paul Hetherington and Polly Gould for their skilful editing of the conference texts and transcripts; Paul Hetherington, Allison Turnbull and Pam Golden for their tenacity in organising the events. The contribution of Andrew Brighton at the Tate Gallery has been indispensable and we thank him for the commitment, encouragement and uninhibited critical perspectives he has provided over the years.

Finally, thanks are due to the speakers, whose ideas, propositions and insights have not only produced some of the most interesting and important conferences arising out of the visual arts and education in recent years, but whose arguments and ideas have resituated the primary themes of the artist as teacher.

William Furlong
Director of Research
Wimbledon School of Art

Fine Art Education and the Museum

Introductory address

RICHARD HUMPHREYS

Head of Education, Tate Gallery, London

A gallery such as the Tate that is devoted to fine art must look very carefully at its duties towards the education, not only of its general public, but also of those art students who will become the producers of the art for which we are responsible. The relationship between fine art education and the activities of the museum is an extremely close one – the two elements are clearly integrated. Nevertheless, there is still much more we could do to make that relationship stronger and more productive than it has been in the past, as the papers at this conference will discuss.

Welcome

COLIN PAINTER

Principal, Wimbledon School of Art

For those not at the other four conferences organised by Wimbledon School of Art in conjunction with the Tate, it may be worth remembering what their themes were: 'The Role of the Artist as Teacher'; 'The Basis for Making Value Judgements about Art'; 'An Attempt to Identify Ingredients of a Fine Art Curriculum'; 'The Role of Drawing in Fine Art and Fine Art Education'. In addition, a central theme running through all four is the relationship between fine art education and fine art *per se*; today's conference epitomises that particular theme in discussing fine art education and the museum.

In putting together the programme, we soon decided that we were viewing the concept of the Museum as a generic one that also included galleries. Thus we are talking about art of the past and of the present. No doubt our main theme today will be the way in which museums and institutions of higher education can collaborate more effectively to deliver fine art education. We will also look at ways in which galleries and museums can be conceptualised. What is a gallery? What is a museum in the changing and pluralist world of fine art? And what opportunities can galleries and museums offer to graduates of fine art when they leave and are seeking opportunities to progress?

In looking at the list of delegates, I am impressed by the wide range of institutions and functions represented. There are journalists, art educationalists, artists and museum officers. The audience is a kind of representative sample of the professional fine art community and, as with past conferences, the discussion is between colleagues within that particular professional culture. One of my own particular interests in the theme of the conference is the way in which museums act as defining agencies: we could look at museums and galleries as one of the ways through which this professional community defines its values and priorities. There is a sense in which the conference could be seen as addressing quite fundamental, philosophical issues – even the question 'what is art?', which is always rather embarrassing to ask these days: it's not very trendy and one sort of shuffles one's feet if one asks it. But in the context of this particular event, instead of studying that question from a philosophical or a psychological point of view, you could simply say that one way of understanding what art is, is to look at what museums and galleries say it is. A way of apprehending what British art is, is to point to the kind of work that is exhibited in the Tate as the official collection of British art. From that perspective, museums have a very responsible role and in a real sense they define what we understand art to be at a particular time. Furthermore, not only do they define it for us (or we define it together through museums and galleries), but perhaps equally significantly, they define it for other people outside our professional community. In other words, their concept of what art is, how you behave towards it, the ethos of it, the way it feels, the way it looks, is something that we deliver through museums and galleries.

Chair's introduction

CHRISTOPHER FRAYLING

Pro-Rector, Royal College of Art, London

One of the defining features of these conferences is epitomised by the subject today: these conferences are among the few that offer perspectives on art education not just from within art education, but crucially, from outside the bunker as well. The theme of fine art education and the museum is very timely. Since the Arts Council of England currently comes under the Department of National Heritage rather than, say, the Ministry of Culture, heritage equals contemporary art – an interesting conundrum. There is a good deal of talk about museums and the millennium. Interestingly, part of that talk is about upgrading nineteenth-century institutions to take us into the twenty-first century. There is another interesting problem: fine art courses are increasingly building bridges between the works of the art school and the works of the museum, with their own interface problems. Above all, artists such as Joseph Kosuth are exploring the museum as an installation space, as a gallery in itself. This raises a whole spectrum of possibilities and interesting discussion points.

While preparing for today's introduction, I was reading an article on the history of museums, which reminded me that the word museum originates from the Greek, meaning 'seat of the Muses', a word that was further defined in Shakespeare's time as a place dedicated to the Muses and to study, where one engages oneself in noble disciplines. By the end of the nineteenth century, the article goes on, the emphasis had shifted somewhat to the collection, display and conservation of objects or artefacts from the past, a rather different role. 'Through its collection', says the writer, 'a museum came to present the past, that is to say, to present the values of a vanished or vanishing society, or even further, to focus attention on permanent values endangered by modern progress.' The museum came to mark out these values as a heritage because of their importance for the continuity of culture. The values exemplified were moral, religious, aesthetic, historical and biological, and interested visitors and research workers alike were reminded of forgotten ideas and made aware of a starting point for an enhanced life.

So, historically, the shift is from an environment where the noble disciplines are practised, to a place where one observes one's heritage and thinks hard about the setting of the sun. One of the key turning points, in my view, between these two philosophies of the museum – which I believe are battling it out even today – happened at the time of the foundation of the art and design education system to which we, in England at least, all belong. For in 1837, when the Government School of Design opened in Somerset House, and again in the 1850s when it moved to South Kensington and developed links with what were then called 'branch' schools all over the country – when, in other words, the national system of art education was set up – the civil servants and educators who evolved our system saw no disjunction, no discontinuity at all, between the idea of the museum and the idea of contemporary practice. Indeed, these ideas were part of one continuum. The museum was there as an important element in providing a visual stimulus and a series of exemplars for the artist of tomorrow.

Of course, the exemplars, and their relationship with contemporary art, were somewhat remote by today's standards. You can see some of them in the Cast Court at the Victoria & Albert Museum: casts of Trajan's Column, or letter-forms, or pieces of Renaissance metalwork and so on. These works were by definition, to use the critically correct word of the moment, canonical. They were, in other words, thought to be the greatest hits of Western art. But they were there in a dynamic relationship with the students, and that is the point.

The Victoria & Albert Museum started life as the Visual Aids Department of the Government School of Design: the objects stored there eventually took up so much space that they had to be moved out into premises of their own. What became known as the Victoria & Albert Museum therefore started out within art education and grew into something else. The Select Committee of 1836 which founded our system, saw no problem in simultaneously concluding on the one hand that an institution ought to be founded 'to afford an opportunity of acquiring a practical knowledge of the fine arts', and on the other that the same institution ought to remedy 'the want of knowledge of the arts among our manufacturing population'. Indeed, the money was granted following the Select Committee's report because it was felt the museum might feed into the future. In those days, we were not in the business of putting money into heritage. On the other side of the Channel, the writer Anatole France could say of an equivalent experiment that took place shortly afterwards, 'the man who builds himself a hut out of marble fragments of a temple in Palmyra is more philosophical, more enlightened, than all the curators in the museums in London, Munich or Paris'. At that time, the main philosophical point was the interface between fine art and museum: only later in the century was 'heritage' invented.

By the turn of the century all this had changed. Heritage went in one direction, the practitioners went in another. Indeed, some saw the museum as a cosy, comforting place from which to view the dangerous developments of contemporary art in relative safety; a place where the eyes in the portrait, as it were, still reassuringly followed you round the room; or a place where the established canon could be viewed at a time when no new canon seemed to be emerging. It was as if to say, 'The present is rather confusing so let's go to a canonical past'. It's rather like the tourists in the *New Yorker* cartoon in the 1950s, who rush into the Louvre and ask the attendant 'Where's the *Mona Lisa*? We're double-parked'.

Today, such issues are high on the agenda. Is the museum a place for visual stimulus, for learning lessons from the past, for giving exemplars to copy? Or is it a club we all want to join, a place to see originals, which we can compare with our takeaway versions at home, in slides and CD-ROMs and photocopies; a catalyst, a treasure-house, or what? To the young Henry Moore, arriving in South Kensington in the autumn of 1921, the museum was all of these things. In fact, coming as he did from Leeds Art School, it was the South Kensington museums, rather than the college, that really blew his head off. I would like to read an extract from his journals:

When I rode on the open top of a bus, I felt that I was travelling in heaven almost, and that the bus was floating in the air. And it was heaven all over again in the evening in the little room that I had in Sydney Street, Chelsea. It was a dreadful room, actually, the most horrible little room you could imagine, and the landlady gave me the most awful haddock for breakfast every morning. But at night I had my books and the coffee stall on the Embankment if I wanted to go out and eat, and I knew that not far away I had the National Gallery and the British Museum and the Victoria & Albert with the reference library, where I could get any book I wanted. I could learn about all the sculptures that had ever been made in the world, it seemed to me. One room after another in the British Museum took my enthusiasm. The Royal College of Art meant nothing in comparison. But not until after three months did things begin to settle into any pattern of reality, as opposed to heaven, for me. Till then, everything was wonderful, a new world at every turn.

And of course Moore spent the first two years of his sculpture course making transcriptions of the sculptures he had seen. *The Virgin and Child* in the Victoria & Albert Museum turns into Moore's famous *Mother and Child* sculpture and so on. He had previously only seen these sculptures reproduced in black and white in well-thumbed art-history books. The museum for him contained all the elements mentioned above: visual stimulus, lessons from the past, things to copy. His was a very positive view of the museum.

To help us through these intriguing issues, and indeed to add much more, we have an excellent and fascinating range of speakers, both from inside and outside art education.

The emerging artist and the museum

VICTORIA MIRO

Director, Victoria Miro Gallery, London

With some of their peers rocketing to stardom, the expectations of emerging artists are running high. The swift escalation of a whole new generation of artists from the gallery to the museum and ultimately international fame does not escape the notice of countless art students all over Britain. The austere image of Bankside, site of the new Tate Gallery of Modern Art, has swiftly been implanted in young minds as yet another focus for their dreams and aspirations.

When the speculative bubble of the late 1980s art market burst, a new generation was waiting in the wings, poised to take centre stage. Deluded by the falling investment value of established artists, collectors either dropped out or turned their attention to new and inexpensive work. Unsanctioned by museums and sometimes even by galleries, the collector could use his or her own judgement to support a new school as yet untainted by the market. I know several collectors who have sold off classic works of the 1960s, 70s and 80s in order to reinvest in the 1990s. The collapse of the 1980s heralded a nightmare for many established artists and a great wave of optimism for the young.

Nowhere was this change of sentiment so strongly felt as in London, thrusting it into full focus as a budding art capital, much as Cologne had been some years earlier. The recession had resulted in a vast supply of possible exhibition spaces, and young artists, inspired by Damien Hirst and such shows as *Freeze* and *Modern Medicine*, grouped together and mounted their own shows. Not all of those artists have made it into the mid-1990s, but undoubtedly a sense of excitement was generated.

The art schools too, and evidently the calibre of the teaching, fuelled the fire. Goldsmiths dominated, but looking at the CVs of the young artists I represent, the Royal College, the Slade, Chelsea, Wimbledon, Glasgow and Brighton all played a part. The emergence of a new wave of artists coincided with a new generation of writers and curators, who together formed a new network, questioning former aesthetic and moral judgements. In 1991, a new magazine, *Frieze*, appeared on the scene. Everyone on the original team was twenty-two and their fresh approach played a main part in the internationalisation of the new work. A form of cultural plunder started taking place, with curators flying in from all over the world, rushing around artists' studios and departing a few days later with rapidly cobbled-together plans for new shows.

Some institutions were quite happy to take on the new work and make judgements without the comfort of established categories and fixed rules. Among these, the ICA held a solo show of Damien Hirst's work, the Serpentine made a group show entitled *Broken English* and last year Damien Hirst curated *Some Went Mad, Some Ran Away* for the same gallery. The current show at the ICA, entitled *Institute of Cultural Anxiety* and curated by the twenty-four year old Jeremy Millar, includes many of the new names.

Here at the Tate, there is more caution. As a museum, it is in a far more difficult position, having to perform a constant balancing act. Although it must be involved with the art of the present, it also has to be a great museum of the history and origins of the modern movement. Museums are strongly determined by the passions of their directors, and I think this is particularly so in the case of Nicholas Serota, the present Director. Without doubt, he has reinvented the Tate, and has come to the realisation that the successes of its past history do not constitute templates from which to stamp out rules for the future. The use of the space and the memorable shows and installations have made this place truly alive and contemporary. Seeing such contemporary art in the context of a collection of great masterworks of early modern art gives students a different kind of framework through which to approach new art. The periodic rehangs emphasise this, and current art students are reading classic modern art very differently now from ten or twenty years ago.

Although the Tate is well visited by the emerging artists, there is a certain hesitation when they are asked to comment on its activities. To quote one opinion, 'The museum has to bear a lot of guilt. It has to be concerned with heritage, yet so much new art is against heritage. It has to present documentary evidence of cultural idealism. It has to promote a moral ideal and legitimise public funding'.

The majority of my young artists feel that more risks could be taken and that the museum could become more of a forum for work that has not yet found its place or may never find its place. After all, very new art is always changing our vision of where art is going. I imagine that many of the problems relating to showing our emerging artists is not only due to the current lack of physical space, but also to the enormous amount of hype, which really has to die down before rational judgements can be made. Estimations of worth in the art world have grown much closer to those of the entertainment industry as represented by film and popular music. Susan Sontag said that a 'significant role of the artist of the future may be to keep alive the idea of seriousness, to understand that in the late twentieth century seriousness itself could be the question'. Perhaps things will have settled down in five years time so that the Tate at Bankside can open with a clearer picture of the contemporary scene.

Unlike the 1960s and 1970s, when artists such as Robert Smithson, Richard Serra, Hans Haacke and Lawrence Weiner were seriously questioning the siting of work and resisting the 'disintegration of culture into commodities', in the 1990s our young artists no longer seek to avoid representation and commodification. The anti-institutional revolt has not been sustained and there is a change of attitude. Much of the work now produced is well suited to the museum and I would like to talk about some of the younger artists I represent in this context.

Last year, the figurative painter Peter Doig was nominated for the Turner Prize. Since his graduation from Chelsea in 1990, Peter has taught part time at the Royal College, the Slade and Goldsmiths, among others. The distribution of the Turner Prize nomination forms to art colleges gave Peter's students the opportunity to put forward his name. The eventual choice of Peter as one of the finalists drew many students closer to the Tate in that they felt they had taken part in some aesthetic decision-making. A great part of the younger art network had recognised in Peter's work a very current sensibility: that undertow and latency that runs though so much work at present. Peter

Doig's work depicts landscapes, but it is impossible to think of them as landscapes. They are risky paintings, treading a fine line between attraction and repulsion.

In Doig's painting *Cabin Essence* (1993–4), the severe geometry of Corbusier's *Unité d'Habitation* in Briey is seen through a dense clump of trees. Areas of tree-trunk are plastered white; the mood is uneasy. We can see that Peter consistently pays homage to film as a primary source. In some ways, the obvious relationship of this work to current cinematic practices helps narrow the gap between popular culture and art.

A painting such as *Ski Jacket* (1994) could be a real problem to a contemporary art audience. A vast mountainscape dotted with skiers, covered with a veil of pastel-coloured snow, would hardly seem an appropriate subject for current taste. Some people felt betrayed when I exhibited these large-scale figurative paintings, finding them an affront to their contemporary sensibilities. It was mainly the younger viewers who were free enough from the accepted forms of modern art to acknowledge the quality of the work. Many older people had trouble absorbing the work and allowing Peter's point of view to co-exist.

The opening reception at the Tate for the Turner Prize installation gathered together many committed members of the younger art network, helping to narrow the gap between the institution and the avant-garde. There is a period during which many young artists go through rejection of the institution, rather like rejection of the parents, but they really enjoyed that opening, which was the opportunity to meet outside the inevitable white cube and be involved in another dimension.

Looking forward to the new Tate Gallery of Modern Art at Bankside, I hope it will find more occasions, as with the Turner Prize, to challenge the status quo, whether relating to such issues as violence, gender, beauty or racial identity. It has the potential to become a place for a real contest of ideas and values, where students who are questioning their own identity, their own values, their sense of belonging and sexual preference, can feel at ease. I also like the idea of a museum as a place to rub up against ideas that may offend. Contemporary arguments should at least acknowledge the desire to transgress, which is obvious in much new work, and defend that impulse as a worthwhile one. We need to develop new ideas of education.

In April 1993, I made an exhibition with two young brothers, Jake and Dinos Chapman, who have a considerable relationship to current popular culture, representing terrorist-aesthetic rather than anti-aesthetic. In their work, *Disasters of War*, small sculptures with separate bases were packed together on a large plinth in the middle of the gallery. The poses were taken directly from Goya's etchings *Disasters of War*, and the figures were made from toy soldiers, which the brothers cut up and remodelled. The work portrays a spectacle of unbelievable violence, all the more disturbing because of the evident toy-shop associations.

Last September, they made their second show. Included in it was the piece *Great Deeds Against The Dead* (1994). This time, just one of Goya's eighty-three etchings had been chosen and shown in the form of remodelled shop mannequins. Again, the work was presented on a large plinth in the middle of the gallery. Human scale had altered the meaning and its prominent shop-window presentation often resulted in an angry reaction, only to be silenced when the Goya source was discovered. Mismatching technique and subject matter, Jake and Dinos have made it their business to disgust. The brothers' critique of their own work is severe. To quote them, 'We have always been functions of a discourse. In short, our labour deserves professional interpretation, our mental agitation demands a limitless expressionism, our contractual teleology demonstrates our servility to a cultural climax never to be experienced. The Future remains excluded. But sometimes against the freedom of work, we fantasise emancipation from this liberal polity into a super heavy-weight, no-holds-barred, all-in mud-wrestling league, a scatological aesthetic for the tired of seeing.'

Peter Doig's paintings and Jake and Dinos Chapman's sculptures are highly regarded by their own generation, but I think they have a quality that takes them beyond the merely fashionable and represents the kind of artists who will help to develop a young audience. If the Tate Gallery of Modern Art is to reflect the current activity in art, it must hold a close dialogue with younger artists. This discourse is the way to learn and the way to move forward in thinking about how a museum should progress. A successful new Tate at Bankside will have to draw its strengths from the inspiration of young artists. The Director will have to reinvent the Tate yet again.

Sometimes there is a feeling that the contemporary scene is drifting away from museums. Bankside, with all its potential resources, could draw it back again. The verbal descriptions of Herzog and de Meuron's plans for Bankside promise a space that moves away from the museums of the 1980s and is able to offer a versatility suited to a large range of activities. I noted that the central space would be large enough to hold Rachel Whiteread's *House*. Young artists are already aware of the possibilities and some of them, with a particular interest in architecture, are looking forward to seeing the plans and models for the new museum. One such artist is Alex Hartley.

Alex's wall works, *Untitled*, are comprised of etched glass boxes, the front plane set at an angle. Incorporated within these boxes are photographic images. In most cases the photograph depicts another type of box – the empty white cube of a modern art gallery – the type of space within which the work is usually shown. In this work, Alex has created an ideal gallery that appears spacious, but exists only as a cardboard model.

In *Untitled* (1993), he made a work that consists of a series of installation shots of well-known galleries, such as Conrad Fischer in Düsseldorf, Portikus in Frankfurt and Leo Castelli in New York. The images were enlarged from the pages of art magazines, and the work on show, by artists such as Bruce Nauman and Carl Andre, were touched out. It would seem that Alex is suggesting his own work should be shown in these spaces and that he advocates the replacement of the older generation by the new one. 'Buildings', says Alex, 'are both physical and mental spaces. A museum lends credibility to its work through its ambience as well as through its name.'

Bankside will have to broaden its appeal and recognise a socially and culturally mixed society. At this moment, there is a great deal of confusion about where art fits into society, what function it serves and where its emphasis should be placed. We have to ask if art should be for a community and if so, who constitutes that community? I notice a large number of mixed-race art students, but I see no indication of that in the art audience. The exposure and encouragement of young artists from different ethnic backgrounds could be used to make Bankside more accessible to minority groups. One young artist who interests me is Chris Ofili, a black artist who was born here, but whose family came from Nigeria. In works such as *Elephantastic* his paintings are enhanced by montaged elephant dung. Some works include the name of the elephant from whom the dung came, spelt out in coloured beads. His work in some ways caricatures clichés of exoticism and ethnicity, but when exhibited, it attracted a black audience.

I dislike the current obsession with numbers of visitors as a measure of success, like some kind of popularity contest, but it would be good to broaden the audience by presenting different agendas under one roof. As art becomes more technologically oriented, new spaces can be set up and equipped to accommodate it. Willie Doherty's installation, shown in last year's Turner Prize exhibition, was a brilliant example of the possibilities of video, but the Tate was a difficult place to exhibit this piece in practical terms.

In his show last September, Stephen Pippin chose to show three sculptures, each employing a high degree of technological proficiency, which involved concealing a large amount of equipment. In *Flat Field*, a small television set is suspended at the centre of a circular aluminium framework and is driven, via a toothed wheel, by an electric motor. The television rotates at a speed of approximately one revolution per minute. Playing on the television is an image of the world. The horizon of the globe on the screen remains in a horizontal position and aligns itself with the horizontal plane of the table. In *Vacuum*, a television is placed inside a plastic bubble. The air is sucked out of the bubble to create a vacuum. Although the volume of the television is turned up, the vacuum allows only a muffled sound to be heard.

The recent introduction of the audio-guide at the Tate is a step forward in that it is able to relay information about specific works without the need for distracting wall-texts. The Tate at Bankside will have to rely heavily on computerisation and who knows what advances will be made in the next few years. Artists too, are experimenting with the computer and this is quite clearly seen in the work of the painter Brad Lochore. In *Shadow Painting* the image seems at first sight to be a record of an actual shadow. However, it has in fact been arrived at from a projection of a photographic slide of a shadow, which has itself been computer generated, not from light, but from the logical manipulation of abstract data by a computer. By creating images of presences that, despite being the product of a computer, could never actually exist, Lochore cuts away the ground from the viewer's feet. We think we know what we are looking at but we cannot be sure, nothing can be precisely placed.

If the Tate can put so much time and energy into the Patrons of New Art, then surely the Tate at Bankside can put the same effort into the encouragement and involvement of the new generation. Perhaps thought could be given to the possibility of internships, allowing students to gain close familiarity with a collection of modern art. At the Guggenheim Museum in Venice, students are given internships of between one and three months. They help staff the galleries as well as assisting with the periodic exhibition installations. Twice-weekly seminars are held to discuss aspects of modern art with special reference to works in the collection. Young curators too, such as those on the Royal College course, could be involved in various aspects of museology. In the same way that forms are distributed in art schools for Turner Prize nominations, they could be used to invite students to put forward their ideas for Bankside. Discussion groups could be held at the Tate for young artists and curators. The middle generation, which has done so much for the present Tate, must resist using the same templates as before and move on to the next era. Speaking for that middle generation, it is only as a result of developing close relationships with art-students and young artists that my gallery has been able to move forward. Although I value the opinions of artists of my own generation, most of them would be much happier to have their own era reaffirmed. Young artists have a clear vision free from the cynicism that often creeps in as time goes by. In the case of the young artists I know, their seriousness is not in question.

Alfred Barr, a former director of the Museum of Modern Art in New York said, 'The Museum's collection ought to be like a torpedo advancing through time, with the leading edge in the present and a narrow trailing end in the past. The great commitment of energy and buying should be to what is going on now'. With all the optimism and excitement building up towards the new millennium, now is the time to engage our emerging artists in a dialogue ensuring that the vision of a new generation is incorporated into this incredible project.

Locations and strategies

WILLIAM FURLONG

Vice-Principal, Wimbledon School of Art

I would like to start by reading an epigraph by Walter Pater from a book published in 1943 to celebrate the first ten years of the Museum of Modern Art in New York: 'Where one's curiosity is deficient, when one is not eager for new impressions and new pleasures, one is liable to value mere academic proprieties too highly; to find the most stimulating products a mere irritation'.[1]

Now I would like to present sections from three sound works that you won't find in a museum. First, an extract from a work by Jean Tinguely, a sculpture entitled *Meta – Harmonie II*, in which the primary material is sound, presented at the Tate Gallery in 1982.[2] Secondly, a social sculpture by Joseph Beuys, which he recorded at the Institute of Contemporary Arts in 1974 for his blackboard installation called *Art into Society, Society into Art*. And thirdly, my sound work, *What Are You Doing Taping?*, 1986.[3]

Returning to the theme of this conference and the question of what contribution the museum can make to fine art education in the twentieth and twenty-first centuries, I begin with a historical preamble. Were the underlying assumptions that originally led to the concept of the 'museum' the same as they might be today? Clearly they were not. We are told that the origin of the museum dates back to Classical times. An early model, often given in the literature of museology, is the Ptolemaic Mouseion at Alexandria, which was primarily a study collection with a library attached, a repository of knowledge, a place of scholars, philosophers and historians. It is the study element that I think is important, both in terms of a definition and as the primary thread in my analysis.

In Renaissance Europe, those with power and wealth looked beyond the boundaries of the city-state, beyond Europe itself, for domination over nature and their fellow man. One objective was to attain a more complete understanding of both man and the world. The collections they amassed, not merely of art but of artefacts, antiquities, scientific instruments, minerals, fossils, human and animal remains, objects of every conceivable kind, became the contents of the studios and cabinets of curiosity. They were displays of wealth but also objects of study. We have inherited the dual function of places of study and places of display both as justification and dilemma. But museums are, of course, far more than places of study, or education, or entertainment. The very act of collecting has a political, ideological and aesthetic dimension as well as perpetuating established museum practices, which cannot be overlooked. According to what criteria are works of art judged to be historically significant? What makes certain objects as opposed to others worth preserving and collecting for posterity? The original intention behind the establishment of museums was that artefacts should be removed from their current context of ownership and use, from their circulation in the world of private property, and inserted into a new environment that would provide them with a different meaning or indeed, as happens over time, erode and reorientate meaning completely. This can be seen vividly in the ambitious and excellent exhibition called *The Time Machine* currently at the British Museum, where these elusive tensions and issues are explored by contemporary artists in the Egyptian Gallery.

What was the initial and primary motivation of the early museum collectors? Museums, in the sense in which the word is commonly understood today, are of course a relatively recent phenomenon. The foundation of institutions even as grand as the Louvre and the British Museum goes back no more than a couple of hundred years. The first usage of the word 'museum' in English was employed not just to describe an antique institution dedicated to the study of the Muses, but as a modern institution that might contribute to the advancement of learning. This usage is recorded in the *Oxford English Dictionary* of 1683, when Alan Ashmole's collection was referred to in the Philosophical Transactions of the Royal Society as a 'museum'. It formed the core of the collection of the Ashmolean Museum, Oxford. The museum here had a dynamic and functional interface in relation to study in the associated disciplines of the collection. The traditional museum is in a sense a definition of cultural identity, but, of course, the 'culture' is a 'high culture', a 'formal culture', culture disassociated from everyday contemporary life.

However, objects and artefacts have a complex presence and are subject to multiple readings and interpretations. When we look at artefacts in a museum, what in fact are we seeing? Do we see the process by which they have been appropriated to arrive at the museum? Or do we see the objects' shell, which is of course always available to superficial and stylistic readings? Most museums are still structured according to late nineteenth-century ideas of rigid taxonomies. This linear, unitary and consistent mode of presentation surely is in conflict with the way in which intellectual ideas have moved away from a belief in a single overriding linear and theoretical system. The idea that objects are not neutral but complex and subject to changing meanings should compel museums to adjust their activities.

There are examples of the museum as a construction of illusion: the Museum of Childhood in Bethnal Green, for instance, is a museum that presents the toys of children of a hundred years ago. But which children? Very few in fact. The majority of children in the nineteenth century left school at an early age and didn't have much of a childhood, let alone toys. Here is an example of the museum as a powerful fiction constructed and perpetuated.

Anthropologists who sought to demonstrate that ethnographic artefacts had no significance outside their physical and social contexts have now realised that a consideration of the world of materials and artefacts is essential to the understanding of social institutions and practices. It is clearly important that museums are more reflexive about their practices. Historical perspectives can, however, play an important role by provoking questions. Questions that treat politics, epistemology and aesthetics are necessarily intertwined.

Art has a complex relationship to its socio-political and cultural context, made manifest, for instance, when it is considered politically incorrect and subversive by the state, which might move to discredit the work, or remove it, or the artist, altogether. An example of this was the exhibition of *Degenerate Art* as titled by the Nazi regime in 1937. In this instance, the politically motivated contextualising process wished to divest a group of artists' work of its value and relevance. It failed, of course, because the work in question had already established its interactive meanings and challenges in relation to an audience hungry for art that embodied alternative non-totalitarian political resonance and social meaning.

Once the official museum had been created, key works became sequestered from society and everyday life. The museum becomes the terminal destination for art. Art goes there to die. The white-walled gallery becomes the tomb, the museum, the mausoleum. The museum therefore came to represent the separation of the artist from society. The traditional museum is a nineteenth-century model and its contents correspond to those of an ecclesiastical institution and the philosophy behind it. On the one side was the church/museum, the repository of the sacred, and on the other was life. In the church were the curates, and in the museum were the curators; a copy of the ecclesiastical hierarchy. Whoever crossed the threshold of a church or museum was virtually sacralised, whether it was men and their deeds or artists and their paintings. The artist who remained outside was automatically 'excommunicated'. Like the Church, the museum thought itself to be eternal and immune to temporary things. But as art realises its temporality and has more to do with social and everyday things, the museum is challenged to treat it in a different way. Do works enter the museum when they have already lost their provocativeness and power to arouse questioning, when they have become accepted? Museums such as the Louvre were originally where artists went to learn their trade – where do they go now?

Objects and artefacts articulate our values and aspirations as well as substantiating our position within the culture. Artworks invest meaning in their own materiality, and meaning is invested by social attention. The first anti-museum initiatives developed in the eighteenth century, when artists in Rome, Paris and London began to defy official exhibitions or patronage by setting up alternative galleries or inviting the public into their own studios. From the beginning, museums such as the Louvre and the National Gallery have generated political and aesthetic opposition that expressed itself in articulated terms. Gustave Moreau, for instance, stipulated in his will that his works be hung together in a studio devoted solely to that purpose, thus becoming the first posthumous director of his own museum, which exists today in Paris. J.M.W. Turner also wrote several detailed, impassioned wills leaving the paintings to the National Gallery, stipulating exactly when and how they should be installed and demanding a Turner Gallery. Throughout the twentieth century, artists have proposed alternatives and extensions to the museum so as to prevent their work from being subsumed. Marcel Duchamp and Joseph Beuys provide further primary examples.

The conference notes ask 'to what extent should art education reflect the institutionalised values of the museum and to what extent should the museum constitute the ultimate goal of the emerging practitioner?' If art education does reflect the current institutionalised values of the museum and if the museum does constitute the ultimate goal for the practitioner, then the practitioner is surely denying him or herself the opportunity of making any meaningful intervention into their own culture.

During the 1930s in the United States (a country without a long artistic tradition to weigh it down), the static museum became dynamic. It began to live. The unchanging display of permanent collections gave way to a systematic policy of mounting exhibitions devoted to modern movements and retrospectives of living artists under the inspired curatorship of Alfred Barr. The Museum of Modern Art (MoMA) was born. Here was an important moment for the museum facing the inevitable question of marginalisation. As a result of the creative, as well as the political, social and cultural upheavals taking place in the early and mid twentieth century, artists were released from art's traditional categories of object making, media and craft practices. Easel painting had ceased to rule the roost. One might well ask how the museum is coping with all of this? Is there a drift starting to occur; has art got away from the museum?

New languages have arisen that are a synthesis of other languages, and they are validating the use of all techniques, all materials, all combinations (whether random or planned) of all expressive systems. A new language is linking itself to a new everyday world by its incorporation of banal elements of reality, mass media, ephemera and actual experience. The new museum is perhaps the artists' place of work. It is a laboratory where new theories of art are being examined and tried out; a laboratory where artist and observer may come into contact. It is a meeting point between the artist and the observer, who may be another artist, between the museum and society. For the museum should now be considered a school, which does not offer models for imitation but rather an open workshop. In this redefinition of the museum, Beuys was a highly visionary artist.

Early Dada exhibitions and performances were deliberately staged under rough circumstances in beer halls, factories and parks. Later, younger artists, curators and irreverent collectors in New York favoured abandoned industrial lofts, schools and even virtually inaccessible ranch lands, mountains and stretches of desert (Walter De Maria's *Lightning Field* for example – a work involving metal rods mounted in the New Mexico desert). The neutrality of the new spaces became a component of style. In America the tradition of the 'retinal', appropriated by the Greenbergian tradition of object making, led to painting such as Abstract Expressionism and Hard Edge, being made primarily for the museum. These works were inappropriate for small spaces. Here, the museum as such, legitimised and validated the current art practice. However, in the 1960s and early 1970s, artists were reacting against what was perceived as a reductive art-making philosophy, and began to challenge and take issue with the very tenets of the Greenbergian theory.

With this change in attitude and the new alternative spaces, the role and location of the museum began to drift, a movement that has gained in momentum since the early 1960s. Alternative spaces flourished throughout Europe and the USA from the 1960s onwards. The energy of open alternative spaces in the 1960s and 70s was not only inspired by the desire to exhibit work that might have otherwise gone unseen, as Reynolds and Manet did, but also to de-aestheticise art – to free it from the suffocating envelope of grand traditional culture or the museum. Holly and Howard Soloman opened a ground-floor loft space in SoHo, a warehouse district of New York. They did not control what the artists did in the space; even the title was neutral: 98 Green Street. Geoffrey Lew founded an even larger, looser space: the 112 Green Street Workshop.

The raw industrial vitality of these unfinished surroundings gave rise to the Minimal-ism of the late 1960s.

PSI opened in June 1976 in an abandoned school building on Long Island. The first exhibition was entitled *Rooms*. In each of the twenty-eight vacant classrooms there was no intervention by architect or curator. It was not only a space for exhibiting art but also for making it. Alanna Heiss, an American who worked extensively in London in the 1960s and founded the original Institute of Art and Urban Resources, preferred the term 'experimental workspace' to gallery or museum, which again continued a signifi-cant thread.

In Europe, the Pompidou Centre, Paris, designed by Piano/Rogers, opened in the late 1970s. Most critics found it intolerable as a museum in the conventional sense. Bereft of the traditional ornamentation, this steel-and-glass skeleton was built between 1975 and 1978 on a drab five-acre site in the heart of Paris. There was no tidy sequence of rooms arranged around a predictable access, but rather a giant five-storey atrium. The building contained not only art, but a library, films, a video centre, and was acces-sible seven days a week from 10.00 am to 10.00 pm. Displays of architecture and design were exhibited in an adjacent wing, and there was also a centre for new music. When it opened, it averaged 20,000 visitors during the week and more than double that number on Sundays. Figures exceeded original projections by four or five times. It was a large, flexible and highly successful space for art.

Now the new Tate Gallery of Modern Art is about to be developed in London with the conversion of a decommissioned power station on a site at Bankside between Black-friars and Southwark bridge. It is not surprising that disappointment has been ex-pressed that a completely new building has not been commissioned. However, the new Tate Gallery does provide significant opportunities to revisit fundamental questions concerning function, role and relationships, inevitably facing a new museum of con-temporary art. There are more important questions than that of the physical envelope.

One of those important questions might be of the missing art. Over the past thirty years, the museum has failed significantly to take account of a whole spectrum of pri-mary creative practice in the visual arts because of their drift away from current, 'recog-nisable' practices confirmed by historical precedent. I remember having a conversation with Peter Fuller and a museum curator in Australia in 1984. The curator was express-ing his anxiety about finding it difficult to present contemporary art of the 1970s, such as conceptual art, performance, time-based and mixed-media work. Fuller's advice to the curator was 'Forget it. It's all basically rubbish that should be thrown out. Look for paintings from the period and exhibit them.' This opens up another agenda, which I won't go into now, but has the same outcome: that is of rendering invisible an entire area of contemporary practice as the result of the sudden obsession with painting in the mid-1980s, heralded in by exhibitions like the *New Spirit of Painting*, in 1981, at the Royal Academy. This work was object-based and in the main, made for museums and collec-tors. Unlike much of the work in the late 1960s, 70s and 80s, the new painting once again provided curators and dealers with tangible commodities, thus restoring the linear tra-dition in the museum world. The 'train was back on the rails'; the artistic baton was once again being passed on by those with vested interests.

Contemporary museums therefore came to represent a quadruple dislocation. First-ly, from society; secondly, from an art-historical context; thirdly, from the contempo-rary practitioner; but fourthly, and perhaps most significantly, from the student. Clearly, there is a challenge here for the museum to re-establish these associations. In Britain, the process of disassociation with contemporary ideas, culture and practice can be clear-ly observed but was apparently missed by the museums. This process accelerated when, in the late 1960s under Anthony Caro at St Martins School of Art, a new generation of artists asked one of the very questions posed by this conference: 'to what extent should the museum constitute the ultimate goal for the emerging practitioner?' The answer was as problematic then as it is now. Where is the work from this period of Richard Long, Hamish Fulton, Gilbert & George, and Bruce McLean, whose practice stood against and challenged the production of permanent physical object? Artists were not satisfied with continuing what was increasingly seen as a bankrupt and irrelevant Greenbergian tradition of object making. By the same token, where is the work in the museum of Art & Language, Dan Graham, Joseph Kosuth and Joseph Beuys from the same period? Consequently, at this time, challenges were made, through art that embodied questions, through new ways of interpreting reality, and through art that would live in and inter-act with the real world. As a result, meaningful and relevant practices emerged.

From 1973, my work through Audio Arts has been actively involved in areas of art practice including sound, time-based work, performance, conceptual and collaborative activity. In the main, this work has not been susceptible to museum attention, because the modern museum still echoes its eighteenth- and nineteenth-century counterpart by collecting objects of permanence. A good case in point is the memorable exhibition of work by Jean Tinguely, held at the Tate in 1982. The power of the physical manifesta-tion of the works was matched by the sounds they generated – sounds that were as much part of the work as the physical structures. But unless this recording had been made by Audio Arts, a primary component of the work would have been lost. Audio Arts has also collaborated with a number of artists to make works that could be presented as original artworks using the medium of audio tape and slide, *Nine Works for Tape and Slide Sequence* being one example.[4] For this project, I invited nine artists to produce an orig-inal work of art using six slides and up to five minutes of sound. The resultant works did not depend on the expensive movement of objects, yet were primary artworks, not doc-umentation of works. They were works that could be sent through the post and pre-sented in a variety of spaces from city centres, cinemas (as happened in Brussels), to art centres, galleries, or on a wall in a domestic space. A further series was presented and premiered at the Riverside Studios in London in 1984. These were large-scale presen-tations. Again, the works were made specifically for tape/slide presentation, not as doc-umentation, but as original pieces.

Now I would like to play a series of extracts from Audio Arts to further substantiate my argument:

1. *Everybody Loved Dominic Lynch* by David Cunningham, from 'Live to Air',
   International Artists Soundworks, premiered at the Tate Gallery, London,
   1988.[5]

2. *Lorelei: The Long Distance Piano Sonata* by Dieter Roth with Bjorn Roth.[6]
3. *Just Another Bad Turn Up*, a monologue from the soundtrack of a performance of the same name, Riverside Studios, London, 1986.[7]
4. Richard Long reads word pieces: *A Straight Northward Walk Across Dartmoor*, 1985.[8]
5. *Die Gross Bockwurst*, by Richard Hamilton and Dieter Roth, reading first performed and recorded by Audio Arts in 1977 at the Whitechapel Art Gallery, London.[9]

As a result of the failure of the museum to attend to areas of non-permanent art, there is a considerable spectrum of art activity that is not represented by the museums, although they have become important as a reference for the contemporary practitioner and student. Where then is the time-based and non-object-based work from the 1960s, 70s and 80s of Dan Graham, Joseph Kosuth, Stuart Brisley, Art & Language, Bruce McLean, Daniel Buren, John Hilliard, Mary Kelly, Susan Hiller, Dennis Oppenheim, On Kawara, Douglas Huebler, Seth Seigleb, David Medalla, to name but a few? Secondary documentation, rather than the primary work, has crept into museum collections, as have associated objects, but where is the spirit and substantive manifestation of invention embodied in Lucy Lippard's book, *Six Years: The Dematerialisation of the Art Object from 1962 to 1972*? Where is the work of Germano Celant's Arte Povera? Are we to accept the view of a previous Tate Gallery curator who claimed that artists who made work that did not lead to tangible objects should not expect their work to be represented in museum collections? Where, from the last thirty years, is Live art, Conceptual art, time-based and site-specific work, performance, installation, work in film, video, sound and book form?

In answer to the question raised by this conference: 'What contribution can the museum make to fine art education in the twentieth and twenty-first centuries?', the answer has to be 'a marginal one', since as things stand, so much work is just not available in the museums because it has simply not been retained. The museum that is relevant to art education resides now in the temporary exhibition, in artist-run spaces, in imaginative gallery initiatives such as Interim Art, White Cube, the Cabinet Gallery, Karsten Schubert, Matt's Gallery, City Racing, Victoria Miro Gallery, the *Freeze* show of 1989 and other galleries in London such as the Serpentine, Camden Arts Centre, and MoMA in Oxford; through initiatives such as Locus +, the Public Arts Development Trust and Artangel, who commissioned the extraordinary *House* by Rachel Whiteread. All of these spaces and organisations offer opportunities for students to interact with work that arises out of their own time and can be used and interpreted accordingly.

The Tate recently held a large exhibition of the work of German artist Rebecca Horn. This was a vibrant, provocative exhibition, which attracted so many visitors that the doors had to be closed on a Sunday afternoon to ease the pressure off those in the gallery, as happened with the hugely popular Turner Prize exhibition. Students were there in force. This is an example of the functioning museum.

The international exhibition, such as the Venice Biennale and Documenta in Kassel, Germany, becomes, albeit for a number of months, a highly functional museum event.

In the Venice Biennale of 1993, Hans Haacke created a memorable installation, a work arising out of the fact that Hitler had visited the German Pavilion at the Biennale in 1934. The entire floor was torn up and visitors had to pick their way precariously across an uneven surface, undermining physical stability, but speaking metaphorically of German instability both during the Nazi era and also in the period around unification. This was a powerful work, worthy of any museum presentation. People walked across it to create the sounds of shattered slabs of stone, therefore becoming part of the dynamic of the exhibition rather than passive observers. The museum needs to take account of the site-specific: the artwork created for a particular physical, social and geographical context, which may be well away from the museum. Other examples are the Munster Sculpture Project and *Chambres d'Amis* by Jan Hoet. Richard Hamilton's installation of works in the British Pavilion at the Venice Biennale in 1993 was a powerful display, where the artist had created juxtapositions and sequences far more memorable and convincing than his own curated Tate show a year before. Had the museum stifled the work at the Tate? In short, his works lived in Venice but were asleep in London.

At *Documenta 9* in 1992, sculptor Richard Deacon made a work that related to a specific environment, which brought the artist into contact with other artists, curators, critics, children and passers by. Why is it that Britain doesn't have a Documenta or a Biennale? In financial terms, Documenta broke all records of attendance and ended up making a profit – an exhibition of challenging contemporary art. Could not the new Tate programme a large-scale event that builds on the undoubted success of Venice and Documenta? It has also to be borne in mind that Documenta is held in the small provincial German town of Kassel, which is rather like Farnham in Surrey.

The museum therefore has to cease to be a monolithic institution. It has to start to live and interact dynamically with its various constituencies, and I'm not talking here about token education departments with their limited budgets and facilities, which are rather like the children's room in a pub, often cold and begrudging. For instance, in which art venue in London can you present work of a multi-media nature? Where in London can you arrange to record or video a live event without having to start from scratch and phone up Audio Arts for the equipment? How many major arts venues even have sound-recording facilities? This lecture theatre at the Tate Gallery, for instance, is in mono; it has no stereo sound.

I would like to ask a fundamental question, which to me is probably the most important issue to arise out of this conference. Up until now, I haven't spoken of the most significant dislocation: that is, between the museum and the art school. Of course, students on fine art courses visit museums, but the relationship is passive. With the establishment of a new museum of modern art in England at Bankside, isn't this the moment to grasp, to bring into a more productive relationship, the activities of fine art education and the new museum? Could not, for instance, students of fine art and the staff be relocated to the new museum, where they would work and interact with artists, curators, the public and each other? I believe this to be a dynamic and challenging model, which should be addressed. It is generally acknowledged internationally that Britain has one of the, if not *the*, best art school systems in the world, yet it seems isolated and separate from so many cultural infrastructures of support. Young artists normally have to go abroad to have museum shows: to Germany, Holland or France. The separation of fine art education and the museum is clearly an unsatisfactory state of affairs.

The final question in this conference raised the issue of new technologies and to what extent the museum is a redundant institution, given current technology and the capacity for the reproduction and transmission of images electronically. This is an important area, but, given that so much work has been overlooked over the past three decades, even with appropriate technologies for its retention and presentation, I cannot be over-confident. How many more versions of the Old Masters do we need? In the Tate Gallery shop we have jigsaws, ashtrays, tea-towels and soon CD-ROM versions and eventually, no doubt, the Old Masters theme park. Where is the contemporary artist and student in all of this? Their museum is the industrial loft, the self-help exhibition, not least, the art school. We now have a golden opportunity with the new Tate, not to argue over the architecture, but to review in its totality the opportunity to establish a new, dynamic, interactive and innovative model in which the artist and student are central to the debate and the museum.

Notes

1. Epigraph by Walter Pater from a book, published in 1943, by Conger Goodyear, the first Chairman of the Trustees of the Museum of Modern Art, New York, to celebrate the tenth anniversary of the Museum.
2. 'Jean Tinguely, Sculpture at the Tate Gallery', *Audio Arts Supplement*, 1982.
3. *What Are You Doing Taping?*, a soundwork by William Furlong, presented by the Institute of Contemporary Arts, London, at St James' Church, Piccadilly, London, 1986. Published by the ICA/Audio Arts as part of its public works series, 1986.
4. Audio extract from *What Are You Doing Taping?*
5. 'Live to Air', *Audio Arts Magazine*, 1988.
6. Audio Arts with Edition Hans Jörg Meyer, 1982.
7. A soundtrack for the performance by Bruce McLean, *Just Another Bad Turn Up*, recorded and produced by William Furlong/Audio Arts, 1984.
8. 'Richard Long', *Audio Arts Supplement*, 1985.
9. 'Collaborations, Readings', *Audio Arts Supplement*, 1987.

The museum as a catalyst

Sutapa Biswas
Artist and Teacher

In the introduction to his essay 'On the Museum's Ruins',[1] Douglas Crimp quotes Theodor Adorno, who writes, 'The German word museal [*Museumiikel*] ... describes objects to which the observer no longer has a vital relationship and which are in the process of dying. They owe preservation more to historical respect than to the needs of the present'. To paraphrase: museums are the family tombs of works of art. The intention of my paper is not to attempt to resurrect the museum, but rather to acknowledge that within its confines, some truly anarchic and sublime activities are taking place.

In his paper delivered at an inIVA Symposium in 1994, the artist Fred Wilson described a series of projects that he had curated in the United States.[2] One that particularly comes to mind was a collaboration with the Museum of Contemporary Art, Baltimore, which had invited Wilson to organise an exhibition anywhere in that city. Wilson chose to work at the Maryland Historical Society, which he describes as one of the most conservative environments in Baltimore. Nonetheless, his strategy was to intervene somehow in the normal activities of the museum. After a year's research and a six-week residency period, the culmination of the project was an installation, bringing together various archival objects and artefacts from the museum's collection, and allowing a subtle new reading of the context for these works. For example, part of the installation constituted a silver globe found in the silver storage with the word 'truth' inscribed upon it. In the same area, he positioned six pedestals, three with busts of people who had been influential in Maryland: Napoleon, Henry Clay and Andrew Jackson – none of whom were from Maryland – and the other three without busts but labelled Harriet Tubman, Benjamin Banneker and Frederick Douglas. These were three important African-Americans from the nineteenth century, all from Maryland, but barely recognised in the Maryland Historical Society's collection.

What I find most intriguing about this project was the title of the installation itself – *Mining the Museum*. Wilson arrived at this name because it could mean one of many things: 'mining' as in gold mining; or as in land mine – exploding myths and perceptions; or, to quote Wilson, 'it could mean making it mine'. It is the latter interpretation that I find most compelling.

The act of resuscitation is never straightforward, and sometimes fruitless. Nonetheless, many museums, particularly, it seems in North America, are becoming catalysts for potential intervention of this nature. In my view, this is something from which fine art institutions can learn. In December 1990, I found myself in Canada through a Fellowship at the Banff Centre for the Arts, in Alberta. Judith Mastai, who was then Education Programmer at Vancouver Art Gallery – a major municipal gallery with a permanent collection, library and so forth – approached me with the idea of collaborating on a project that would coincide with an exhibition called *Fabled Territories: New*

Asian Photography in Britain. This was organised by the City Art Gallery in Leeds, and was to travel to the Vancouver Art Gallery in November 1992. The nature of the project was left to me, but the Vancouver Art Gallery undertook to assist me in any way possible.

I had decided early on that if I were to accept the offer, I didn't want to parachute down into Vancouver for a few days, and then simply disappear. We agreed that I would do some initial research on aspects of the history of Vancouver before making any concrete decisions. In doing this, one of the things I focused on was that Canada presented itself as an interesting phenomenon in the sense that everyone who lived there was displaced. This was a potentially good starting point for a project. With the assistance of the Vancouver Art Gallery and a group of independent and recent friends, I began to network with a number of locally based arts and other organisations.

Given the time limitation of most residencies, I decided it would only be workable if we kept things as uncomplicated as possible. I chose to work with a small group comprised of up to twelve women who should be of various ages and racial backgrounds (in the end the youngest turned out to be twenty-two, and the oldest seventy-eight) and who could either be practising artists or novices to art. The theme for the project was 'Memory and Desire'; open enough to allow many readings, and at the same time inviting the participants to think around personal subjects.

Over a period of one year, I corresponded with the Vancouver Art Gallery and a list of women, some of whom I had met with already. The project was not without its problems. Unfortunately, by the time I arrived in Vancouver, members of the local community, calling themselves The Coalition for Color, were up in arms with the Vancouver Art Gallery for importing issues of race, accusing them of not acknowledging artists of colour on their own doorstep. Does this sound familiar? It was inevitably a complicated situation. Whilst there was some justification in the nature of the coalition's grievances, many of their attacks were clearly not thought through. In my view, part of the complaint had its foundation in gender politics, directed by certain male individuals who felt excluded from an all-women's residency group.

Although the local coalition group was ultimately supportive of the work, as a visiting artist I met head-on some of the complexities of working in a new environment and being wedged between the museum and its community. As an artist, I was determined not to allow the politics of the situation to detract from the dynamics of our 'Memory and Desire' residency group.

The group – Ana Chang, Sherida Levy, Alexis Macdonald-Seto, Shani Mootoo, Marianne Nicholson, Linda Ohama, Haruko Okano, Sandra Semchuk, Alfreida Steindi, Kiki Yee and myself – met on a regular basis, averaging twice or three times a week. In our first meeting I presented my work and discussed that of the group, along with their ambitions for the residency and of course some of mine. It was soon established that what we wanted to do was to work collectively. On a budget of $600 Canadian dollars, we set out the following goals:

a) to make a work of art collectively, the starting point for which was to be taken from an idea contained in an earlier work of mine

b) to make this part of a larger exhibition of work by the individual members of the group

c) to use the resources we had to hand

d) to learn how to curate an exhibition by sharing skills

e) to hire out the exhibition to different venues across Canada, including the Vancouver Art Gallery

f) to raise revenue through this that would come back to the individual members of the group, offering remuneration for their artistic work, and assisting them in producing new works.

Finally, we decided that the project showed great potential in terms of its overall package, and so we agreed to try and establish a series of similar residencies across Canada, where a member of our original group would travel with the touring exhibition as artist-in-residence and would set up similar skill-sharing projects.

The exhibition opened at the Vancouver Art Gallery to a packed house. Although the project was not without its difficulties, it was overwhelmingly successful, and full of momentum. Thanks to the commitment of our group – and the Vancouver Art Gallery, who in may ways acted as a catalyst for the project as a whole – with limited funds we produced what in my view is a sublime act of intervention. I receive postcards yearly from members of our original group who still meet to discuss life and art.

Notes

1. Douglas Crimp, *On the Museum's Ruins*, MIT Press, Cambridge, Mass. and London 1993.

2. Fred Wilson, 'The Silent Message of the Museum', paper delivered at 1994 inIVA Symposium *New Internationalism* held at the Tate Gallery, London 1994. Published in Jean Fisher (ed.), *Global Visions: Towards a New Internationalism in the Visual Arts*, Kala Press, London 1994, pp.152–160.

Back to the future

COLIN WIGGINS

Education Officer, National Gallery, London

I feel I should warn you that I'm going to start with a controversial statement. I know that many of you will be shocked by it, so prepare yourselves. I should say that this is my own personal point of view and does not necessarily represent any officially held opinion at the National Gallery: Nicolas Poussin is a greater artist than Rebecca Horn.

The current Rebecca Horn exhibition at the Tate is packed with students. Indeed, on any one day you can watch groups of students making neat little academic-style drawings from these bits of wire and tubing and things. While at the Poussin exhibition, though hugely successful in terms of its attendance, there is not a fine art student in sight.

To me, Education Officer at the National Gallery, this is quite a problem. Because to me, Poussin *is* a greater artist than Rebecca Horn. However, he is an artist who is traditionally presented by art historians as cerebral, as difficult, as an 'academic' artist. Therefore, by the time his reputation gets through to students, he's 'boring', and worse, 'irrelevant'. Having spoken to several groups of fine art students in the past few weeks, I found that *none* of them had seen the Poussin show, and they felt that it was pretty unlikely they would do so. They were all too busy getting excited about Rebecca Horn.

This confirms what Paul Huxley said at a previous conference: 'a young artist's allegiances will be to recent art, where there is something to identify with, rather than with the daunting works of the distant past.' And to quote Huxley again: 'Today's students know that Jackson Pollock threw paint, that Andy Warhol traced around photographs, and that Marcel Duchamp just made choices.'

Yes, they do know that, and we know that. But of course, we also know, to take for example Jackson Pollock, that he did not simply wake up one morning and think 'I'm going to be an artist. How shall I do that? I know, I'll throw paint'. Pollock arrived at his drip paintings after many, many years of constant, intelligent, impassioned and often anguished involvement, debate and engagement with the *tradition* from which he came. Whether we're talking about Cubism or El Greco or Surrealism or Navajo sand painting, Pollock was fully aware that he was working within a tradition.

The problem I have when convincing young art students to visit the National Gallery, is that the word 'tradition' has become synonymous with 'boring'. This is perhaps the fault of art history and art historians and I think we can certainly point an accusing finger at Vasari for the idea that, first of all 'classical' art is somehow superior and intellectual, and secondly that art 'develops': Giotto influences Masaccio … Masaccio influences Michelangelo … Michelangelo influences … etc. Art history continues this idea into our own time: Cézanne influences Picasso … etc. This 'linear development' idea about art history is what is usually taught to fine art students and it is not a helpful one. But it's the one we've been stuck with since Vasari.

So why don't we look at art history from a different point of view and see the 'tradition' as a series of radical and extreme revolutions against the established canon of the previous generation? Whether we're talking of Mexican muralists, of Michelangelo, or Caravaggio, or even Constable, they're actively undermining what went before. Yes, Constable was a great subversive.

But that introduces another problem for the young artist of today. We're living at the end of the twentieth century, a century that has seen both Picasso and Duchamp. And virtually every worthwhile artistic idea of our century comes from those two. So what do we do next, when everything seems to have been done? We can't even be subversive any more, for heaven's sake, because even that has become part of tradition.

These are problems that we cannot possibly solve for art students. We can only hope to open their eyes to them and to help them confront them. The next Picassos will have to crack these things for themselves. We must recognise that the role of the 'teacher' is of necessity limited. All we can do is direct.

Art is a very sophisticated language. If we dive into it by just thinking about the recent past, then we're in very shallow waters indeed and in danger of cracking our heads on the bottom. Maybe we can just paddle about a bit, splash around on the Rebecca Horn shores. But students have to be shown that to take oneself seriously as an artist, it's essential to engage the whole tradition. It's essential to look at the despised Dead White European Males – Michelangelo, Rembrandt, and what about Joseph Beuys? What is he? A Dead White European Male. Even Beuys has succumbed to tradition.

Now I'm going to shock you again with another slide. A self-portrait of Sir Joshua Reynolds. Reynolds! The very name strikes boredom into the heart of any self-respecting art student. And yet without Sir Joshua, it could be argued that we wouldn't actually be sitting here today. It was Sir Joshua who established the idea that if you are born in these rainy, windswept isles, it is not necessarily an obstacle to becoming an artist. Sir Joshua laboured passionately throughout his life, despite the handicap of being a hopeless draughtsman – one of the world's worst in fact. But I consider him a very great artist.

One reason for putting Sir Joshua on the screen is that I wanted to ask the question 'Why does the National Gallery exist?' It exists partly as a result of Sir Joshua's beliefs. The Gallery was founded in 1824, largely as a result of the bloody-mindedness and hard work of a man called Sir George Beaumont. Beaumont was a wealthy amateur artist and collector and friend of Reynolds. He presented his marvellous collection to the nation, which really was a major factor behind the establishment of today's National Gallery. Before this happened, he opened his house, where he had his collection, to young artists. Where do you go if you're a young artist – let's say Constable – in 1815, to see Old Master paintings? You have to knock on Sir George's door and say, 'Excuse me. I wonder if you'd be so kind ...' And Beaumont, to his eternal credit, encouraged artists to look at his pictures and based this encouragement on Sir Joshua's principle that young artists must learn what he called 'the grammar of painting'. But the very last thing one should tell an art student is 'have a look at the work of Sir Joshua Reynolds and then learn the grammar of painting and then you too will be an artist'. As you all know, it doesn't quite work like that.

Reynolds and Beaumont shared a passionate belief that new art could only be inspired by the establishment of a national gallery. Beaumont wanted his gesture of giving away his collection to be of benefit to young artists in this country at the threshold of their careers. But not everyone agreed with him. Constable, for example, thought it a dreadful idea. He thought it was retrogressive, reactionary and would only result in the production of hundreds of bad pastiches. Which is, of course, a very valid point to make.

So the argument that we have today, about whether or not it's beneficial to send students off to study Old Masters, the Dead White European Males, is not a new argument at all. It goes back a very long way.

What we arre trying to do at the National Gallery, as a continuation of the beliefs of Reynolds and Beaumont, is to prevent the collection from becoming seen as a Museum of Dead Cultural Artefacts. And if there are those among you who do seriously think that the National Gallery is where art goes to die, I would ask you to go and look at the Caravaggio painting that we currently have on loan from Dublin, which was recently discovered in Ireland. A painting from the seventeenth century will, I promise, shock you.

The National Gallery is a place full of living works of art. We might put labels next to them and say 'possibly painted in Parma about 1527', but that's not the only way of thinking about the paintings in the Gallery.

We have for many years been initiating and developing schemes to involve contemporary artists in the life of the Gallery. This started with the Artist-in-Residence scheme, the first Artist-in-Residence being Maggi Hambling, sixteen years ago. We also hold a series of exhibitions called *Artist's Eye*, for which a contemporary artist is invited to make a selection of works from the ollection and to display it in whatever way they wish together with examples of their own work, in order to make whatever points they want. A reason for doing these things of course, is to demonstrate that living artists can use the Gallery. Not that living artists *must* use the Gallery. But that they *can* use it.

But I would argue very strongly that art students *must* use the Gallery. I think it should be a compulsory thing for them to do, in the same way that it is compulsory at school to learn to read. You can do what you want with it afterwards. It is incumbent on us, as educators, to show all of the options. It is our responsibility.

Apart from these schemes, we have recently gone a bit more long term. In 1990 we invited Paula Rego to work in the National Gallery for two years, under a scheme we call the Associate Artist. This is continuing today with Peter Blake, who'll be there for another two years. Part of the deal of having a studio in the Gallery is that you can open your door to groups of art students and talk to them about the problems of being an artist in the late part of the twentieth century, when we have to come to terms with Rembrandt, Raphael, Michelangelo etc, as well as with Picasso and Duchamp. Art students can have a direct and personal contact with a successful and well-known artist whom they see using the Gallery. This is not a replacement of the Artist-in-Residence scheme, which functioned with much younger artists, four or five years out of college.

We do not want to give the impression that we are just backing the 'established' figures, so one new scheme on which we're currently working actively involves fine art students in the life of the Gallery.

In 1997 we are holding an exhibition of students' work, transcriptions of the National Gallery paintings. And I want to stress that this is not a token exhibition, downstairs in a corridor by the toilets, but a proper, main-floor National Gallery exhibition with the full backing of the Director and Trustees.

I want to finish by showing you some examples of student work already produced as a result of this project. You all know Titian's *Bacchus and Ariadne*. This slide shows a very beautiful painting made by a Wimbledon student. We could talk about it as conventional, yes. But he has looked at the Titian and transcribed it into his own language. I talked to him about two weeks ago and he told me how excited he is by Jasper Johns. And you can see how he's actually using Johns as well at Titian. It's a painting that excited me and made me think that here we've got a student who can paint, who isn't frightened by five hundred years or more of 'tradition', who isn't frightened of being called old-fashioned for taking a squarish piece of canvas and putting oil paint on it. It's a courageous painting, a more than competent painting that shows how valuable it has been for this particular student to sit in front of *Bacchus and Ariadne*, to think about it for a long time and to make a work that is ultimately independent of it.

The Munch show three years ago was the National Gallery's biggest success with the student audience. This is a painting made by a Camberwell student, after visiting the Munch show. And you can see what painting she has transcribed, can't you? The beautiful, relaxed, calm, ordered, oh what a sunny day *Bathers* by Seurat. But instead of sitting around being calm, ordered and relaxed, they're now all suffering from a terrible Nordic angst, thinking 'Oh no, sex, death, how awful!' This is a wonderful transcription of Seurat out of Munch, made with a sense of humour, wickedness and, a vital ingredient: subversion.

Accelerated architecture:
the new museum and electronic culture

SEAN CUBITT

Reader in Film and Media Studies, Liverpool John Moores University

I heard recently on the radio a broadcast about a new museum opening in the West of Ireland dedicated to the memory of the Great Famine. The curator, an articulate and passionate apostle for the enterprise, was faced with a curatorial problem of immense difficulty: the peasants of Ireland were so poor that they had no possessions. What they might once have owned had been sold in the vain attempt to find food, and most of that was lost, discarded, melted down or broken. Even the written word was scarce since the painstaking assault on the speaking Gaelic had left the population largely illiterate. There were virtually no artefacts from the world outside the big houses. Her solution was to provide models of those conditions, and to expand on the handful of diaries and letters from the emigrants to provide some memorial of that ghastly time.

Similar problems have confronted the museums dedicated to the Holocaust, or the new Museum of Transatlantic Slavery at the Maritime Museum in Liverpool. It would be wrong to compare the difficult work of remembering a past that has been wilfully obliterated with the simpler problems that confront us when considering the impact of new media on the form and function of the museum. But it may give a sense of what I understand the purpose of the museum to be: to remember, on behalf of a culture, what needs to be recalled, even counter to the currents of history. I will be here concentrating on the art gallery, but I hope that many of the observations will be applicable to the historical museum too, and that it will be remembered that the gallery performs a task in essence the same as that of the museum: the task of commemoration.

There are a series of elements that can be gathered under the general rubric of 'the new media and the museum': the use of new technologies in the provision of guide services to visitors; the curation and exhibition of electronic media arts in museums and galleries; the creation of 'virtual museums' on computer media; recourse to electronic media dealing with the impact of the production and appreciation of art, history and culture.

I want here to attempt to speculate on the wider impact of electronic cultures – not just of the new media – most especially on the visitor to the museum. First, a distinction: a *medium* can be defined as a material process that we employ to mediate between ourselves, like these words I'm using now, physically manipulating voicebox, air and eardrum to mediate between you and me. A *culture* is, in Raymond Williams' famous phrase, 'a whole way of life', embracing not only relationships between people, but between people and things, and including such human attributes as belief and hope as well as technology, cooking and toilet training. In this sense, the study of media forms a subset of the study of cultures.

The study of art theory belongs within the study of culture, and overlaps with media studies, because there is that quality of art that is medium-specific. This quality is celebrated by the most influential of modern critics, Clement Greenberg, and differently, but just as centrally, by the Courtauld approach to art history, which is so important to the traditions of curatorial practice in Britain. On the frieze over the central door of the Tate's main building, that medium specificity is celebrated in the figure of the two Muses who preside over the nineteenth century's conception of art: Painting with her easel and Sculpture with her small, bronze cast of a classical sculpture. This is a wonderfully self-referential image for Sculpture, whom you would expect to see with the tools of the trade, the mallet and chisel, but who is instead supplied with the central teaching device of the academic tradition. Sculpture in particular is represented as a concept, not a practice. Perhaps that is why the notorious reluctance of the early twentieth-century British art establishment to accept the new European art of the previous thirty years did not extend to sculpture, so that Epstein and Gaudier-Brzeska could chip away, while Cézanne was still anathema. That art is a quality specific to painting and sculpture is a statement about the medium specificity of art. It is not, however, a full statement of the cultural practices of art, which would need to extend to curation, the architecture of galleries, the culture of gallery-going, the commercial markets, the principles of display, the ancillary cultures of slides, art training, art history, art books, art holidays, festivals, magazines and conferences like this one. So my first argument is that, if we are to understand the relationship between art and the mew media, we need also to understand that both take place within and as wider cultures, that they are linked by their role in mediating between people, and that they share as much as they are divided by.

The metaphor I want to employ is one shared by the museum and the computer: the metaphor of architecture. The gallery is not its architecture; nor is the computer restricted to the current logic architectures that, especially in the major families of operating systems, currently dominate the human/computer interface. As you approach the main facade of the Tate, you notice an extraordinary blending (that's a kind word) of styles. The main entrance columns seem to draw simultaneously on Greek and Egyptian architecture; there are Celtic griffins and Egyptian sphinxes above a Palladian terrace. And surmounting all, in the place where a god might be, there is Britannia, flanked by her heraldic beasts. The message is clear – a message from the height of the British Empire – that all the aeons of preceding civilisations have found their apogee in this civilisation. The ascent to the level of art via those forbidding steps is undertaken under the triumphal shadow of Empire. Today, a curiously similar claim is being made for the convergence of media in the new information technologies. The confluence of computing, television, photography, text, sound, music, voice with a communications network comprising microwave, telephone, telegraph, satellite and who knows what else is a technological delight. But its celebrants claim far more for it: that it is bringing about a fundamental change in society, in psychology, in the fabric of what it is to be alive and human. For just as the preceding civilisations can be subsumed in the Tate's facade under Britannia, in the worlds of *Wired* and *Mondo 2000* they can be subsumed under the mighty microchip.

It would be too simple to argue that the analogy can be stretched much further: that, for instance, as Empire denies the value of colonised cultures, so digital media can erase the differences between the media and cultures they reproduce. It is easy enough to imagine (though not, I'm afraid, to purchase) CD-ROMs as fascinating as the National Gallery's remarkable series of books, *Art in the Making*, which, with their scholarly articles from the archives and their amazing X-ray, raking light, spectrographic and micrographic images, illuminate the practice of art in ways that might even be enhanced in interactive media (chasing the use of a particular pigment, for example). Microsoft's disc featuring works from the National's collection is a sad disappointment compared to that possibility – and it has to be said that the National sold the electronic rights to Microsoft's Bill Gates for a song, and that they will regret it.

What interests me far more is the notion of an architecture. Some of you may have been lucky enough to catch Susan Collins' installation for the *V-Topia* exhibition at the Tramway in Glasgow. Collins' work was engaged in helping the visitor not to understand, but to experience the works, and since most were installations, to provide a kind of spatial counter-discourse to the themes of both the show as a whole and the individual works within it. It made you aware, with its altering sonorities and first-person address, of the architecture through which you moved; an architecture as much of light as of stone and steel. Some of you may have seen the major retrospectives of Bill Viola, Stan Douglas and Gary Hill over the last couple of years, and been as amazed as I was by the complexity of the ways in which they reorganised space as well as time; the germs of an architecture in which every aspect is a potential threshold.

It's no bad thing to try to learn from artists what we can understand about the gallery as an architectural domain. We have a tendency to see the gallery itself as a kind of transparency, and to design it accordingly, so that light, wall colours and furnishings are arranged in order to heighten the autonomy of the artworks. In doing so, we tend to work on the aesthetic principle that the apprehension of art is the matter of an instant. But watching people moving through galleries, it's clear that art isn't instantaneous, that visitors like to look at a favoured piece for – well, as long as it takes. Thinking about the gallery architecturally allows us to understand art temporally. Art takes place, and it takes time. For centuries, that spatio-temporal, architectural experience has been central to aesthetes: in the caves at Lascaux, in the approach to Stonehenge, in the medieval warrens surrounding the great cathedrals.

That fundamental reorientation of space and time, so profoundly divided by the Kantian separation of duration and extension, is to my mind central to the experience of modernity. So much of what has been undertaken in art concerns that dialectic, from the search for the sublime to Analytic Cubism, and it is a dialectic pursued with increasing urgency and pace in the twentieth century. What I believe we are living through is not a 'post' modernity, marked off from the modernity of the Enlightenment by some arcane epistemological break, but an acceleration of modernity, an acceleration already written into the concept of modernity (*modes*) itself. Architecture, for we accelerated moderns, is the art and science of place, of turning space into place, into something that can be experienced. Certainly building had been core to its development, but it has as much to do with how we configure ourselves in landscapes and in relation to the stars.

Much of the art of last hundred and fifty years has devoted itself to exploring what happens on the flat surface of the picture plane, confirming, denying and toying with the illusions of depth and projection. The new media of broadcasting and cinema, though ostensibly time-based media, were likewise experienced as miracles of spatial congruity; voices and images of distant relatives or famous figures delivered to you, not necessarily instantaneously, but across time and space as across a single dimension. This approximation of how here interacts with there evoked a wholly new architectural understanding of place, of now with then. Artists plunged themselves into this new architecture; it is as visible in the architectonics of Ezra Pound's *Cantos* as it is in the murals of Diego Rivera. It is an understanding fundamental to the operations of digital media, and to the acceleration of such characteristic operations of modernity as globalisation of business, mobility of labour, suburbanisation, private and public transport and electoral democracy. It is ironic, then, that the art gallery in particular has had such a difficult time coming to terms with so basic a property of modernity, even though, as an institution, it is itself a product of the same forces.

There is something wonderful about having to go to a gallery; about arriving in New York or Paris, with the prospect of seeing the actual works you have seen a thousand times in books and on slides. It is not so much the presence of the objects, the 'aura' Water Benjamin observed. I think it has more to do with the possibility of seeing the fact of the works in a way that none of our electronic media can recapture. But that is only a part of the culture of art. Even a jobbing critic will rarely write an article in the actual gallery itself; he or she will refer to the catalogue and the press pack for illustrations to spur the memory on, and often find ideas that hadn't been there in front of the works themselves. It's exceptionally rare that the experience of an artwork is so powerful it blots out all memory of other artworks and other human culture. I'm not sure that, on the rare occasions when it does happen – in some of Gyorgi Ligeti's compositions, perhaps, or possibly in the cinema – it's altogether a good thing: it's too Wagnerian, too overwhelming, too totalitarian.

The experiences of aesthetic delight I've had of late – the Pissarros at the Musée d'Orsay, or the young Irish artist Daphne Wright's *Domestic Shrubbery* installation, or the current Sigmar Polke show at Tate Gallery Liverpool – depend for their full power on your entire humanity, all you perceive, all you know, all you remember, all you feel, all you forget. I think it would be a treat to work up a concatenation of ideas, quotations, technical details, dimly recalled scents, fragments of old songs that might comment on works like these. Of course, we cannot render scents, and more importantly textures, reprographically, and it is texture, the sense of touch, to which the actual art object appeals so directly. Even the great experience of cinema – a good print, well-projected on a big screen – is poorly served by electronic reproduction, losing not just its detail but its sheen: the satins of Renoir's *La Règle du jeu*, the oleaginous iridescence of Kurosawa's *Dodes'ka-den*. Some element of the aesthetic remains tied to the medium through which it is perceived, but that also goes for perception through glasses or contact lenses, the prosthetic media with which we have become so familiar that they seem almost a part of ourselves. They too are filters; as much so as the panoply of skills, memories and dreams that we bring to bear in the act of looking at a piece of art.

What is at stake, in the end, is not the quality of the art, but the quality of the experience. What the gallery is about is mediating between people. As architecture, the gallery is a medium. Now, we are all pretty familiar with the media critiques that argue the case for mediation as an ideological and therefore suspect activity, but as Louis Althusser once said, there is no 'outside' of ideology. We must accept that mediation precisely because what goes on between people is full of hidden and not-so-hidden agendas. That should not, however, drive us to silence and introspection, as if there were a way of communicating without mediation; as if there were a world composed only of 'myself' without the need to communicate. Mediation is a site of struggle – of compromise and conflict, of tyranny and love. No one ever said that communication was unambiguous or uncomplicated. The most straightforward statement can be misunderstood a dozen ways, by the person for whom it was destined, or by anybody else who happens to overhear it.

In this enormous and enormously complicated conversation of mankind, it matters profoundly what the physical make-up of the medium is, as do the protocols and regimes of sense-making specific to different cultures. But if Kant got the severance of space from time wrong, he did at least specify the universality of the two, at odds or in unison. The challenge that faces us concerns the impact of acceleration on a scale poor Immanuel, with his enormous appetite for walking, could never have countenanced – what acceleration does to perception and conception, how the passion for speed has produced the speed of passion.

It is as if we are impatient with buildings. We want buildings that move, either externally like airliners and trains, or internally, like homes, shops, schools, hospitals and offices equipped with monitors and terminals, radio and playback. We want an environment as fully and comprehensively alive as we feel ourselves to be.

That is what we want. What we get is the shopping mall and Crinkley Bottom. I wouldn't want to argue the toss with dedicated culturalists who seek out the popular pleasures of consumerism. What I feel sad about is the paucity of reach entailed by these kinds of products, how little they demand from us, how little we give in return, how thin their concerns, and how afraid they are of the great circle of darkness that surrounds our brief moment in the light. They don't improve life, they just help it pass by quicker.

What we need is a new art culture that will take as its object not the things but the people in the gallery, and that perceives that the value of things is not intrinsic but communicative, deriving from their place as interstices of the endless journeyings of our species, as that through which we communicate, not artist to viewer, but person to person, in the common experience of them. The relationship of the museum to the new media is then one of articulation, as an articulated truck is constructed, flexibly linked into a synthetic unity. In the end, this is no different from the way in which art has functioned throughout the modern era, differentially articulated through the web of art-related language and communications, buildings and commerce, to the wider culture. It is simply that with the new media, that process of articulation is accelerated. There's no need to expect the 'end' of anything; the textures we so prize in art are already virtual, in the sense that we don't usually get to run our hands over the surfaces of paintings and sculptures.

We don't need to fear new media: people won't stop going to museums because they've got Microsoft's gallery at home. On the contrary, it's now clear that people who rent and record films on video are also the keenest cinema-goers, and that home tapers are also the biggest record buyers.

The curation of electronic media arts is of abiding importance to museum culture and art education. Here, faced with the unique opportunity to witness how a new medium comes into being (and of intervening in its development), we have some of the keenest and most passionate minds of the generation that grew up with video and digital media working through, as critically and aesthetically as any other artists, the issues raised by, among other things, interactivity and networked communications. We have an enormous amount to learn, both from them and from the mistakes they're making on our behalf.

Education, after all, is not just about what we can teach: it is about what we, as well as our students, can learn together.

Pirates in the museum:
new strategies for fine art

JILL MORGAN

Head of Fine Art, Leeds Metropolitan University

I talk to you today as someone who has worked in an art gallery outside London, and whose views and perspectives were nurtured through the debates and ideas of the early 1980s. For many of us working with artists on new strategies for contemporary practice in galleries outside London, changes in the rules rendered new initiatives impossible. We watched as public funding was rerouted and recentralised to the South Bank to fund touring exhibitions organised by a curatorial quango. Fear entered the picture and curators were under pressure to conform to the new cultural dictates. We are now invited to participate, rather than taking our own regional initiatives – which were often radically conceived in collaboration with artists and educators and very often with local people – to those guardians of funding.

Means of Escape

The overriding theme in the work of Lubaina Himid in 1989 was the liberation of the black object from the white museum, an idea that is going to grow increasingly real for Western scholarship as people in the rest of the world begin to demand the return of their own cultural artefacts from the stockpiles of European and American museums. It is very uncomfortable for the curator – the *keeper*, to think about this notion of the imprisonment and liberation of the object – to concede that perhaps a Ming vase would be better off in the heart of the battle in Tiananmen Square than on the Duke of Westminster's mantelpiece. This brings us to a key question: who decided that art is made to be saved or preserved for perpetuity, particularly the outrageously beautiful artefacts made for the privileged class in the face of inequality, poverty and oppression?

Are we then discomforted enough by the secret histories of the museum to become cultural iconoclasts, like the early nineteenth-century masked Luddites in Rochdale, who swept through the industrial valleys breaking up or threatening to destroy the wool-spinning and winding machines that were putting them out of work, cutting their wages and forcing them into conditions of slave labour and starvation? In a powerful political irony, the tools the Luddites carried, their rakes, spades, hammers and scythes, which became their symbols in the violent struggle against industrialisation, are now mutely present in the museum, lying next to the fragments of the 1830s machines they destroyed. Not many of these implements exist in the museum, because they were used for a lifetime. One spinning wheel, one table, two linen chests, one stool, one bread crock, one spade: inventories of the possessions of yeoman families are a testament to the value of objects in the struggles of people during the Industrial Revolution.

Testimony, rewriting of history, re-memory: those of us marginalised by the dominant culture and history can, through a process of rediscovery and reworking of the meaning of cultural objects, recover our memories, and therefore our place, power, and traditions in the human cultural experience. One could even manage to recover Joseph Beuys from his tradition.

Within this discipline, the reclaiming of objects hidden within the museum is essential, and to allow this to happen we need an approach to curatorship that is focused on access, sharing knowledge, questioning truth and concepts of history, which I would say are all equally important issues for students of art.

In looking at history, it's interesting, and absolutely vital, to challenge and to contradict, through a number of strategies, that which tends to represent itself unilaterally as incontestable law – either the laws of history, the laws of modernism, or now the laws, or lawlessness, of postmodernism. These certitudes are negated by the articulation of new cultural demands, leanings and strategies in the political present. The enunciation of cultural difference problematises the division of past and present at the level of cultural representation and its authoritative address.

The notion or rewriting history can be clearly seen in specific reference to the short work by Virginia Woolf, *A Room of One's Own* (1929), based around the construction of Shakespeare's sister. This rewriting of history and its radical consequences has been discussed usefully by Tony McGleskie. In the very act of appearing to celebrate the omnipotence of patriarchal authority, Woolf undermines it by claiming prior authority to fiction: her own. She reveals the fictiveness and hence arbitrariness of the patriarchal cultural tradition, i.e. that its authority relies on an artifice of the archaic, on representational strategies, on the guise of a 'pastness' that is not necessarily a faithful sign of historical memory, but a fictive force that gains power though iteration, history repeating itself inaccurately. Woolf stages a conflict with the past, complicating the notion of history and simultaneously demonstrating a commitment to its very absences. And we should restate the importance of looking within the visual culture at history, of radically questioning notions of time, of cultural certitude. We should investigate the transforming possibilities of alternative cultural demands. As Alice Walker has said, 'our mothers and grandmothers moved to music not yet written'.

Of course, romantic concepts of history, feminist as well as traditional ones, need to be approached with care, and I'd like to read a piece by Adrianne Rich, which I think in a sense of radical poetics explains some of the ideas that have continued to come to the surface during this presentation:

Heroines. Exceptional. Even deviant. You draw your long skirts across the nineteenth century. Your mind burns long after death, not like the harbour beacon, but like a pile of driftwood on the beach. You are spared illiteracy, death by pneumonia, teeth which leave the gums, the seamstress's clouded eyes, the mill girl's shortening breath, by a collection of circumstances soon to be known as class privilege. The law says you can possess nothing in a world where property is everything. You belong first to your father, then to him who chooses you. If you fail to marry, you are without recourse, unable to earn a working man's salary, forbidden to vote, forbidden to speak in public. If married, you are legally dead.

The law says you may not bequeath property, save to your children, or male kin, that your husband has the right of a slave holder to hunt down and repossess you should you escape. You may inherit slaves, but have no power to free them. Your skin is fair. You have been taught that light came to the dark continent with white power, that the Indians live in filth and occult animal rites. Your mother wore corsets to choke her spirit, which if you refuse, you are jeered for refusing. You have heard many sermons and have carried your own interpretations locked in your heart. You are a woman strong in health through a collection of circumstances, soon to be known as class privilege, which if you break the social compact you lose outright.

When you open your mouth in public, human excrement is flung at you. You are exceptional in personal circumstance, in indignation. You give up believing in protection, in scripture, in man-made laws. Respectable as you look, you are an outlaw. Your mind burns, not like the harbour beacon, but like a fire of fierce origin. You begin speaking out and a great gust of freedom rushes in with your words, yet you still speak in a shattered language of a partial vision. You draw your long skirts, deviant, across the nineteenth century, registering injustice, failing to make it whole. How can I fail to love your clarity? How can I give you all your due? Take courage from your courage. Honour your exact legacy as it is, recognising as well that it is not enough.

Critically re-examining the role of the museum and the possibilities of contemporary practice has been a continuing project. And as Jane Beckett comments, these institutional spaces and master narratives appear to control our cultural knowledge. Establishments that can invest in the long-term view see feminist interventions as minor interruptions. However, she suggests that women have taken up different spaces such as the transient wing museum, which challenge our very notions of what an institution is. Even by taking up spaces within existing institutions, she sees a transformation as possible. We establish new sites, disrupt old meanings, and thus make new spaces.

Echo

In 1991, the artist Maud Sulter was invited to select works from the collection of the Tate Gallery to be shown at Tate Gallery Liverpool alongside her exhibition *Hysteria*, which represented the work she had completed as Artist-in-Residence in Liverpool. The exhibition, *Echo: Women Artists from the Tate Gallery, 1850–1940*, represented the first real opportunity to review and critically consider historic work by women artists in our major national collection of twentieth-century art. The exhibition did not tour to London. In the introduction to the catalogue, Nicholas Serota, Director of the Tate Gallery, and Lewis Biggs, Curator of Tate Gallery Liverpool, wrote:

A collection is a history of sorts, partial and provisional. The Tate Gallery's collections of British and modern art have been acquired for the nation over the last hundred years and continue to grow. Maud Sulter has drawn attention to the absences as well as the presences within the collections. Her enterprise will generate further research and debate into the cultural values which underwrite these works and the strategies behind them. Scholars and art lovers will find familiar and less familiar paintings enriched with new meaning and value.

It would be nice to see, some four years later, the evidence of progress beyond these declared intentions about this kind of exhibition. And I wish I could be more positive about the 'golden opportunity' of the Tate Gallery of Modern Art. In their Conclusion in *Old Mistresses: Women, Art and Ideology* (1981) Rozsika Parker and Griselda Pollock stated:

> Women's practice in art has never been absolutely forbidden, discouraged or refused, but rather contained and limited to its function as the means by which masculinity gains and sustains its supremacy in the important sphere of cultural production.
>
> The mapping out of a new framework and our revisions are relevant to both feminist historians and artists. We must understand the historical process and practices that have determined the current situation of women artists if we are to confront the role of cultural production and representations in the systems of sexual domination and power.

And this contestation remains true. Within the *Echo* catalogue is an illustration of a tiny watercolour by Georgina Macdonald entitled *Dead Bird* (1857), 'presented by Mrs J.W. Mackail 1938'. It's interesting to note that the vast majority of women's work in the Tate Collection was in fact bequeathed during the 1920s and 1930s, at a time when the Trustees were more polite about receiving often unwanted gifts. When work by women is in the Collection it is largely there because it was given rather than purchased or acquired. The accompanying catalogue entry reads:

Georgina Macdonald 1840–1920

Georgina Macdonald, the fifth of eleven children, was born into a Methodist family. She attended drawing classes at the School of Design in South Kensington, London and shared, with Emily Seddon, private classes with Ford Maddox Brown, where they painted from a model. These classes came to an end in 1858 when she took time out to care for a sick sister's child.

  She was courted by Ned Jones (later Edward Burne-Jones, Baronet) from 1856 – she was fifteen and he twenty-two – until 1860 when they married. Her artistic career continued to be interrupted, by motherhood, her husband's career, and the complicated web of the Pre-Raphaelite Group's affairs and intrigues. She did however carry out various craft projects with Jane Morris.

  Later she became active in radical politics. In particular she campaigned to establish the South London Art Gallery in Southwark, making art accessible by allowing free admission. The Gallery, still committed to these principles, remains active today, and has recently celebrated its centenary.

The ordering of information and collecting of items based around notions of Victorian taxonomy brings me to a little article, 'Whiskered Bat', which I saw in the *Glasgow Museum and Galleries Preview* magazine:

> An interesting new addition to the Collection is a juvenile female whiskered bat, *myotis mysteceni*. It was found alive in Blanefield, north of Glasgow, by a member of the Central Scotland Bat Group. Unfortunately, it died the following day and was passed on to the museum. The Whiskered Bat is rare in Scotland, with fewer than ten recorded sightings since 1980. It is from the most northerly known locality for the species in Britain, and may be the first Scottish Whiskered Bat ever photographed. Only four species of bats are commonly found in Scotland: Pipistrelle, Brown Long-Eared, Dorbintons and Nutterers, but several others are now turning up, thanks to the work being done by local bat groups. The Whiskered Bat may be more widely distributed than previously thought. If anyone knows [– and here comes the rub –] of the existence of any bat roosts, Richard Sutcliffe at the Art Gallery and Museum, Kelvingrove, would like to hear from you.

A small bat, netted for inanimate conservation in the aspic jar of the twenty-first century. Her prompt expiry followed the political resistance of the working class, the concept of non-participation in life itself, taking Baudrillard's doctrine of the resistance of the masses in the face of cultural manipulation to its natural extreme. To die, to survive. And now she is no doubt pinned up in a trendy conservation display, frozen wings and those ears that have heard messages from afar for ever pinned wide open, listening. Why should the Whiskered Bat with her radar ears echo my concerns about the European museum?

The project is to challenge and change the canon of the museum. A way forward in the liberation of objects into meaning and into language, is to look at the cultural interventions of artists of colour, often those living through border politics where they have been subject to colonising powers, have fought for territory and identity and are on the edge of negotiation for land, human rights, political and cultural change.

In the exhibition *Sin Frontera*, held at the Cornerhouse Gallery in Manchester in 1993, Mexican-American artists made a series of works that presented personal museums of the political and social world, a gathering of objects, some created, some found and collected or passed on, referring to domestic altars, private and public spaces. The artist Domania Baines discussed ideas of cultural identity, narrative and domestic space. The need to circumscribe space in the community is a driving force in the work of women artists, who for example, use neighbourhood walls for their murals. Another kind of reappropriation of territory is found in works that spring from a domestic space. The day-to-day experience of working-class Mexican-Americans circumscribes space within the domestic sphere, through home embellishments, altars, healing traditions and personal feminine styles. The phenomenon of the home altar is perhaps the most prevalent. Like the family life of women, the box form occupies space. Feminist life seeks to gather encircled by interlinked and therefore circumscribed site, location and 'activity'. In this sense, box art and installation work break feminine space and refashion domestic enclosures.

The result of the discourses around practice, gallery site and art education in the 1980s was the setting up of new gallery spaces located in art schools, universities, artists' studios. The potential for these sites to extend the debate around practice, site and audience seemed rich, and furthermore less subject to the increasing central control. However, we now see significant problems with the role of these spaces, trying to compete in the market economy of new universities, striving to meet the new Arts Council's South Bank orthodoxy and beset by the internal conflict directly caused by the Unit 67 research programme. While the advantages of acknowledging the research practice of artists are clear, the effect of Unit 67 is to drive the research direction toward a scramble for points, a commodification of ideas and of issue-based practice. Galleries will become caught up in ratings wars.

How do we avoid polarisation and division and work together academically, politically, in practice and education, recognising our differences, respecting our multiple and connected histories and thereby recovering meaning and the possibilities of art? We may yet see the turning of the tide.

Chair's summing up

CHRISTOPHER FRAYLING

Pro-Rector, Royal College of Art, London

I'll start with some general points before going on to talk about the individual papers. The day centred on the interface between contemporary artists and the museum, rather than the interface between the curriculum and museum (although we came nearer to this aspect in the discussions as the day progressed). It also focused on what exactly the function of the museum is – a store of exemplars, a repository of values, a treasure-house, a source of visual stimuli, or what? There were different and rival expectations from the contemporary artists and the museum, and rival stereotypes to some extent. I think that the biggest polarity of the day was between Jill Morgan's Ming vase and Bill Furlong's audio tapes as images of this problem.

Events versus things was an issue that came up, certainly in the two discussions. The question of whether museums should document or select emerged in both discussions. Should art schools teach more about presentation, and, indeed, curation? We had a spectrum of suggestions for interventions by artists in museums. The facsimile versus the real object was touched upon. The gallery and the museum were discussed as different places generating different expectations. Great expectations of Bankside were expressed, which the Tate must find scary, but which makes this an interesting moment to be having the conference.

The perceived disjunction between the aims of the museum and the aspirations of young artists is clearly a key issue. I thought that the changing relationship between the past and the present in a postmodern era would come up more, though it did come up: we have a different attitude to history and therefore a different attitude to the museum as material. What also came up was the fact that, in a very good phrase, museums of art are really 'museums of gallery art'.

We heard about practices that go on outside the gallery, which I think was important from a curricular point of view, because, as we know, so many students are interested in the non-traditional media. There was not much on education, except in the discussions.

Victoria Miro talked about some members of the emerging generation of young artists and how they're beating at the door; a further sense of great expectations. In another nice phrase, she quoted an artist who said that the museum has to 'bear a lot of guilt'. I must say, if some of the expectations that have been piled on museums in the course of the day actually came true, they'd bear a lot of guilt because they'd be turning away an awful lot of people.

She cited a very interesting phrase from Susan Sontag, which identified museums as embodying an 'idea of seriousness'. I do think that is a very important phrase. Clearly, in the past the museum has often been interpreted as a repository of rules, or given some kind of prescriptive role. But there is another kind of seriousness: the scholarship and diligent work of curators. This recalls a remark by Tom Crowe of Sussex, at the recent

Association of Art Historians' conference: 'give me a catalogue raisonné by a very careful scholar in place of ten volumes of cultural theory' he said; this was his interpretation of the idea of seriousness. And I think that's very important, whether we agree with him or not.

Above all, Victoria asked the question, how do we build bridges between members of the emerging generation and museums? How can they transgress? There's a lot of transgression going on as the clock ticks away to the millennium. Can they transgress in museums, please? And where can you put a 'scatological aesthetic for the tired of seeing'? Is there a role for that in museums as well?

Victoria finished on the thought that a collection ought to be like a torpedo: it leaves a trace behind it, but it has a warhead on the front. That came up once or twice later, not as an image, but as an idea.

Bill Furlong made a plea for temporary exhibitions, artists' spaces in galleries and a flexibility that sometimes permanent collections, because they *are* collections, are unable to offer; a space, as he put it, where students can interact with their own times.

What about events as opposed to collectibles? This is a key issue, because it is so important in art education. Sound pieces, time-based work, performance, installation: these, he said, had been rendered invisible by the national, and to some extent regional, galleries, partly because – and I've never really heard this thesis before – of the fashion for figurative work following *The New Spirit in Painting*, which everyone latched on to because they were collectibles, and which blotted out that other history.

Sutapa Biswas took us through a case study of an 'inclusive history'. This was a phrase that came up later, and we were encouraged to use it. She described a group of artists of mixed ability and race, working together on an autobiographical project in what seems to have been a very understanding gallery in Canada. It was a case-study of the sort of things that people hoped would happen more in the future: a collective show, a political show, a show that questioned assumptions about who's in and who's out in the very gallery in which it was situated. And that boiled it down to practicalities.

Colin Wiggins planted a bombshell – talking about Poussin as a much greater artist than Rebecca Horn. Interestingly, when we had a conference on values in art, I think it was three years ago, everyone felt deeply uncomfortable about talking about values of any kind; but he was absolutely right to raise it. And he tried to exorcise the concept of 'tradition', saying we shouldn't tell our students it's boring, and indeed we shouldn't teach history in a linear way based on the Vasari model; we should look rather at tradition as a series of breakthroughs and revolutions, and then history might be a bit more interesting. He took us from Rembrandt to Reynolds to Joseph Beuys – whom you might call the Artist who Mistook his Calling for A Hat. And he finished on the thought that living artists can, not must – although the word 'must' was used with reference to students – *can* use museums, and should do so more; they shouldn't be so scared of them because actually museum people are quite nice, welcoming people. It's just that perhaps we don't ask enough, which I thought was a useful observation.

Sean Cubitt talked about the acceleration of architecture with the acceleration of culture generally, and the impact of electronic culture, which he interpreted as a whole way of life. And – if I understood him correctly – how the culture of art is not as far removed from the virtual world of digital technology as we sometimes think. This is very often presented as a polarity between 'facsimiles' and 'things with auras'. The distinction was broken down in his presentation, although there were some irreducible aspects of the art object, such as texture, which can never be reproduced by a CD-ROM.

Jill Morgan gave us what she called an exercise in radical poetics from a feminist point of view, and took us from the Antiques Roadshow to the Internet and beyond. She talked of how the Victorian heritage has cast a baleful shadow over museums, weighed down as they are by basements and reserve collections. She said that museums and galleries were places where one wanted to be able to talk, understand, interact and converse, not wander round in hushed silence as if one is in a mausoleum. She also claimed that they're too obsessed with aesthetics, methods of production, and above all with mapping, with categorising people and artists in boxes, which puts young people off and is patriarchal to boot. Why, Jill asks, in the most radical statement of the day, should outrageously beautiful objects be preserved at all? And there's logic here, after all, for they embody the social and economic rules of yesterday. Why is it that we value them so much? And it seemed to me that that's about as far as one can go, theoretically, without advocating the blowing up of museums completely – which is, of course, what some artists may wish! Jill finished by throwing down that gauntlet: what sort of strategies can one have to disrupt, to intervene, to redefine, to get rid of the maps and basically to break the flow of museums and make them question their own assumptions?

I'd like to end with the quote from Fred Wilson that Sutapa Biswas cited in her paper: the concept of 'mining the museum'. I like this idea very much: that you can think of the museum as a gold-mine, a treasure-house – as a lock-up for very expensive things, where basically the role of the museum is to conserve them. You can also think of the museum as a land-mine, which I think, was edging towards Jill's idea. But you can also think about making it 'mine' and Sutapa's case study was intended to show that happening. It seems to me that for teachers, the challenge is a two-way process: to make young artists think of museums as places where they feel at home, but equally to make museums places where young artists *will* feel at home. Making the museum a place to dig seems to me to be the punchline.

What Art School Did and Didn't Do for Me

Introductory address

ANDREW BRIGHTON

Head of Public Events, Tate Gallery, London

This is the sixth conference on which the Tate Gallery has collaborated with Wimbledon School of Art, and the reason we do it is because they're extremely good to work
with. The other reason why we do these conferences is because of you. To put it in a
slightly jocular form, if a bomb were to be dropped in this room, there would be an awful
lot of important jobs going in art schools throughout the country! I venture no view as
to whether that would be a good or bad thing. In other words, it is very important for us
to have this event, which sees so many distinguished members of the fine art academic
community gathered together to discuss issues that concern us all. I would hope very
much that we can be some kind of clearing house for ideas and events that concern art
schools, and of course, deal with the ramifications of issues around art.

Welcome

COLIN PAINTER

Principal, Wimbledon School of Art

It is important that to say that the themes for these conferences have always grown out of collective concerns at Wimbledon, which we feel are a kind of touchstone for issues of fine art education in general. About two years ago, we ran a conference called 'Essential Ingredients of the Fine Art Curriculum'. We tried to create a situation in which people would put themselves on the line about what students should do on fine art courses. It was not an unsuccessful event, but we didn't actually come away with a list of essential ingredients.

One of the characteristics of fine art education over recent years has been the lack of desire to prescribe what should and should not be done; in the days of the CNEA, we used to have the opportunity to see more fine art curricula presented and shared. Those days were largely characterised by an attempt to create an environment in which people could develop, rather than prescribing a curriculum – dare I say it, a syllabus? – which students should actually address and undertake. In a sense, today's conference comes at the issue from a different direction, through the back door if you like. While people may feel diffident about being prescriptive, we hope that they will be more relaxed when put in a position in which they're simply discussing in a critical way the experiences they had in art school: saying which ingredients were positive, which were negative and which were absent. We have adopted a slightly different format from previous years, when we had half a dozen speakers more or less delivering papers. Today, we have mixed approaches, and, in particular, we're using conversational formats or interviews. So having thanked everybody, it remains for me hand over to Christopher Frayling.

Chair's introduction

Christopher Frayling

Pro-Rector, Royal College of Art, London

This series of conferences dealing with the relationship between fine art and education is unique. Over the years, the series has dealt with many different aspects of the relationship: the practitioner as teacher, the learning of drawing, the establishment of standards – that was quite a hairy one! – the fine art curriculum, and today, what art school did and didn't do for me. That's not '*to* me', that's '*for* me'. But I expect we'll also hear quite a lot about what it did '*to* me'!

Instead of a neat series of six formal presentations followed by discussions, we have two papers and three interviews with artists – three autobiographical reminiscences of the experience of art school in interview form.

When Paul Hetherington sent the title to me a month or two ago, given the pressure on resources in art schools at the moment and the expansion of student numbers, I immediately had a mental image of a Victorian painting showing a young student before a severe-looking group of academic auditors in top hats saying, 'And when did you last see your tutor?' There may be a discussion on that as well.

A few years ago, in 1987, when I was researching my 150-year history of the Royal College of Art, I asked quite a number of professional artists and designers of various age groups what the college experience meant to them; people who had been there between the late 1920s and the mid-1980s. (Not consecutively, you understand – various generations who were there between those dates.) Their replies were interesting. Some, sad to report, said the college experience meant very little, and bristled when I asked, as if the admission that it had taught them anything would in some way diminish them as artists and designers; as if it were an admission of direct influence. Even talking about it seemed to dent their self-image. And some became quite aggressive: 'Of course it didn't do any good, my genius sprang Minerva-like out of my head.' I found that a very interesting response: in fact, it was the majority response among well-known artists. They would perhaps have agreed with Courbet when he wrote in response to being asked his views on the value of the Academy: 'I deny that art can be taught, or in other words maintain that art is completely individual and that the talent of each artist is but the result of his own inspiration and his own chosen study of past tradition.' So there is the 'Courbet tendency'.

Others said there were moments or experiences that hadn't seemed much at the time, but in retrospect took on a much larger significance: individual lectures, images, comments, people. They said that at the time they didn't appreciate the experience, but as they grew older they valued these moments more and more. Others stressed the social value of the experiences, the network of people into which they were launched, the entrée into the world of artists and galleries and critics, and one called his time 'pre-professional training'; an experience of socialisation as much as education. Others found nourishment in particular theoretical perspectives that they were offered at college, which sometimes seemed like a bore at the time but in retrospect had become part of a survival kit.

Others still – and this was the second biggest group – stressed that college provided something to fight against, a way of defining oneself in opposition to what was on offer. They would perhaps have agreed with Géricault – this is the 'Géricault tendency' – when he wrote, 'It is obstacles which incite genius. Opportunity spells mediocrity. Neither Athens nor Rome needed it'. Surprisingly few could pinpoint any specific skills or techniques. Now this goes back to what was said about our difficulties in discussing the fine art curriculum: very few could pinpoint any specific skills or techniques they could admit to having learnt. They preferred to talk of studio space, being left alone, having access to resources, and generally self-help. Mention of John Constable's famous line, 'Any artist who claims to be self-taught is taught by a very ignorant person indeed', was almost invariably a conversation stopper.

These were all ex-postgraduate students and many of them dated from a period (the 1950s and 1960s), when undergraduate courses were said to equal diagnosis and skills, and postgraduate courses were said to be finding your voice. So you'd expect a particular take on this issue. Nevertheless, I think it would be interesting to compare their comments with an equivalent range of traditional university students. My sense is that the university students would tend to be much more misty-eyed in retrospect about their college days, rather than hard-nosed, or even dismissive.

Has anyone here, I wonder, tried to put together a group of college alumni or ex-students from an art school? I have, on various occasions, and it's almost impossible. When they do meet, it's rather like Tony Hancock's regimental reunion. There's a lot of looking at the floor and paper-shuffling. Alumni associations in traditional universities, however, here and especially in the States, are large, well-organised and economically significant; they contribute to appeals and play a key part in nourishing college culture. With artists and designers, I've found, two is very often a crowd. Maybe it has something to do with the romantic self-image of the artist, whom, as I say, is Minerva-like, and as we know, refuses to belong to any club that will accept him or her as a member. Maybe it also has something to do with class. I think this could be important. Alumni associations are perceived to be very middle-class, the educational equivalent of dinner-dances. But I suspect it goes a little bit deeper than this. The attitude of artists and designers to their art schools, is often not about education, but about having been in an environment, having been in a greenhouse for a certain moment in their lives, and then growing out of it.

As I say, it's quite difficult to find a positive comment, looking through all these files of famous artists, of exactly what their experience of college was. Of course, perceptions of art schools are related to what the schools have set out to achieve. This has shifted dramatically over the years. A huge exhibition on *150 Years of Royal College Design* opens at the Royal College very shortly: what has come over very strongly in preparing that show is just how radically the philosophy of art education has changed in a century and a half. In Victorian times, the summit of everyone's ambition was to make things well, preferably designed by one's tutor. In the inter-war years, it was to absorb the first delayed waves of modernism, well, Cézanne anyway. So, you look at different moments in art education and you get a completely different atmosphere. Clearly people's perceptions relate to the prevailing atmosphere at the time they were at college.

The scale of art education has of course expanded beyond all recognition. When the Royal College opened in 1837, there were sixteen students. Their average age was about thirteen. If you add together all the graduates in England and America from the art and design education sectors in a single year, it comes to more than the population of Florence in the Renaissance. So the scale has been changed somewhat.

Going through the files and accentuating the positive, I found a paragraph about art education that in my view is the best riposte I've ever read to the claim that 'I went to art school to be self-taught'. It was written by a man called William Cory in 1891, who was a bit of a historian, an ex-schoolmaster and a sometime art teacher. He was, to be sure, writing about a certain kind of education, in a certain kind of society at a certain moment in history, a hundred years ago, but his reflections are not without relevance to today's event. He wrote:

> At college you are engaged, not so much in acquiring knowledge, as in making efforts under criticism. A certain amount of knowledge you can indeed, with average faculties, acquire so as to retain. Nor need you regret the hours you spend on much that is forgotten, for the shadow of lost knowledge at least protects you from any illusions. But you go to a great college, not so much for knowledge as for arts and habits; for the habit of attention, for the art of expression, for the art of assuming at a moment's notice a new intellectual position, for the art of entering quickly into another person's thoughts, for the habit of submitting to reputation, for the art of indicating assent or dissent in graduated terms, for the habit of regarding minute points of accuracy, for the art of working out what is possible in a given time, for discrimination, for mental courage, and for mental soberness. And above all, you go to a great college for self-knowledge.

Now it sounds idealistic, of course. Words like 'soberness', 'discrimination', 'minute points of accuracy' have that ring of late-Victorian times. But I love that line, 'above all, you go to a great college for self-knowledge'. It's idealistic, but it's a terrific description of a creative environment where what's learned, what's digested, is, if anything, much more important to the individual than what's taught; another distinction that I think we might find of value.

A peculiarity of constitution or temperament

Stephen Farthing

The Ruskin Master, The Ruskin School of Art, Oxford

As a student, thinking that being an artist was all about idiosyncrasy conditioned by received opinion and fashion which was then embodied in a lifestyle, it seemed logical to start by identifying the artist that I could share a liking for with my peer group and teachers. Then, by watching and talking and looking at their work, and perhaps gradually acquiring skills, confidence and knowledge, I would become an artist. This places me as a kind of shadow apprentice and suggests an uncomfortable relationship between ideas about the self and received ideas of what an artist might be.

Now, putting to one side the problems of what was or was not on the curriculum, it is a problem for would-be artists, of how much of yourself you need to expose, and how much of your role models you need to mix in, in order to serve yourself up as an artist. That is, an artist who is both acceptable and radical.

Now, this case study of an artist is told in words that describe a film, the story of an artist's career, an artist who was in fact self-taught, and who worked in an art school without walls, a sort of Malrauxian art school.

Journey 6,833 starts on a suburban railway platform located nineteen minutes to the south of London. A bowler-hatted traveller immediately marks himself out from his fellow commuters by adopting a novel approach to boarding the 8.32 to Waterloo. He crosses the packed station to the empty downline platform and enters the 8.32 by walking through the downline train, which is empty and has just pulled in on the adjacent track, and settles himself into an empty carriage whilst his fellow travellers enter via the more conventional route. Throughout the journey, his silent thoughts in the form of value judgements on his fellow travellers are shared with us, the audience.

In the next scene, our hero is pictured at his place of work, an open-plan *Metropolis* office. This *Modern Times* office offers a valuable insight into both his lifestyle and his sense of order. The camera moves us away from the regular pattern made by the rows of clerks sitting at their identical desks and lingers on a perfect row of bowler hats hung on cloakroom hooks. On each of these hooks also hang, at about 300 degrees from the vertical because of the asymmetry of their handles, a row of tightly rolled umbrellas. This symmetry is disrupted by one umbrella, which is hung in the mirror direction, so that the pattern is corrupted and the two parallel diagonals become a V. On passing, the office supervisor corrects the deviant motif and with a filmic glance and reaction shot, the culprit, its author, is identified. It is of course our commuter and hero.

It must be clear by now, that our hero is something of a rebel, or in 1950s-speak, a kind of angry young man. On his return journey that evening, he almost skips from the railway station to his suburban lodgings. It is clear that he is elated to be returning from work. Without time to acknowledge his landlady, he dives into his room, whips off his suit and replaces it with a paint-splattered smock and beret. He then throws open the door to his back bedroom and reveals an artist's studio. In the centre is a massive part-finished post-Cubist, sub-Picasso stone carving of a woman. As he sets about reshaping the face with a mason's hammer and chisel, from the top of a stepladder, we learn that *Aphrodite at the Waterhole* has been carved in secrecy from blocks of stone smuggled into his lodgings by night. But the suspicious tap, tap, tap of steel on stone finally boosts his landlady's curiosity to a pitch with which she can no longer live. She bursts into his room and stumbles upon something far more shocking than a tenant carrying out unauthorised building works. What she sees is *Aphrodite at the Waterhole*. And what follows is an amusing but clichéd exchange between the landlady and her artist lodger.

In order to explain Aphrodite's presence to this landlady, the artist immediately goes on the defensive. 'It's not doing any harm. It's a work of art', he explains. The angry landlady then turns her attention to one of his paintings, a modernist picture of birds. This time, in defence, our artist titles the picture as a way of explaining its existence: 'I call that *Ducks in Flight*'. Quick as a flash, the landlady doubles the attack, 'I've never seen beetroot-coloured ducks before'. In desperation, the artist explains something of the making process, 'They fly at a fair lick, those ducks. They're up and out of the water and away. You just have to whack on whatever colour you've got on the brush at the time'. Desperately in need of praise, exhausted by this unwanted criticism, and depressed by the lack of understanding, we cut to a coffee bar to consider the situation and catch our breath. Unable to purchase his favourite beverage, a cup of tea, he settles for a cappuccino with no froth, and a soliloquy: 'What a life. Where does an artist like me go to get accepted? There must be somewhere. Wait a minute. Where did the others go? Rembrandt, Gauguin, Vermeer and all that mob? Where did they go to get appreciated?' His eyes fall on a poster of the Eiffel Tower. 'That's it. Paris!'

A steam-train whistles its way through Kent. The camera switches from an interior shot of the rebel dressed in a dark suit in the dining car to an open truck containing his crated worldly goods, just in time to see Aphrodite, whom he's decided to take along with him as a calling card, decapitated by a passing bridge.

It is at this point that the audience's imagination goes into overdrive. We've been introduced to a maker of modern art, his thoughts on painting duck have given us some feel of his understanding of the relationship between chance and order, and we realise that the suburbs of south London do not provide a sufficiently developed critical platform for an artist to thrive. But, could it be that this yet undiscovered and unproven talent will have a chance of critical acclaim in Paris as a result of the chance decapitation? Or has a masterpiece been destroyed? We're not left to play with this question for long. In the next scene, whilst being loaded aboard a cross-channel ferry, the decapitated Aphrodite slips through the bottom of a cargo net and disappears into Dover Harbour.

For the first time, a sadness falls over the audience. Not so much for the loss of the object, but for the loss of a chance. Our imagination has leapt ahead, taken us beyond the quality of the object that we believe the rebel really is able the achieve, and tried to embrace the accident as a way forward. In fact, I suspect we believe in the ability of chance to add value to his work more than we did in his traditional skills. Without Aphrodite, he seems lost. All he has left are his wits and ambition. As the ferry pulls away towards France, the rebel throws his bowler hat and umbrella from the stern into the wake that drags back to Dover. In Calais it is pouring with rain, and as the English disembark in files with their hats and umbrellas, the drenched rebel, now dressed in a jumper and a beret, sets about hitching to Paris.

At an artists' café, amongst the gingham tablecloths and the grey smoke from black tobacco, our hero introduces himself as Anthony Hancock. When he chances upon another English artist, Paul Ashby, he quizzes Paul on what really makes him click as an artist. They swap notes about how they make pictures. Anthony says, when asked if he has any work with him, 'I'll paint one tomorrow. Once I get an inspiration I'm away. I once had a canvas fifteen by eight, filled in, framed and flogged before the first dab of paint dried'. Paul says, 'It's quite different for me. With me, every brushstroke is torn out of my body'. Then he rather thoughtfully adds, 'Your work. Was it misunderstood?' Anthony's reply: 'No. They just came straight out with it. They said it was a load of rubbish'.

Now, in his early days, Anthony Hancock was ever-flexible in his ideology. In conversations with other artists he was intelligently hungry to accommodate the new. As a complete naive, he brought freshness to the scene. His simplicity was irreproachable. In fact, he soon had a cult following of action painters and Existentialists and was personally deeply involved in a kind of Conceptual art.

Later in the film, a tutorial takes place between Anthony and his new friend Paul Ashby. It's one of those no-holds-barred tutorials, where standing in front of a large life-study in monochrome, Anthony identifies a small area of paint in the middle of the picture with an authoritative index finger and declares, 'That's where the picture is, there!' He totally ignores the carefully painted figure, which is the point and the subject of the painting in the artist's mind.

The tutorial is over when Paul exclaims, 'That is incredible. An entirely new concept of art!' Anthony is delighted to have helped a fellow artist reorientate his theoretical base, and shortly afterwards Paul introduces Anthony to the avant-garde art scene in Paris, which he takes to like a duck to water. He is particularly charmed by Chelsea, a beautiful Existentialist with a black jumper and blue lipstick. He becomes a regular visitor to her parties and joins the cultural hub of the Paris scene. In her company, he discovers action painting and fearlessly contributes to the intellectual artistic community. 'When I paint a chair', he says, 'it isn't a chair that I actually paint. I try and get inside the chair and paint what can't be seen'. As he gets the measure of this kind of explanation, he dispenses with the easel and begins to use his whole body as a brush. His success drives his friend Paul, a more conventional artist, back to England, and it also attracts a very important art dealer, who introduces himself by saying, 'If I like your paintings, you're made. You've got nothing more to worry about'.

Anthony becomes a cigar-smoking success, changing his paint-splashed check shirt and jeans for a red waistcoat, beige suit and black fedora. Unfortunately, his success has been based on a misunderstanding over the authorship of his paintings, which are in fact, Paul's. So, finally our hero leaves Paris and flies back to England and suburbia.

In the final scene, he's back at his studio wearing a checked shirt and chipping away at version three of *Aphrodite at the Waterhole*. Not so much out in the cold but back in front of the gas fire.

The station, the studio, the artist, the umbrellas, Aphrodite falling into the harbour, the departure, the café, the criticism, the action painting, the dealer and the gallery: the story takes us stage by stage through the artist's self-directed learning programme, through a kind of art school without walls. He wears the right clothes, has the right studio, eventually the right friends and dealer. He's also blessed with bags of self-confidence, a survival instinct and an uncanny understanding of modern art and criticism, a kind of 1950s Damien Hirst. What's intriguing is why, with all these attributes, the rebel doesn't succeed as an artist. At the start of *The Story of Art*, Gombrich puts his trust in the notion that we don't really need to worry about what art is. We should only worry about who the artists are. I think that is probably the reason why Anthony Hancock did not succeed: he never was an artist. What he was, was a frustrated clerk and a bit of a rebel. And of course, as we know, rebels are rebels and very few of them are artists.

A short time ago, we invited Gregory Green to come to the Ruskin School in Oxford to talk to the students about his recent work, functional but non-operational nuclear devices, rockets, bombs and drug-making factories in tableau, and functional pirate radio and TV stations. He started his talk by setting out a programme, which he finalised by saying, 'Do interrupt at any point, I think I respond well to questions. But there's one question I won't answer: why is it art?' Janine Antoni, of chocolate fame and also currently showing at the Saatchi Gallery, also operates this principle of warm non-co-operation.

There's an illusion that contemporary art practice requires an increasingly controlled theoretical atmosphere for its making, exhibition and survival. But it seems to me that whether it's Janine Antoni or Damien Hirst who provide models for today's students, they present no greater or lesser theoretical problem, nor do they require substantially more theoretical support for their work to survive than the models that served me twenty-five years ago when I was a student at St Martins. These models were perhaps John Walker or Jim Dine.

I don't know what art school did for me or to me. Something I've thought about all the way through preparing this talk is what would have happened if I hadn't gone to the Royal College and I'd gone off to New York? A question I can never answer. In 1989 I was an external examiner at the art college in Dundee when one of a pair of twins exhibited her final work, the other one exhibiting identical work in Newcastle. I believe they ended up with the same result. What had art school done for them?

Art schools can provide an opportunity for would-be artists to try their hand at the act of creation. In most cases, this act is derived from a fairly cursory knowledge of history and an enormous appetite for contemporary practice. As time passes, the output of art schools may look different, and the way it's talked about may sound different. But I believe the essence of the experience today is exactly the same as the one I had twenty-five years ago. Art schools are rather like restaurants. There may be more of them now, the menus may have changed, as have the staff, the decor and the prices, but their primary function has remained the same: to feed.

Sarah Kent (art critic) in conversation with Jake and Dinos Chapman (artists)

SK: I have with me the brothers Jake and Dinos Chapman who, hopefully, need no introduction. They work together, which is an examiner's nightmare, and probably embody everything that art schools most fear and hate in their students. They also embody, I think, a paradox about art education. As an external examiner, I often find myself in argument with members of staff over what exactly it is that we are assessing. Is it people or products? Are we assessing studentship and the way that, in some sense, it mirrors teaching: a good student proves that good teaching is possible? Or are we measuring creativity and what the students produce? I remember a student who was the worst possible person to have in art school. He was never there, he didn't turn up for seminars, he didn't do any work, he was stroppy, difficult and so on. Then at the last minute, he produced an extraordinary body of work that deserved a First. Terrible arguments ensued with members of staff who, understandably, were irate at the notion that this person who, in every sense, had made a mockery of the establishment in which they worked, could be applauded for having behaved badly. This is one of the ironies of art school education; it raises the question of whether art schools are training good students or hoping to produce good artists. The two things are often not the same. First, lets tackle the issues of working together, acting as two people making one body of work. Jake and Dinos, you went to the Royal College of Art at the same time but you were in different departments. Did you start working together at the college?

JC: No, we began to work together about two years after we left college; but we were actively engaged in talking about each other's work, which was more interesting than the work itself. As a consequence, we decided to work together.

SK: So you didn't present the kind of problem I've described?

DC: Not that problem, no.

SK: What problems did you present, and what problems did you come up against at art school?

JC: Ignorance, trenchant thought, the claim that all criteria for judging works of art can be reduced to transcendent values, as the last speaker implied by citing Damien Hirst, as though the criteria for judging a Damien Hirst were the same as those for judging a Jackson Pollock. I'm not sure if that's true. For me, one of the interesting things about working in the Sculpture Department at the Royal College was that the ideological position of the college was written in wrought iron over the gates. I remember that, in the syllabus, the head of department wrote a description of his view of the course. It said, 'A sculptor is born, not made', which begged the question: if innate values determine how students 'evolve', then how does a tutor qualify to receive a pay cheque? The question seems to be avoided, repeatedly, yet it remains problematic for every member of staff at every college I've been to. In some senses, the experience of being at college became a dramatic game-playing about how the question was a problem, and various ways to make the staff earn their pay cheques.

SK: Did the staff that you came across earn their pay cheques?

DC: Generally not, though they thought they did. This form of teaching has been in place for such a long time that, rather than offering a set of variable attitudes, it has ossified into a procedure. I don't think we belong to the Courbet school of resentment; I don't think it's personal. The most interesting thing about being at art school was being introduced to that neurotic white unit.

SK: What neurotic white unit?

DC: One's little space.

SK: I thought you were describing a member of staff!

JC: No! Neurotic, white, middle-class units are slightly different! In colleges, you have strange territorial divisions, little spaces each occupied by a worker-being who is supposedly expressing some inner necessity. The problem is that if you have no inner necessity, you have no art practice, so you have deluded art students oscillating between psychosis and neurosis. Neurosis the week before a seminar and psychosis the day before, because of an inability to produce expressionistic evidence of inner necessity or angst. One of the funniest experiences was being led round the Royal College of Art, shown different spaces and told, 'This is where Tony Cragg worked, this is where Bill Woodrow worked', as though some trace of their angst might rub off. Luckily it didn't.

SK: Dinos, do you think that art schools should give students a hard time? Should they question them, challenge them, analyse their work, force them into a position where they become good at verbalising what they're doing? Or should they embrace them, help them, soften the blow? Do students want a confrontational or a nurturing situation?

DC: To make anything happen, I think it would have to be more confrontational. Being in the Painting Department of the Royal College was very strange; I never quite worked out why I was there. Occasionally, someone came round and suggested that you might work in a different medium, then wandered off when you refused. That doesn't seem very confrontational to me, or very 'nurturing'.

SK: Your remark implies that you were expecting somebody to explain why you were there, rather than having your own idea.

JC: It's not a question of explanation, but of encouraging speculation. We didn't think that art school was about being self-taught. But there are certain practices, certain discourses and conversations that are current and available and part of the business of thinking about making art, and these were absent, or even repressed, at art school.

DC: There was a feeling in both departments, I think, that everything that happened outside of those little beehive cells was irrelevant, that all you needed to do was to make sure that you were in there working and everything would be fine. There was a lot of talk about not worrying about what went on outside, when the one thing we really needed to worry about was what was happening outside!

SK: When you say 'what was happening outside', are you talking about other artists' work or what you need to do in order to function in relation to the art market, the art establishment and the whole circus?

DC: All those things. I was working for Gilbert and George at the same time as being a student, so I was splitting my time. And the most profitable time was when I wasn't at college; this manifestation of the outside world was quite powerful.

SK: You could argue that one of the most important things about art school is that it provides a cocoon, which gives you the time and space in which to explore ideas without having those pressures.

JC: That presupposes that you uphold the bourgeois values of artistic contemplation and appreciation. One of my experiences at art school was seeing a range of people from different backgrounds being able to cope with, and to articulate (or not), positions within art school. Without being too vulgar, it was class-based, gender-based and race-based.

SK: I'm not sure what point you're making.

JC: I'm saying that the idea, or the will, to become an artist (whatever that is) was not examined. It seems that you're propelled into some kind of presuppositional orbit – assuming, because as a human organism you're familiar with the idea of looking, that somehow looking is the only prerequisite needed for looking at art, and that other kinds of discourse are only complementary to the situation. Theory and practice are constantly divided.

SK: You must have had some kind of theoretical back-up to your practice.

DC: Not at college.

SK: No art history? No art theory?

DC: We used to talk at home and walking around the streets, but not at college. College seemed to be entirely practical. I think the idea of most college practice is that it offers technical assistance, helps you to make something. Prior to that process, there doesn't seem to be any involvement, no questioning about why you're making something.

SK: And those questions aren't asked in tutorials or seminar situations?

JC: Well, the art school is a microcosm of the wider critical situation. After you leave college, critical reactions to works of art are as uninteresting as critical responses at college. In some ways, that's because of a historical delineation between philosophical and aesthetic thought. It seems to me that if these two things are brought together and the separation between painting, sculpture and film is dissolved, which is the bias towards the modernist autonomy of materials, then things may become more interesting. I suspect that most people teaching in art schools now could simply not cope with that theoretical position. They would be inarticulate.

SK: One problem is that staff are being forced to decide between being artists or teachers; it's becoming more and more difficult to teach part-time, and full-time staff are required to take on so many hours of teaching that they have no time to pursue their own practice. The question that subtends this situation is whether it's possible to be a good teacher without being a good artist?

DC: Yes, definitely.

SK: So you don't think the problem is structural?

JC: No, it's an intellectual problem. We live in the grand old tradition of anti-intellectualism, which is responsible for the Hancockian anecdotes that we've heard today; the play of the bourgeois artists and the plebeian. If Hancock, the rebel, is the basis of a theoretical approach to a critique of art schools, it's soft, English post-structuralist discourse.

SK: Presumably, your criticisms are levelled mainly at MA courses?

JC: No. BA as well, and Foundation, primary school, infant school, the crèche – it's genetic.

DC: More is expected by a student entering an MA course than a BA course; you start a BA course when you're eighteen. There's also nothing coincidental about the fact that there are no students here today to represent their demands.

SK: This isn't a conference about student demands.

DC: Well, we're talking about the people who have views about how art schools should function.

SK: There are some students here.

JC: Yes, but are they going to come and speak?

SK: If you were setting up the ideal art school, how would you structure the course? Would you have structured courses?

DC: It would be like the Maze Block. I think that art can be taught by example. I'm constantly saying to people 'Go and work for somebody, for however long you can take it. Work for somebody you don't necessarily like; see someone in practice'. There are art schools and there are artists and it doesn't seem as though they're mixing, naturally anyway, so it's preferable to go and see the artist at work, rather than get him or her into college, because it's a different environment.

SK: There are enormous dangers, though, in the studio-based notion of teaching. I'm thinking, for instance, of the Slade, where there's still a Euston Road studio that churns out Euston Road painters year after year. Then there's the Joseph Beuys phenomenon, producing clones of the master. Do you think there's anything to be said for this system?

DC: Yes.

JC: Yes, no. I think it's dangerous. I wouldn't say that it was advisable, necessarily, to send students to work for artists because, in my experience, artists are as dumb as lecturers. But I think you have to find some way of addressing the notion that theory and practice are divorced, which seems to me to be absurd. To produce a work of art is to know how to produce a work of art; to know where the frame of a work of art exists; to know where the support for a work of art exists. These are conceptual concerns. You can't imagine someone stretching a canvas, attempting to paint on it and missing it.

SK: Jake, when you left the Royal College you went and studied European thought, didn't you? What kind of course was that?

JC: It was theoretical. It was about continental philosophy, which, ironically, excludes English thought; so it was European.

SK: What made you decide to do that?

JC: I would be reluctant to say lack, loss and melancholia, but, from my experience of being at art school, there was certainly a need to 'up the stakes', to raise questions about what was interesting about aesthetics.

SK: You felt you needed a theoretical base?

JC: No, I didn't see it like that. I don't think it's about base and superstructure or base and practice. I think the two are indissoluble; you can't take one from the other. So it wasn't that I needed to learn about Kant in order to sharpen a pencil correctly; it's not like that.

SK: I know it's difficult to talk about, but can you say how studying Kant, for instance, has or has not informed your work?

JC: If you think about looking at works of art, the experience of looking at a piece is not exclusive to the solitary viewer of that work. Their position in relation to the work is already presuppositional; concepts of beauty exist prior to our appreciation of it. When you view a work of art, Mr Kant is already there. It's not just a question of finding some theoretical explanation of the experience. When we look at a work of art, we project value onto it; we're involved in something that is historically grounded in a way that our experience is not necessarily conscious of. It's not just a question of finding a master text to explain works of art. It's a question of trying to examine the modes and conditions under which we look at, think about, and make works of art.

SK: In order to make a work of art, how necessary is it, though, to intellectualise or to be aware of the process?

JC: It's not necessary but, from my point of view, it makes things more interesting.

SK: How do these studies in European thought affect your contribution to the work?

JC: *He* studied American thought.

DC: Well, I'm doing my own studies as well. It's not that he's the brain and I'm the hands. We each do everything; we're symbiotic, like the Wilson twins.

SK: How much verbal dialogue is there when you're working?

DC: When we haven't got gas masks on, it's constant. Part of the process of our production is about ego conflict; it's about presenting ideas and being as adversarial to each other as possible. The work is a product of a chaotic kind of exchange.

SK: One of the things that strikes me is that you each had two-year foundation courses, then BA, then MA, without a break.

DC: I had an enormous break between BA and MA. I only went to the Royal College because everybody else around me decided to go, so I thought I'd join in.

SK: How many years were you out of college?

DC: Five.

SK: Was that useful?

DC: Immensely.

SK: What were you doing? Were you being an artist?

DC: Yes. I had a succession of studios and, as I said, I was working for Gilbert and George and moseying around the art world, seeing what was around.

SK: The question I was going to ask was: if you go from school to art school and stay in art school all those years, don't you get a peculiarly distorted view of life through that process?

JC: Well my experience was equally distorted, but from a different point of view. I don't think there's a norm. Look at our work. In some ways we were suspicious of being invited here because, looking at the list of speakers, it seemed that we were invited as symptomatic of a bad art school education and that there was some correlation between our work and our putative dysfunctional abnormality. But there are certain lecturers responsible for that.

SK: But you could argue, couldn't you, that in order to be a successful artist, you have to be dysfunctionally abnormal – since our notion of good art practice is, in some way or other, that it breaks the norm? It destroys, questions or appropriates what has been done before.

JC: I don't think you have to be that avant-gardist about it. The idea of producing art already involves failure. You have a set of expectations, you produce an object, that object goes beyond your intentions, and you carry on. That's what making art is like. I don't see anyone who's ever produced an object that can be fully possessed, for which there's a definitive interpretation, or whose relation to the object is completely viable, understood and happy. Making art is already an engagement with failure.

SK: I suppose the question, then, is how, within an establishment structure – an art school – can you organise failure?

DC: I can only speak from the ridiculously long experience of being at art school, which, I suppose, qualifies me in some way. My experience of tutorship was that it was repressive, the flip-side of being exhilarating, encouraging, speculative, open and generous.

SK: Have you had any experiences that were stimulating, in terms of your work?

JC: I went on holiday to ...

SK: Within an art school.

JC: Oh yes, a school trip; it was great. The bar was quite good. No, there were good people like Michael O'Craig, to name names. And there were people who were really interesting, but they were not involved in practical tutorials. They were responsible for trying to describe or produce a critical debate about art generally; and that critical position was dragged into the studios. The hiatus was being at the Royal College, where the list of invited tutors consisted of friends of friends, and you had no choice in whom you spoke to. There was resistance to certain people that you wanted to speak to. We wanted Griselda Pollock, and others. But they weren't allowed in.

SK: What about contact with fellow students? Was there useful discourse there?

DC: Yes, occasionally. But it was muttered whisperings out of sight of tutors, away from the studio or the establishment; because we didn't think it was wanted there. The best thing about college must be that you meet a few people whom you hang around with and talk to after college. The worst thing, and this sounds immensely Oedipal, is that your relationship to tutors is necessarily to do with lack of power in relation to those who have ultimate power, because art schools are a place of unequal power.

SK: That's a structural fact, isn't it?

JC: Well, I don't see why we have to slip into the position of patriarchy in every institutional situation.

SK: It's generational as well, though; most tutors are considerably older than the students.

DC: I don't think it need be ageist if there were more turnover of part-time and visiting lecturers. It seems very strange that in these places where people are supposed to be open to outside influence, they have a very small pool of people whom they invite in. Consequently, anybody invited gets completely over-subscribed with people who want to see them, to the extent that you find that someone has crossed your name off the list, and it's not another student. There should be more turnover. People should be in and out of those places.

SK: Have you been into art schools as tutors?

DC: A little, yes.

SK: Do you feel you have any contribution to make?

JC: Yes definitely; to destabilise.

SK: To destabilise the institution, or the values that apply in it?

DC: No, don't say that, we'll never get invited again! Just to be fanatically encouraging. I think we get invited in for that reason. You have friends who would like to shake their college up a bit, so they invite people whom they think might do the job ... friends of friends of friends!

SK: I think at this point, we might invite a few friends up onto the platform ...

Sacha Craddock (art critic) in conversation with Richard Wentworth (artist)

RW: I've written a lot of things down since I came in this morning and the phrase that is sitting at the top of my piece of paper most prominently is 'Fear and Hate'. I don't even know who said it. And I think it's worth saying that Sacha and I have a commitment to trying to offer something that makes it's way round those two words.

There was a suggestion that 90 per cent of the people who arrive in an art school want to be artists. I'm not at all sure that this is verifiable. I certainly wasn't in that 90 per cent. So I want to ask you, Sacha, who I know arrived at art school late, what were your expectations? What did you want? What did you think you were doing?

SC: I'm sorry but I'm going to have to give you a bit of a story, although there is a point to it. It's a slightly political point. It's boring to have people constantly label me this thing called 'critic and artist'. Actually, I don't do much art anymore. I have a studio, but I've just sub-let it. So forget the idea of managing to balance these two things.

During the 1970s, I did a lot of extremely serious political work: housing work, trade-union work, branch secretary, you name it ... I always thought in the back of my mind that I was good at art, but because it seemed to be an irresponsible, rather decadent pursuit, I left the idea. But when the Tories suddenly came in, I thought, in a naive or perhaps sensible way, that unless I did something about this thing, I'd never get the chance to get a grant or go to art school again. So I applied to St Martins and got in.

As somebody who'd existed in the world outside art, not knowing any artists at all, I came from a very different position, which has strongly affected my understanding of art. I found, to my utter horror, that the people teaching me were insanely naive about this thing called 'politics'. I came from a position of doing things, like the Birmingham bomb appeals, or working as a clerk doing legal work, and found myself with a bunch of tutors saying things like, 'God, the Pope's not a bad guy, is he?' And I thought this was unbelievable.

When I first went to art school to do a foundation course, I still thought I couldn't really be a painter, which of course has worked out to be sort of true at the moment. But I had this feeling that perhaps I should do something more graphic because it was 'more useful', but thank goodness, my politics got more sophisticated as time went on and I realised that there wasn't this kind of problem. I soon became – and this is important, and forms my attitude to the way I write about art – deeply unmoralistic about what art should or should not deal with. And from then on, I've maintained the belief that I could pursue any kind of art, even rather sad, miserable forms of escapism. I believed very strongly that I could stay and make my paintings. I never really read anything about formalism whatsoever, and I should think the kind of work I did looked a bit like that. I was very involved in the excitement and the pleasure of starting to make paintings. I wanted to be a painter eventually, but I also needed to do other things. I really don't like the idea that most people think art schools didn't do anything for them. I found my experience extraordinarily brilliant and exciting and useful. But what about you? Can you explain where you went to art school?

RW: I have a very strange history because I went to what was then Hornsey only for one year, on the foundation course. And at that time the Royal College ran foundation courses in some of its departments, so I spent a year in the Furniture School at the Royal College and, for reasons that would be far too elaborate to explain here, I then went into the Sculpture School, and at that point the place turned into a university. So my main claim to fame during my time at the Royal College is that I have a letter that declines to offer me a degree, and I also have a letter that gives me an MA, which is a kind of reflection of how the bureaucracy of the school might work. I've never used either letter.

I've always felt incredibly anxious about those parts of schools that are called the 'Sculpture Department', because they always seem to me to be where all the dirty tools get left. There's a sort of principle that goes: painting is clean and quiet, and then there's this other thing that goes on, which is somehow rather more vividly artisanal, and involves grinders and things. And that all gets put somewhere and then there's a sign on the door that says 'Sculpture'. I've never felt able to belong to either club.

A better way of thinking about my art school experience is to think about people – those people whom I cherish and would never have met otherwise, most of whom have either died or I don't see anymore; but nonetheless they were people who were unbelievably nourishing. I think that was quite typical, in that period, and maybe it stays with people forever.

SC: Can you say what the period is?

RW: The period of being nineteen-and-three-quarters, in considerable emotional turmoil. Adrian Searle made a very interesting point about using art school as if it were National Service, to kind of get him away from his family, as if it helped him to travel or something. He also used the expression 'growing up'.

It occurred to me this morning that perhaps the title of this conference is a mistake. Obviously, in order to organise a conference, you have to title it. But maybe what I would ask myself is, what did I do for art school? And what have I done for it since, as somebody who's been involved in schools and has been a student in a school? And it fills me with shame, actually, when I think of some of the things that were on offer to me as a student, that I simply didn't recognise, that I was arrogant about – blind. I could easily say that the school communicated very poorly and that somebody wonderful came to give a talk somewhere and I missed it. But nonetheless, I sense that what I got was far more by, let's say, serendipity, than programme.

I'd like to name two people whom I think were crucial. One of them was a very young sculptor called John Panting, whom, I suppose, can only have been four or five years older than me. What was it that John provided? For a start, he was teaching part-time, but he would be there after hours, working. That was extraordinary, you know. I think the department shut at ten o'clock at night, and John was around till then when he had something to do. Maybe this is my version of working with Gilbert and George. It was a kind of energetic vigorousness: there aren't many hours in the day and I want to do this thing, which is quite different from the tutorial – the luxury of somebody spending some time with your work and discussing it with you.

The other person was somebody whom we all speculated about. We never knew what he did and we all wanted to know. We suspected he never made anything at all! He was a man called Peter Atkins. And he terrified us, I mean, absolutely terrified us, because there was a quality to Peter's teaching that was so bloody demanding. There was a mixture of the authoritarian and authoritative. You really had to work to Peter's timetable. He kept the timetable and he remembered exactly what he'd said to you the last time. He picked you up on absolutely everything and it was extremely demanding and exercising. In a way I think that what happened to me in the space between Peter and John was really very special. And I don't suppose Peter and John ever had a plan about teaching me. And I think there is a way in which it's very hard to teach students to, if you like, learn to ask the questions the right way or ask the right people the right questions. I know from teaching that you see those ones who come in who just know how to learn. They know how to nourish themselves. It's probably something to do with how they were brought up; it's some trick of personality. There are other people whom one thinks are totally wonderful, but after three, five, seven years, they still haven't really mastered this essential thing, which is to do with addressing what's around them.

SC: Many people have talked about how, almost despite the fact that they were at art school, these fantastic things accidentally happened. That's missing the point, because of course there's something clever about teachers who imply to you that they're your friends and they're meeting you round by the bike sheds rather than actually in the classroom. In other words, you get this sense of being privy to something. But that's a clever teaching method. We all do it.

I'd also like to be slightly critical of the acceptance that has been going on through-out the day of the notion of somebody being the kind of student that a school doesn't want. Art schools will fall over backwards for naughty students who are kind of inter-esting, who work hard. Most art schools are trying their best in some way. It is rather off-key politically to start seeing the Establishment in terms of the institute, or some institution.

RW: An Italian student of mine once said that when they were at Goldsmiths doing fine art, they didn't realise there was anything else that you could study. Now this may be connected to some of the things Jake and Dinos were talking about: that there is a way in which the art school can be so successfully encapsulating that you don't even realise there are other connected or related disciplines. I have to say, I thought it was an extraordinary feat that they'd managed to keep this distance. But nonetheless, I think there are things within schools that, if you like, are permitted and things that are not permitted. And I know a lot of people who have struggled very long and hard to dismantle themselves, or the sense of themselves, as a painter or a film-maker or what-have-you, and become something else. I think it would be very useful, Sacha, if you could describe whether you felt there were forces sitting on your shoulder that have discouraged you from writing or that have encouraged you to write?

SC: You mean, if there is such a thing as an authority or an institution that stops you doing what you want ?

RW: Yes, and try and characterise those forces.

SC: Well it's a very complicated characterisation, isn't it? The answer is yes, but I wouldn't say that, in terms of St Martins and then Chelsea MA, the forces were not necessarily strong enough to make one feel encouraged or discouraged. It was the real interaction, the time where the 1970s died their final death. There were a lot of paint-ings of teapots jumping round the room; the sort of stuff where the kitchen would come alive. Then there would be a lot of history-type stuff. So it was a kind of turning point. That is such a big question because it is a big political question.

RW: Are you saying you couldn't paint jumping teapots?

SC: Well, I wouldn't dream of painting a teapot if it fell on my head. I think it's a horrendous thought. In other words, when you've run demonstrations for ten whole years, you don't go and paint a teapot.

RW: But where did the writing fit in?

SC: But the writing is different because it's ... it's ... it's just verbal.

RW: Is there no history of your writing within art school?

SC: No, none at all. I would never write anything. I never wrote anything ever. I've only written about two letters.

RW: All right, we'll treat this as a dead end. My question was connected to this ficti-tious 90 per cent of people who want to be an artist. It seems to me that the people who remain interesting to me are the people who are, I don't know another word for it except 'creative'. There are people who are functioning creatively and they're not nec-essarily doing those activities that we characterise, broadly speaking, as painting and sculpture. They're sometimes very involved in film, sometimes they're involved in high commerce, but that's not to say that they don't have a set of values and a set of possibilities that they could only have acquired in an art school.

SC: I think that's true. One can get terribly sentimental about one's gang and how they're all doing different things like programming music in railway stations and things like that, as opposed to putting art in railway stations.

I just want to say a couple of things that haven't been mentioned: some pretty basic stuff about what's happening now. It's true that things have changed very much and the kind of education people get in other schools before they come to art school has changed, because in the 1980s there was strong anti-abstraction. I don't mean 'abstract' in terms of painting, but notions about politics with a small 'p' and the abstract with a small 'a'. And so when one's teaching now, it's much more to do with tangibility and realism, not in terms of the way something is represented, but the fact that people often want to kick their paintings. This is because they haven't done any art history and they don't know how ineffectual paintings actually are. Secondly, they want things to move or to function in some way. So, in other words, there's this strange fear of a lack of function for art. This comes from a change in the kind of rationale people are given, which is a Tory-type self-help rationale.

RW: One of the things that seems to me to be an obvious change is that art schools must be definitively tied to some idea of product. Going back to this thing about whether you did or didn't have permission to do something, I don't recall there being the same sense of product twenty years ago, because there wasn't the same sense of opportunity. There is now, or I imagine there is, a sense in which young artists and young art students have a lot of models before them. I'm not old enough to know what effect, let's say, the marketing of early 1960s British Pop art has had – whether there's a correlation there – but it seems to me that there's a sense now of product, the like of which I've never seen before. I don't know how you make a programme to deal with that; I don't know how you go underneath that or around that in teaching. It's like the air that is breathed. If you're twenty-five now, you were nourished briefly on punk, and then you had eighteen years of one government. This is a very extraordinary set of perceptions, which are mostly not true for this audience.

Andrew Brighton (Head of Public Events, Tate Gallery)
in conversation with Helen Chadwick (artist)

AB: Helen, can I begin by asking you to tell us which art schools you went to, a little of your personal history, and, to ask how was it for you?

HC: I don't know how, from the point of view of the personal, this is going to have value in terms of how one considers art education now, but I will begin with a potted biography. I went through four art schools: Bristol Foundation; Croydon, which, after a kind of psychotic year I dumped to go to Brighton for three years to do a BA; followed by an MA at Chelsea. I was very young. I went straight from school and I don't know what my expectations were. In a sense, I disappointed my school by jettisoning a university place to go to art school. I don't know why, but the process of making, the kind of concentration and focusing that it drew from me was something that started to become a bit of a fix. So I decided to pursue it.

I think, in a way, I was quite a trusting subject, and I thought I'd continue to pursue this activity. In that passage from school to art school you have certain expectations. What I realised was that there was a distinct difference between school and the institution of an art school. What became most valuable during this passage of six years was developing an attitude to the institution that, painful though it was, could be a way of using it, despite its negativity. I had somehow to glean together enough of a platform of support, albeit through a kind of DIY, which would allow me to continue to pursue what I wanted to do. I didn't even know what I wanted to do, except just continue some kind of process and activity that was in some way compulsive. I suppose it's obvious, and naively, I should have internalised the fact that one went to art school to be an artist, but that was really not my intention. It was really to carry on doing something. And I must admit I found it rather farcical when I heard rather heroic posturings about how being an artist was important and one suffered and it was painful. This kind of vision just seemed completely absurd. And right up until the point of leaving art school, it seemed irrelevant. This term 'artist' just somehow felt alien.

AB: Would it be true to say that at the time you were at art school, the term 'artist' implied a notion of somebody who was heroic, and by implication, somebody who was male; a sort of male hero as the model, and that this was inscribed almost habitually, without notice, in the culture?

HC: I guess, without doing a feminist rap ...

AB: Well, I'll do that.

HC: Yes, much has been said about the law of the father and the kind of Oedipal relationship, and one of the things I had to circumnavigate was the fact that I was offered, not an Oedipal complex, but an Electra complex; and I was encouraged to sleep with rather than learn from a father. Though maybe that was very useful, because, in a sense, it reinforced a desire to pursue one's course. And sadly – I'm not proud of it – my experience of being at art school was of a continuing process of isolation, not from my peers, but from the institution, the structure.

AB: And was that a personal thing or was it because of the character of the work you were making?

HC: I think they were synonymous, really. The schools were still rigidly divided up between painting departments and sculpture departments. There wasn't really that phenomenon of a broad fine art course that somehow embraced all, or an experimental area. And it wasn't until the last year of my BA that I was rather unceremoniously shunted off into the sort of Conceptual area, although I was allowed to keep my little geographical base in sculpture. So in a sense I suppose what I was doing was rather anomalous, but therefore I think I was somewhat sheltered.

AB: But then you did get into a postgraduate course?

HC: To Painting.

AB: They took you on a misapprehension? You must have slopped the paint around in some way or other at Chelsea?

HC: Well, as a non-painter, I rather appreciated the risk that the Head of the school then took, in that he acknowledged that my position was maverick. I couldn't be accommodated within sculpture because of, I guess, ideological differences; therefore a place was found for me.

AB: So that's an example of somebody who you think acknowledged what you were doing and was willing to bend the rules to give you space. Were there other people who did those kind of things?

HC: Yes, but I mean, as far as it goes, to give one space is the baseline. And I don't know whether one should have more expectations from art school. In a sense I was very happy. One of the things I would fight for is the fact that art school gives time and a kind of place of shelter where you can pursue something even though you don't know what that's going to be or what direction it might take. It's sort of going too far to say it's an educational oasis, but a sense of a student at the water hole – rather than Aphrodite – is, I think, one way of looking at it.

AB: Was your practice partly formed by rejection of the models that you were being offered, or was it partly formed by, maybe, looking at models beyond the ones that were normally paraded before students?

HC: It was a synthesis of the two. There were no precedents or role models, so to speak, that one could position oneself against. So in a sense I suppose it became quite difficult to identify what I was doing with some kind of art history. And again, survival partly necessitated dumping art history and looking for other information: in fashion or film, a polyglot of popular influences, rather than taking a belief in history as a model.

AB: Were there any texts or theoretical approaches that made it possible for you to look at these alternative models?

HC: No, it was a very anti-intellectual time. We're talking early to mid-1970s.

AB: You see, one of the things that I felt the Chapmans were saying – I'd better speak carefully here or I'll get done over, I'll get a flaying if I get this wrong – is that if they had been at the Royal College when Peter de Francia and the intellectual set were still there, it would have been very different. And for me ... I was at St Martins in the early 1960s. I think I'm the oldest art student to be on the platform today!

HC: But a survivor.

AB: A survivor. There were people like Peter de Francia who introduced you to all that Marxist stuff. I can remember the moment when there was a clunk in my head and I suddenly intuited what a Hegelian view of the world was. And that thing of not thinking of the world as being constituted as 'you' and 'other', but of the individual in a total historical process – that there was an interconnectedness between things – was like a big shift in my head, which I gained an awful lot from intellectually, theoretically. Then, being taught by someone like John Latham, where you got put though all sorts of strange gyrations of making, which shifted around the furniture in your head. I want to say that I think our experiences are very various. I'm picking up the point you started with: can we take the personal and universalise? I think one of the problems is that art schools are actually various. And people's passage in the same art school at the same time can be very various, because there are people that you happen to be students with or people you're taught by. I know plenty of people who will praise art school teachers who were at St Martins when I was there, and I had nothing to do with them, or alternatively was fucked up by them. It's a very difficult thing to generalise about. What it does tell you is that there are, and perhaps should be, very pluralistic institutions both internally and across the board. Do you think that is so?

HC: Well, I think that is something to be preserved, as much as it can be. I would question quite how pluralist institutions can be, but at best, if they can support the kind of variation of potential that people want to explore, that is obviously a Utopian vision.

AB: But you have subsequently taught in art schools?

HC: Oh yes. I mean, I've never left the damn places. I still teach, albeit not very regularly. And I ask myself why I do this. Initially it was a financial imperative. I now find it quite difficult to give up that role. I realise I value it, surprisingly, and I think that it can become a kind of opiate: the possibility of having an intimate exchange with another person, where you really don't know anything about their personal lives or them as people, but you share this conversation around their projection of what they want to realise. For some reason, that to me is what has the most value in art school. That seems to be the kernel of art education. I don't like the word 'education'. The experience of art school, and how that dialogue can be preserved, is, I think, something that I'd like to address to all the people working in art schools and who are, in a way, in a position to lobby for resources for art schools.

AB: If we were to put forward the proposition that it's more difficult to run an art school on the resources we have now than it was in the past, then I think the problem with that proposition today is that nobody is going to oppose it.

HC: On that financial issue, I'd rather look at it another way. There's something I very much want to say. I woke up this morning and heard on the radio about the £300 surcharge that vice-chancellors are wanting to impose on students. It's all very well talking about the fact that the institutions don't have the kind of resources they require, but I'm very concerned about the position of poverty that students are being pushed into. I'm very ill at ease with the fact that institutions will offer places to students without guaranteeing them some kind of base support through a grant system. I know there's a passage across the board into a kind of marketing, whether it's in the Health Service or whether it's in education, but I don't know how an individual can be expected to study full time while working semi-full time in order to finance being there.

AB: I think you're right there. One has to look at, say, the German or American art schools, where the tradition is that people work and then come in, leave for a time of work, and then come back in again. So it is possible. But there is also something else that may be getting the label 'Thatcherite'. One of the things that Dinos talked about, is the power relationship that exists in art school. I think one of the problems with students having grants is that they don't see themselves as economically providing for their education – they don't see that those teachers are really employed by them. The fact that it's done by local authority grants or whatever, means that students underestimate their actual economic power. I partly say this from having run an MA course where students were paying for themselves, and they were, I think, more willing to say, 'Look, we're not getting what we bloody paid for'. And that, in a sense, helped to equalise the situation. But that disadvantages more impoverished students. There is obviously no objection to that whatsoever, but I'd like at least to put that argument in there.

HC: As a Marxist?

AB: As a Marxist. I remain a Marxist, at least in one way: I think you should always look at the economic base, though I don't see the economic base as determining all things. But I'd like to go back again to your art school. You see in a sense, you've done what Chris suggested might happen, in his experience of interviewing students about the Royal College: the picture you form is, on the whole, of you emerging, in spite of, rather than because of, that institution. You haven't said 'these people were important to me'.

HC: I think there is a degree of friction. I don't necessarily see that as being an antagonistic situation, but rather the inevitable role that an institution serves, in its inability to provide the very particular possibilities that individuals need in their rite of passage from late childhood through to being adults and having a sense of what direction they want from their life.

AB: But you've also mentioned your peer group. That would seem to me to be something that hasn't been talked about sufficiently: that one's fellow students can be incredibly important. For example, for me, running an MA course, which seemed to me a good MA course, 60 to 70 per cent of what was good about that course was what students did for each other and not what staff did. Do you look back at certain crucial relationships, intellectual or otherwise, that you had when you were at Brighton, for example?

HC: I think one of the most stimulating factors was that there was the situation where one helped another student realise something in some way. It wasn't collaboration in the sense of two individuals working together towards a common aim, but whether you were a model or whether you were a cameraman, you helped another student in some way; perhaps less on the intellectual front, but that was a peculiarity of those times. Certainly in an ad hoc way there was a kind of hands-on desire to help one another. That's not really a true collectivity towards common aims, but certainly there was a sense of responsibility, of being involved with one another's chosen area of work.

AB: Another thing I want to ask you about is technical assistance. Some people got an immense amount from certain technicians. That is to say, the information base is not just the teaching staff but the technical staff too. Did you encounter that at all?

HC: In one individual. It's true to say that I think the people I've learnt most from in my life were technical people; they were makers. I was learning a kind of attitude in order to be able to make something; not just understanding what the material can do, how you do it to the material, but a kind of – I don't know how to put it – a kind of empathy with working. It was through people who made, but they were a minority, given how many there were at those institutions. It's a very particular individual that you might meet who enables you … who gives you a depth of … you can't really describe how it operates … who gives you a perception into things. That is not education. It exists in a more profound dimension. I don't think one can expect that from teachers or anyone you encounter, but it does happen occasionally. And that's quite precious. If that is an exchange that can happen in education, if there are possibilities for that, then that is an absolute gain.

AB: Were they people who showed you things, not by telling you, but by showing you how it might be done?

HC: Kind of Zen, almost, being able to cope with situations.

AB: Could you make it more specific? What sort of things are you talking about ?

HC. No, I can't make it specific. It's not academic.

AB: It's a quality of engagement or something like that?

HC: Yes. It's a kind of understanding of how to interpret conditions or situations. I don't know how you square that with practice and theory. It's something else. But it is kind of vital.

AB: I'm thinking back to when we were trying to talk about the curriculum in a generalised way. We've come here today and we're talking among the right people about their particular experiences, and somehow or other the two things haven't matched. That is to say, this is somehow an intellectual failure. But I think I would want to argue that this is what is at the core of fine art education and that this is art practice. And art practice is a contested area – that which constitutes art is a contested concept and therefore you can't have a settlement; you can't have a consensus. It is intrinsic to it, that there are these arguments. Furthermore, the experience, or these part-experiences, are intuitive ones rather than conceptual ones. I'm not talking about a historical natural response. This core characteristic of what we're about means that there isn't some easy enmeshment from which you can start talking clearly about aims and objectives. At the core is this principle. Obviously you couldn't put this in a course document, but I think art education at the core has to say, 'We do not know what the fuck we're doing'. This is because, if you knew what you were doing, that would presuppose you knew what art was, and once you know what art is, then in a sense you're no longer doing it, certainly in the modern tradition. You're going back to, say, some notion of academic tradition, which there may be arguments for. The cultural energy of art in modern times has been around the idea that art is not something that you can entirely conceptualise and have rules for; the incoherence of this conference demonstrates this to a certain extent!

HC: There's a kind of quantum energy rather than a quantifiability. Something like that.

AB: Yes. And I don't think that's something I would want to manage out of the art school system. Would you want to disagree?

HC: Absolutely not.

AB: Good.

HC: On the other side, I ask myself what the role of art schools has been, in what is seen as the flowering of contemporary British art at the moment. Everywhere I travel, people go 'Oh, it's so exciting, Britain, and what's happening in London and Glasgow, and where should I go and where can I see all this stuff?' Eyes are on Britain as an interesting place in the contemporary arts. Frankly, I don't see this as being a particularly unique period, but if it is, then presumably the art schools have a place in having enabled that to happen. So certainly one isn't being negative, but I think one has to acknowledge the kind of resistance you need as an individual to go through a system.

AB: Yes. But I would argue that that kind of resistance is required of you in the system. Maybe it's an unhappy phrase for thinking for yourself, or at least making for yourself, or even the clichéd heroic thing about having an artistic personality, which still exists. Often there are people who can't sustain it, but you're asked to be a rebel. Some people can't keep that up or can't perform in that sort of way. Also, there is acceptable rebellion and unacceptable rebellion.

HC: I think there are grades between resistance and rebellion. I don't see resistance as Liberty at the barricades or anything necessarily as conspicuous as that. I think it can be implicit in how someone chooses to develop a programme that seems appropriate, and how that is stitched together from a variety of sources. It's organic, isn't it?

AB: You've got a new plateau of support. I do agree with that idea of little communities that give people courage, which I think you find at art schools.

HC: And a place to do it.

AB: Yes. Which is most vital. The two things are enmeshed. But that giving of courage, I think, is important, in the sense of giving one arrogance.

HC: Yes.

AB: Because I sort of gave up being an artist partly because I lack that particular kind of arrogance. I've got other sorts of arrogance.

HC: Yes, but something my technician taught me was a simultaneous humility that enables you to glide through.

AB: Then there's this question that haunts us: are we general educationalists, or are we training artists to be artists? Training people – assuming that people are already artists? I think that's a false distinction. What you say is 'we will treat what you make as if it is art', from which would follow that a whole lot of critical things would go. To say somebody is an artist, we would have to say that they have a special gland or something.

HC: Yes, it's a horrible, horrible word.

AB: You started by saying that your fascination was with making.

HC: It was a kind of drive, an obsession, an opiate, you know. Someone mentioned Prozac, but it's the wrong drug to describe the condition.

AB: There have been some studies on competent and incompetent generals. And one of the arguments is that good generals had to be fascinated with the technicalities of generalship. I think I went into art school because I wanted … what did Freud say: 'You want fame, fortune, and the love of beautiful women'.

HC: Well, that's why you're at the Tate.

AB: People have been talking again! I remember David Hockney saying that if somebody gave him a paint pot and a brush, he'd paint his bicycle, because he just loved putting the stuff on. And actually putting the stuff on ultimately bored me shitless.

HC: That's the real difference.

AB: The real difference. But you've got the fame and the fortune and the love of beautiful persons. Is there a question you'd like to ask me? I had certain traumatic experiences at art school that I can report. One was sort of suddenly intuiting what the art stuff was about. One was when I had a job in the holidays. I worked in an art shop in Charing Cross Road. It sold materials and reproductions. And a man came in and he said, 'Have you got any paintings of snow-capped mountains?' The idea that you choose a painting on the basis of its subject without specifying the artist was an incredible shock to my system, from which I never recovered. I became interested in popular painting and the popular use of it; painting images from that trauma. It was an entirely different use of art. It was about just what it depicted rather than who it was by, all that sort of stuff. The other experience was when I went to the Royal Academy Schools. I was full of John Hoyland-type painting at that time. I'd come from St Martins and the Head of Fine Art used to come out and actually bait the students by saying, 'Oh this is rubbish, this is rubbish', and it was a fairly lively sort of contact. But the Royal Academy Schools were very Tory and decent in that sort of Church of England way. Peter Greenham was the Head. I was full of rage. Royal Academy Schools were full of people from Kennington and from Kensington. Kennington was very working class; Kensington was very upper class. And the upper classes and the working classes got together and drank and fornicated and really enjoyed themselves. I was this suffering middle-class intellectual in the middle. But the great trauma was that I was being extremely rude about Peter Greenham and one of the lads from Yorkshire lifted me up and said, 'You go fucking look, lad'. So I went, partly because I knew he'd beat my head in if I didn't, and I looked at this guy's painting and he could put the stuff on like nobody, you know, they were beautiful!

HC: Snow-capped mountains?

AB: No it wasn't, it was the paint – the painterliness – that I was admiring. It was a painting of the Queen, actually. What I'm saying here is that there are models of practice that always troubled me, which are not generally admitted within the art school culture: popular painting, traditionalist painting. That's one of the things that I think shouldn't go by in our discussions. I remember when I was teaching at Goldsmiths, there was a girl who came in and she wanted to paint horses. So you start with the usual stuff: 'Have you looked at Stubbs?', etc., etc. She wasn't interested in Stubbs. She wanted to paint horses. She was interested in horses. She had no interest in anything other than horses. I was made her tutor because I was vaguely interested in that sort of stuff. I was a total failure and she left after six months. Now, what I'm saying is that the art school culture doesn't encompass the totality of uses of painting, sculpture or image-making. And I wonder whether you would go along with me by at least wanting to question the conservatism or the restrictions within us?

HC: Well it's a conservative radicalism, isn't it?

AB: Mmm. Mmm. Nobody, it seems to me, is running an art school that is saying, 'All we're going to teach you is conventional skills'. And those art schools that try to drift in that direction are usually seen as using it as an excuse for being pretty dumb.

HC: That's a good way to end.

Chair's summing up

CHRISTOPHER FRAYLING

Pro-Rector, Royal College of Art

It's my job now to summarise the day's proceedings, and I'd like to put in your mind two images that have emerged in the course of the day. One of them is David Hockney's defaced diploma certificate, which he turned into a print. You probably know the image. It has a royal coat-of-arms (this being the Royal College of Art), and a hapless young art student perched on the head of the college principal, having his head bumped against the coat-of-arms. Below the principal, whose old Etonian tie is flapping in the wind, are all these other students, who are being crushed by the weight of bureaucracy. It's an image of that tension between the institution, with its inevitable sluggishness and bureaucracy, and the individuals, who bash against it in order to define themselves. I think this has been one of the strong themes of the day.

The other image is not a visual one at all. About two years ago I wrote a paper about research in art and design (picking up the gauntlet that was thrown down by Colin Painter). At the end of this paper, I said there should be much more debate among fine artists about the range of practices they undertake: in what sense do they constitute research, and what kinds of exhibiting are appropriate to what kinds of activity? Afterwards, a senior member of the Fine Art staff of the Royal College took me aside and said, 'That's a disgraceful thing to say. You're really letting the side down by suggesting there should be a debate'. I became very upset about these unquestioned assumptions and the idea that if you talk about something it's dangerous. I get very upset about that because we're supposed to be in a lively, intellectual, creative environment where all things are open to discussion. The idea of there being no-go areas, that if we open the black box we're somehow going to give something away about ourselves that might be dangerous, is a pernicious attitude. That was the second image of today. We haven't necessarily jumped into the boxes enough, but we have looked into several. One of the themes has been how one should always question and examine one's own assumptions, and that the implicit handing on of values is not really very useful, neither to students nor staff.

We started with Stephen Farthing's 'A Peculiarity of Constitution or Temperament'. He chose as his case-study the film *The Rebel*. It's surprising in a way that an image from the late 1950s is still – and everyone seemed to recognise it – very much in the ether. It's the story of someone who has no critical standards and only rudimentary skills. At least, the film suggests he has only rudimentary skills. The sculpture he is working on looks rather like an Epstein, which I think was meant to be satirical because it was thought by the writers Simpson and Galton that Epstein had only rudimentary skills. He hasn't met any other artists. He wants to wear the trappings of an artist – a beret, smock, a palette as a sort of piece of jewellery – but on the other hand it's the railway cuttings, East Cheam tendency. Against this, Stephen talked of art schools providing, as he put it, a 'shadow apprenticeship', of peer-group teaching; of how important it is to be among other young artists in order to define oneself, and to find one's own voice in an environment of other artists. In that project, the trappings of the artist, the self-image of the artist, perhaps weren't as important as some people thought. That's what I took from his talk.

Then we had the first of our interviews: Sarah Kent with the Chapmans. It's very difficult to summarise, but a few points emerged strongly from this session. Firstly, that we place too much emphasis on art as a transcendent value, and not enough on debate, discussion, questioning, breaking the flow and actually examining the whole notion that we hold of art. There is not enough bringing out of these implicit assumptions instead of this rather defensive handing on by institutions. Secondly, that art schools could be an environment of confrontation, something to fight against. Art schools, it was said, ought to be more confrontational and passionate places than they are, and they ought to encourage more speculation. I suppose the punchline was a belief in what we're doing, and standing by certain positions. In other words, 'By thy works shall ye be judged'; an environment doesn't really get anybody anywhere. Thirdly, there was the feeling in art schools that, 'everything outside is irrelevant', as they put it. When they were at college, there was a sense of anti-intellectualism, and allied to that, the monotechnic versus the university model. As you might say, not so much Herbert Read as Jake doing some reading. Then fourthly, the question of the possibility of being a teacher without being an artist was raised. The answer was resoundingly 'yes, it is possible'. I was glad to hear it because I don't know whether I'm a good teacher, but I'm definitely not an artist. Then fifthly, the social world of the art teacher was discussed, again, handing on assumptions and prejudices, in particular the torch of modernism, from generation to generation in an unquestioning way. Now, it's become a cliché to attack that, but there is still that unquestioned assumption in certain enclaves.

Then we had Richard Wentworth in conversation with Sacha Craddock and the very interesting issue of politics came up. I remember once meeting a well-known designer who said that all design students should read the *Economist*, not for the financial figures, but to tell them something about what was going on in the world they are going to inhabit as designers. Sacha was saying something similar. I thought, 'I wonder what young artists should read, just to open their minds to the fact that tunnel vision isn't good for you?' There is a hell of a lot of tunnel vision, not just in autobiographical presentations, but today, we tend to reduce to the white cube and the studio. So it is interesting to wonder what journals should be folded up in the pocket of an artist, if a designer should be reading the *Economist*. I found the false idea of radicalism an interesting thought: somehow we all seem terribly radical – conservative radical, that is – but the closer one looks in political terms, we aren't, although within our little world we sometimes are. The issue on collectivity versus the genius individual came up a lot in reference to collective action, both students and staff getting together to make a point. Richard rather movingly talked about the individuals you meet and cherish when at art school, even if you never keep in contact with them again, and how that can be a life-changing experience. Then he said, to paraphrase President Kennedy, 'Ask not what art schools can do for you, ask what you can do for art schools'. I thought that was an excellent question, and it came up again with Helen when she said how valuable she found it to go back to art schools as an established artist, and derive some nourishment from the company of young people, experiencing intimate exchanges with students, as she put it, and how that dialogue can be preserved. It was very nice to hear established people talking about college as something that they could put something back into. You don't hear that very often and I thought that was a very valuable contribution. Art school is a place, Richard said, to learn to ask people the right question.

Then there was the last session, with Andrew and Helen. Helen started off by talking about the transition from school to art school in the pre-diploma era, like BC and AD. Was it that significant? I suppose it was. What is the value of an art school? To develop an attitude to the institution, to use it despite its negativity, and to develop a platform of support through a kind of DIY. This is a model of the art school as a kind of build-your-own pizza, but you've got to have the ingredients. The important thing is to provide the ingredients without being dirigiste about which pizza you want people to eat. Helen also talked about how she felt the term 'artist' was quite alien when she was at art school. There was this notion of the struggling artist, which seemed very remote for someone who was interested, in quite a humble way, in developing her own practice. So it was a case of: 'Happy the land that has no need for heroes'. Here was the role of art schools as a baseline, a kind of shelter in which to produce something even if you don't know what it is you're pursuing. And then there was the image of the waterhole, which has had quite a bit of mileage since: not so much Aphrodite at the waterhole, as somewhere that people can go to but are not necessarily forced to do so. Then there was the way in which the artist values the contact with young students; Helen doesn't have to teach but does so for the nourishment. Subsequently, Andrew brought up an interesting point about art being a contested area by definition, therefore we're never going to get a consensus. Some of us may be disappointed that it is not all neatly wrapped up in a bow by the end of the day, but it is in the nature of art that this never happens. I'm sure that's true, and that at a very deep level, the students' experience is intuitive rather than conceptual. So, again, it's incredibly difficult to generalise. In a way, the anecdotal approach is the only way into this on some level, because each student is a special kind of artist. So intuition was important and not easy to mesh with the language of aims and objectives, because at a fairly deep level, we don't quite know where we're going. But isn't that the point?

What sort of themes arose from the day, from which one can generalise? I think there was a sense of convergence between practically informed theory and theoretically informed practice. In other words, bringing together two things that have too often been seen as antithetical. There was a very strong sense of convergence of the reflection on practice and practice itself; a sense that art schools are not as passionate as they used to be; a sense of being up front, of 'Don't let the buggers grind you down' – that was a big theme of the day – a sense that art schools should be both a shadow apprenticeship and a place of learning through art. Not all graduates will be professional artists. Why should they be? There was a sense of peer-group teaching; having other artists in a greenhouse environment is every bit as important as the tuition of professional teachers. In other words, the density of that relationship is very much part of the art school experience, which I'm sure is true. I'm spoiled where that's concerned, because in the wholly postgraduate college in which I operate, that density is very high, and everyone is roughly on the same starting line. It's much more difficult at an undergraduate level, but still clearly very important. There was also a sense that art schools were being asked to do too much: professional training, all the disciplines of the university, an adventure playground, a place to socialise artists, all that puts a lot on the shoulders of one set of institutions. There is a sense, as Helen put it, that institutions cannot provide for all individuals. The individual must find his or her own path, but the path must have certain sign posts, or things on it that the individual can go along with.

Going back to where I began, I said that when I was writing the history of the Royal College I spoke to a lot of people, and I said that if an established artist admitted that art school had taught them anything, it would somehow diminish them as artists, like an admission of direct influence; it was a challenge to authorship. Now if we put that side by side with what Andrew said from the floor about acts of creation being acts of destruction at some level, and to be critical of the art school experience is part of what we give our students, I think that explains something of the tone of the day. It is in the nature of reminiscence that you remember the bad things. It is also in the nature of reminiscence that there is a certain sadness about lost opportunity. In other words, things I wish I'd done, which in retrospect I see as a missed opportunity; you need a resistance to institutions to be built in to students for them at some level to be art students.

I hope there have been memorable moments in the day: Richard talking about the artist putting something back into art school; Helen talking about the role of the institution in bringing on the individual. There have been moments in which the positive has emerged: a sense that art schools are very valuable places, and I hope that enough of the positive has come out of the day to nourish us all in what we do, because we certainly need it at the moment. I hope this conference, like its predecessors, has managed to reach the parts that other conferences haven't reached.

What Do You Think You Are Doing? Intention in Making, Understanding and Teaching Art

Introductory address

ANDREW BRIGHTON

Head of Public Events, Tate Gallery

Welcome to the Tate Gallery. I was particularly enthusiastic about the topic of today's event because it seems to me to be important that those things that are peculiar to disciplines in education dealing with aesthetic practices are in some way articulated. I've always found it difficult when writing course documents, or seeing the sort of requirements that are put upon one as an academic, to 'state criteria for assessment'. I've felt when teaching that if a student says to me, 'What are your criteria for assessment?' the most sophisticated reply is, 'I do not fucking know'. The business of addressing the particularity of a work of art and assembling some sort of understanding of it seems to be so much tied to that particular work of art that the idea that one could have some stated criteria seems to militate against the character of art school teaching, and indeed to falsify how we deal with works of art outside of the academic situation. So, in a way, this conference addresses that area of unknowing.

Welcome

COLIN PAINTER

Principal, Wimbledon School of Art

This is the seventh conference we have organised at the Tate. I would like to thank the Tate again for this continuing collaboration and I think this particular conference is more collaborative than most. We owe the ingenious title to Andrew, who agreed the theme in discussion with colleagues at the School. Normally, in introducing these conferences, I've been able to make a connection between the last and the next and so on, but there have now been so many I've lost track. Each one is an entity in its own right. We could hardly say there's a continuing theme, except that they all address issues common to the making of connections between fine art *per se*, the fine art world and the education and teaching of fine art.

Chair's introduction

CHRISTOPHER FRAYLING

Pro-Rector, Royal College of Art

I was reading a book the other day called *A Pot of Paint*,[1] which is about the celebrated lawsuit of 1878, of Whistler v. Ruskin, in which, as we all know, Whistler sought damages for libel from the critic John Ruskin for writing a review that said he was 'A coxcomb who'd asked two hundred guineas for flinging a pot of paint in the public face'. 'His *Nocturnes*', said Ruskin, were 'slapdash, unfinished, they look like work in progress rather than finished paintings'. Now everyone knows that, but what people perhaps don't know is that one of the witnesses who spoke in Whistler's defence was a man called William Michael Rosetti, who was the brother of the much better-known Dante Gabriel Rosetti, the pre-Raphaelite painter and poet. William Michael Rosetti wrote in his notes for the trial, which are in an archive in America, that the critic – and this is 1878 – the critic, in judging a work of art, should always be mindful of the artist's intentions. Where Whistler was concerned, he said, each of the Thames *Nocturnes* was 'justified to itself by adequately and exquisitely fulfilling its own conditions; and these are essentially aesthetic conditions. Whistler', he concluded, 'produces the exact result he is aiming at. So Ruskin's accusation of randomness completely missed the point.' When it came to the trial, this submission was extremely important in explaining to the judge that it wasn't as slapdash as it looked: actually, Whistler had intended it to look like that and his intention was embodied in the work of art. It was a real turning point in public arguments about art, and it took place over a hundred years ago. We will see today how much or how little the debate has moved on in the last hundred years.

'The artist's intentions', wrote Rosetti in his submission, 'should never, however, be confused with his motives'. An artist might be hungry, or broke, or going through a bad patch in a domestic relationship, but intention, or design, had much more to do with the specific aesthetic questions the artist was answering through the work; not the intention to do something declared in advance, but rather the intention in *doing* it, which might well change during the process. Well, Rosetti wasn't an art teacher, he was in fact a critic and the editor of a journal called *The Germ*, which was about Pre-Raphaelite art. If he had been a teacher, and if he'd been living a century later, the issue of intention would have been even more central to his thinking. I believe it is key to the debate about education at the moment. He was remarkably ahead of his time.

How many times has one asked a student 'What do you think it means?', or, 'How did the meaning emerge?' And how many times has the student replied rather defensively, 'The work speaks for itself'. End of discussion. It's a very common debate and I imagine the whole spectrum of how one responds to that will emerge today.

Well, to help us unpack this complex and very timely issue – timely because, as Andrew has said, we're constantly being asked to be much more explicit about what goes on in that kind of teaching transaction – we have an even more action-packed conference than we've had in the past. Nine speakers in all, as opposed to the usual six, will be bringing a particular take on a linked set of themes. And these themes are, firstly, how important is an awareness of intention to artists in the making of their work? This is a question of self awareness. Secondly, how important is an understanding of the artist's intention to our experience of a work of art? This is a question of the viewer's awareness. And thirdly, how important to teaching and evaluation are students' intentions in the making of their work? This is a question of the teacher's awareness and the vexed issue of criteria and the sort of transaction that I've described.

Notes

1. Linda Merrill, *A Pot of Paint: Aesthetics on Trial in Whistler v. Ruskin*, Smithsonian Institution Press, Washington and London 1992.

Clear intentions and withered promises

Michael Baldwin

Artist working collaboratively as part of Art & Language

What no one has said so far is that intention is not very fashionable. Post-structuralism decidedly looks down its nose at it, which seems odd in the sense that if lecturers and theorists go in for the human sciences, it would make sense for them also to be interested in intention. One would think that it's one of the ways in which we recognise ourselves as being human; in so far as we are intentional.

What I want to do is to set the scene by showing a number of pictures. They represent rather gristly material in relation to intention, which might just be, as Daniel Ceden suggests, 'about-ness', intention as a sense of purpose. The pictures are crippled in a certain way. Once I've quickly set the scene, I also want to talk about some rather strange text works, now lost, which were used later to mask other works.

These are works from 1979–80. One is called *Stalin Contemplating the Body of Lenin*; the other one is called *A Portrait of V.I. Lenin in Disguise in the Style of Jackson Pollock*. I probably don't need to elaborate very much on how calling something a portrait, especially of V.I. Lenin, a Soviet icon, would be intentionally crippled, certainly technically crippled, by being attempted in the style of Jackson Pollock. The work on the left is based on a David in Avignon and part of its title and one of the positive facts about the manner of its execution is that it was executed by mouth. The title it bears is concerned with the idea of the nude, and with violence, so it has an attribution of violence. Painting by mouth robs us, as executors of the painting, of a certain male aggression. The picture on the right is a drawing of a studio, a high genre in which the artist tells you what it's like to be an artist. This was also executed by mouth. We were impaired in some way. A similar version contained all those embarrassing things that we hid under the bed; things that we wouldn't even want to recognise responsibility for. That's the studio again, illuminated by an explosion in the dark, again impaired. Then there followed another group, which was actually inspired by that painting: the least suburban snowstorm I've ever seen, quite extraordinary for a sixteenth-century painting. It really does look lost. We endeavoured to use that sense of something happening to the painting rather than within it. The problem with those snow items was that when they were intellectually complete they were aesthetically hopeless and when they were aesthetically OK they were intellectually hopeless. We're dealing now with a museum, the Whitney Museum, setting our own material in the Whitney Museum, a place that we cannot be in, as it's the Whitney Museum of American Art. And another work is based on the idea of looking in from outside the Whitney. There are various ways in which the painting goes backwards and turns into a mess.

There came a time when we had a problem of where to go and one of the little bits of conversation in the studio was that possibly, a place we could go to was a place that can only exist in intention: the future. And we tried all sorts of things (everybody understands that fascination with things in the future, rocket-powered shoes and all that sort of stuff – I'm a child of the 1950s) but it was a place we couldn't go. Now I'm sorry that these works are lost. We destroyed them in a fit of irresponsibility. They made some promises, declared some intentions, if you like. They were medium-sized canvases on which texts were inscribed, in which we promised to paint various landscapes. These texts had the relatively trivial quality of quasi-contracts, public notices, or planning applications and resembled all of these, at one level, while being quite unlike any of them at another. The difference is only partially covered by the circumstances in which the painting promises were intended to be displayed. They were destined, intended, for the walls of a gallery, to lead separate lives, to act as a companion only in so far as the phantom future might accompany one.

There were those 'promises' that, as it were, matured upon a certain date in the future, and those with no date at all, merely the modal form, 'We shall paint, we shall execute'. One question that might now be asked is: 'did we execute them?' Another might be: 'how do we know we did?' Someone sophisticated might insist on asking: 'Where do these texts stand in relation to any picture that might be thought to satisfy them?' And we could ask if such texts could, without any further speech or action, serve to identify any painting at all. It would seem odd to suggest in 1997, of any painting executed in, say, 1996, that it satisfies a given text uniquely, even if the text promises production of a painting of a certain description in 1996, and the painting later produced answers to the text description in some way. Obviously many possible and actual pictures painted in 1996 might satisfy the description of a painting in the text. We might have attempted to satisfy the text and failed, or changed our minds, or a painting might be thought to satisfy the text on the sole grounds that we had originally intended it to do so, and so on and so on. These texts might be fragments from a possible world, but it remains to be seen whether we are committed to the construction of a possible world, a world in the imagination, in which the text functions. It's not even clear that in writing the text we were required to imagine a painting at all. Nor is it clear that we did in fact imagine a painting at all, let alone one that we intended to paint.

Now someone might argue that the best way to treat these paintings is as specifications for objects to be constructed in the future. The logic is quite familiar. In the form of a contract, for example: I shall supply you with ten black sheep with engaging personalities to be born into my flock in 1996/7/8/9 or whenever. But this doesn't work, or rather it does and it doesn't, because how do we know that a sheep, an intentional thing no doubt, is interchangeable with the apparent description of a painting, an intentional thing in another sense? In our text, we've made no commitment to supply a painting of this or that description.

Consider a well-known statement of intent. Picasso wrote that he intended to execute a painting at some near-future time and that it would be called *Guernica* and that it would have certain characteristics and so forth. All he had to do to redeem the statement of intent was to proclaim, presumably ostensibly, at some later date, 'This is *Guernica*, the painting I intended to do'. Explicit or not, the painting has, in some microscopically ceremonial moment, established some link of intentionality with a text or speech that predicts it. It's not clear that our texts don't contain the same sort of commitments, the same linking ceremony that would be considered a standard realisation of a statement of intent. In the absence of a linking or connecting event between text and possible painting, there might be an imagined circumstance in which there exist multiple candidates for satisfying or redeeming the text. One might also imagine a situation, say, in 1998 or 1999, in which an adequately sensitive onlooker might argue that a painting satisfies the text that predicts a painting better than anything else, even though it is painted a year later. One of the things we used to say while wandering around the studios was 'Wouldn't it be really great if we could be Conceptual artists during the week and amateur landscape painters at the weekend?' Now does this shed any light on things at all? Why did we say that we wanted to be Conceptual artists now and amateur artists in the future? There's no need to discuss in any detail what I mean by 'Conceptual artists', for the time being, think of them as clean-handed professionals with managerial and organisational skills. If this anecdote of desire is true, then it might introduce some kind of connection between the text as statement of intent, or promissory note, and the possible work that would redeem it. In the text, there is a strain or tension between the cultural character of the promising note and what it seems to promise. The sophisticated postmodern text on the wall promises an amateur painting. The tension, which seems to offer some sort of condition for the eventual redemption of the promise, forecloses utterly on the likelihood of that outcome. The cultural form of the promissory note renders the promise implausible, even impossible. One might say that if these texts are promises, they are promises that we couldn't or shouldn't keep; and this, even if one or both of us intended to do so at the time. In finding forbidden margins to write about, we're entering them in make-believe. We were in fact ensuring that the text, conceived solely as a text, could not be meant. Charles Harrison has suggested that the work would be in jeopardy and almost unbearable discomfort. The text seemed to be a dare. In the text, we seemed to propose committing cultural suicide. One might say, however, that this anecdotal cultural analysis is resting on a considerable structural faultline. It's all very well to say, for example, that the text would have no allure if we promised to paint a red circle on a green ground or for that matter something controversial or pornographic, or to suggest that an alternative might have been to promise to paint a picture that we sold at auction for £1,000,000. Then there would be some possible world, which the text might construct, in which we might fail spectacularly or damage our self-image.

But it remains to be seen whether the texts do indeed construct such a possible world. If they seem to construct a possible world that, at the same time, they internally and contextually render non-possible or implausible, the construction itself is an illusion. Of course, in the illusion of a possible world of painting and landscapes, there are scenes with which we are familiar and towards which we feel a certain warmth. The cultural appearance of the text, its presence as artwork, makes recovery implausible, perhaps impossible. But what if someone overcomes this cultural drowning and tries to read the text as part of a book with a foreclosed meta-narrative? Would the text that begins, 'We aim to be amateurs', be an invitation to the viewer to imagine a painting that somehow satisfies the text's description? Is there any need to imagine that the authors of the text were necessarily imagining anything? If a viewer does indeed overcome all these obstacles and imagine a painting of a certain description that matches the text, do we regard this as first-order aesthetic recovery or not? The viewer might certainly be determined on this. Could there ever be a rapprochement between this viewer and a hard-nosed one who merely notices the bare essentials of the text: typeface, words, sentences, grammar etc., and who acknowledges that it is capable of being interpreted this way or that, but who nevertheless refuses or never sees the need to put herself to the trouble of imagining anything that might match the descriptive text? Could the imaginative viewer claim priority for her aesthetic response? And if she did, would there be anything to support it? No doubt the hard-nosed viewer would say that such an aesthetic response was impertinent; that it was akin to being lost in a reverie of imagining the tune played by Sherlock Holmes on the violin as a response to reading the sentence, 'I found Holmes at home playing the violin', when the appropriate response was to note the detail and get on with the book.

But what if it matters to the plot later that you did imagine what it was that he was playing? What is clear is that the picture-imagining viewer cannot easily privilege his imaginary picture over that of anyone else. Of course, the text can provide a reason for us to prefer imagined green paintings over imagined red ones when it says, 'we shall paint a green painting', but it isn't entirely clear why. The detail of these texts, in respect of the appearance of seemingly possible pictures, is patchy and inconsistent. A great deal of this language is figural and allusive. The painting will be a front but no freak. But this is a detail that goes to possible form characterisations as well as pictorial or iconic ones. It's often difficult to separate them. For one reader/beholder, a picture will be no freak, but may conjure up light and joyful brushstrokes, and for another, it might evoke a spring-like apparition for the imagined picture. But a voice off is objecting that these imaginers are missing the point. It is not their job to interrogate the text and then somehow imagine a landscape that might satisfy it. They must do one, or possibly two, things: first, having not tried too hard to find a painting, they should wait and see what the artist eventually does; a second possibility is that the viewer might recover, not what the promised picture might be like, but what the author of the text was imagining. As what? The text as a mental image?

Consider the following historical situation in the studio: One of us has just scribbled down a few lines intended to form the basis of one of the promissory predictive texts. Having completed it in some immediate sense, he hands it to the other to read and to work on. What is the other person being asked to do? Is he being asked to imagine a possible painting so that his object converges with the painting imagined by his colleague? Would that amount to a plausible work on this text in the studio? It seems unlikely that any such attempt at intentional convergence would take place; not for long, anyway. What is most likely is that the writing, the text, would be worked on, so as to create a linguistic entity whose topological remainder at least goes to a possible painting that we cannot paint, cannot or will not execute. In other words, the task will be to write to the project. We must hide behind our speech at this appalling moment.

There was never any realistic possibility that we would execute a painting as promised or predicted in any of those texts. We might say that the landscapes were illusory intentional objects, tautological, pie-in-the-sky. It may be instructive to note that this project could be reanimated, but this would be achieved perhaps not by executing the painting but by retrieving the text and altering the dates. I'll just come to an end here and say that, given that I was starting things off, I thought it best to illustrate some little bits of grit in a conceivably smooth oyster. It might just get people to realise that the discussion of intention may indeed be old-fashioned, but it is something in which we can find interesting intricacies. In many ways, we can make those intricacies reach wide-ranging cultural circumstances.

I need art like I need God

TRACEY EMIN

Artist

The only education I've ever had is an art education. I left school illegally when I was thirteen and I managed to get a place in art school when I was twenty. I left with a First Class Honours Degree from Maidstone College of Art and all the art history and a lot of the art education there was taught with a kind of Marxist bent. So I didn't only leave college as a First Class student, I left as a Socialist with a belief in distribution of wealth and equality.

After Maidstone, I went to the Royal College of Art to do painting and I found out that my beliefs weren't held by the whole of society, which was quite fatal for my art career and my self-worth and everything. After leaving the Royal College, I got myself a little studio, went there every day, tried to get on with my painting, and the last painting I made, which was in 1990, was the *Deposition of Christ*, a copy from the National Gallery. I found out I was pregnant. I was a failure as an artist. I had no money. By the time I'd left college I was £5,000 in debt. I had no future and I was homeless. And I was with someone who didn't love me. And I didn't have the confidence as an artist to be able to look after the child on my own. I had a termination. After the termination I stopped making art. I stopped believing in art. I stopped believing in God. I stopped believing in the future. And I stopped believing in myself, basically. If that happens to you as an artist, you cannot create anymore. It's impossible. And luckily, a couple of years later, I started to get a bit better, and I started slowly to believe again. And the first slide that I want to show is a declaration of that, and gives the title to my talk today and is also the title for my show at the South London Gallery: *I Need Art Like I Need God*. And it's actually in that order. I'm not talking about Christianity, I'm talking about the faith and belief of all things.

Art isn't a game for me. It's not a conceptual phenomenon. It isn't like some intellectual mind fuck. For me, art is the reason why I'm here, the reason I exist now. It's my future.

'I need art like I need God'. This was a declaration to myself. I grew up in Margate by the sea, going for long walks along the beach, and I had a little kind of Instamatic snapshot camera and I wrote this phrase out. I realised the moment I put it down in chalk that I really, really meant it. It was something I totally believed in, something I would fight for. I would fight over this issue with someone physically, morally, mentally, any way.

Can we have the next slide? This is a drawing of me and my twin brother. Yes, I can draw. A lot of my friends who are really fucking good artists, can't draw. For some reason it doesn't seem to be important any more. I spent two years going to life-drawing classes three nights a week because I thought that was important. I thought it would make me a better artist. I still draw. I've been drawing since 1982 and I love it. Before I make a drawing, I come up with the title. I know what I'm going to draw. That's my intention. And that's my responsibility to myself.

Next slide please. This drawing is called something like, *You fucked me in the mouth, you slammed my head against the wall, you dragged me down the stairs, you held my face two inches away from the fire. You're nothing but pure evil.* So what happens is I start off with a memory and then I illustrate it. These drawings are called *Illustrations from memory.*

This is a drawing called, *Me and Prince*, a story about me and my pet dog when I was little, but I won't go into it.

This is *Masturbating*. I forgot I did a whole series of drawings about masturbating. It's not just about masturbating, it's about being alone and only having your mind and travelling through fantasy. If people are honest, you do this from, I don't know, the age of three or something, and because my work is so narcissistic and so much about myself, I thought it would be good to do a pure illustration of this.

This is about me and my twin brother, me masturbating in the bath, my brother masturbating in the toilet; it comes under the masturbation section again.

This one's called, *So What?* and it's about getting kicks watching stuff off the TV when there's no one else in the room.

And this is called, *You slammed your foot against my minge and made me say 'submit'* and this is about me and my twin brother growing up. And actually he used to be aggressively violent when he would do it and I'd usually say, 'You know, everyone did that with their brother', and apparently they didn't. I actually think this drawing is much more sensual, much more sexual, and it's about intimacy. I have a twin brother and it's about that intimacy and about growing apart and knowing when things have to stop.

This is called *My Uncle Colin*. This was shown at Jay Jopling's a few years ago. It is one of the seminal pieces I made from my wall of memorabilia. This is a story about my Uncle Colin who was decapitated in a car crash. The Benson & Hedges cigarette box, which you see, is what he was holding in his hand at the time of the accident, at his moment of death. I think the cigarette box is now like a box of gold; it's like alchemy, as if his moment from life to death passed through this box. The other things are him with his E-Type Jag, him looking out to sea, the seagull he found and put on a rock, the puzzle-box that was on the dashboard of the car, and a newspaper with the story.

A lot of people don't believe that my art is genuine. I don't think I come across as some sort of debutante from the Home Counties. Everything I do has a truism about it. Truth doesn't really exist, especially if you're working with memory, but there is an honesty about what I do. And of course I edit and choose what I want, but everything comes from my own experience and my own life.

This is called *My Abortion*. It's one of my abortion watercolours and text and everything from the hospital. It wasn't one abortion. The abortion didn't actually work and I had to go back and have it done again, like a week later, which was horrendous. And I won't go into this because now isn't the right time, but it was a very important thing for me. The text was written on the wall when I had my show at Jay Jopling's. Saturday afternoons I would be there. It was advertised in *Time Out*. There'd be a couple of hundred people there waiting to see me and a lot of women would read this, or men, and they would come and discuss, not art, not the piece of art I made, but life. Through my experience they then told me about their experiences.

These are my abortion watercolours. After I had the abortion, I couldn't paint or anything. I didn't give a fuck about it, just the idea of belief, the essence, conception, where things really come from. I knew it didn't come from a fucking paint brush or a pencil. I knew it didn't come from wanting to be an artist and having an exhibition and going to my studio every day. I knew it came from inside, like the real belief. I just couldn't make art any more. But I did make these. And there is a series of about fifty of them. It was a friend's birthday. I decided to make her a birthday card, and stayed up till five o'clock in the morning making these watercolours. I'd never made a picture like it before in my life and I've never made an image like it since. I believe that these were a desire to make something beautiful out of something so disastrously terrible. And after I made these, I stopped making art for a couple of years, which doesn't sound very long, but if all you've ever had in life is art and art school and then you stop for two years, there is very little left for you. I wanted to commit suicide, basically.

The next slide please. Sweet, isn't it? I'm an ardent fucking Expressionist; my favourite painter in the whole world is Edvard Munch. I'm aggressive with paint. I've got guts. And here I was, painting these beautiful, delicate little things.

Next slide please. Yes, this is how it should have been: this is the happy world, the happy world that now, looking back on, I know I've never been part of. People used to think I was mad, but I'm not. I've never fitted into society properly. That's because I've always been outside looking in. That's my job as an artist.

Next slide please. *The Radio Listeners*, because I just lay in bed crying, holding onto my womb, crying, listening to the radio.

Next slide please. Ah. If anyone knows my work, this is what you might be more familiar with. I call it my blanket, but it's a quilt. *Hotel International* is the proper title. And it's eight foot by eight. This is the fabric from our sofa from when I was a child, when I was three years old. I kept this piece of fabric. The pink blanket is the blanket, which had holes in, that covered my bed through all my growing-up years. Every piece of fabric on there means something to me. And then I made the blanket. You might have seen it. There's a fantastic picture of me in New York, at Park Hotel, sitting in bed underneath this quilt.

This is my grandmother's armchair. She gave me the chair – my nanny, I call her – and when she gave me the chair she said to me, 'There's a lot of money in chairs'. And by this, she actually meant like, you know, like … by the way, I'm the only woman in my family to have an education, and I'm the only person to have a degree. So my family's incredibly proud of me. But there is no legacy; there is no inheritance, nothing like this. I come from, not a working class background, but a kind of poor, mixed-up, fucked-up, dysfunctional background; but it's exciting, it isn't middle anything. You see, my nan's got no money but she gives me this chair, and she says, 'Trace, there's a lot of money in chairs'. And she was about ninety then. And I thought, this means something. This means that she's telling me something. So I decorated it, did the appliqué. I wrote a book called *Exploration of the Soul*, and sold it for £50 a copy before I'd written it. I sold eighty copies, which paid for the book to be made and for me and my boyfriend at the time to hire a really big, brand-new, fuck-off Cadillac and drive all the way down the Californian coast, to Las Vegas, all the way through Mid-West America, up to New York, Detroit. I took the chair and I did performances with the chair, reading from my book. And the whole trip cost something like five grand and I came home with six and had the most fantastic holiday in America with my boyfriend. And I even had a budget for Las Vegas. And I won as well. I stayed at the Caesar Palace Hotel. We had a gold Jacuzzi, King Caesar suite, mirrors on the ceilings, and I thought, 'yes, art ...' I was sitting in the Jacuzzi with my boyfriend, having a bottle of champagne after my win, and we toasted each other and I said, 'Here's to my nan's chair and here's to art. Art brought us here'. I sold the chair afterwards. I asked my nan, she said, 'Sure'. So I got an amazing inheritance from my grandmother, and I had an amazing time. And also, you know, art, it's a fantastic medium. You can manipulate it and do what you want to actually live your life.

Next slide please. My tent – *Everyone I Have Ever Slept With 1963–1995*. Inside, there are about 102 names. It's a dome-shaped tent. Last year it showed in America in a museum and people said, 'Gee, kind of looks like a Mario Merz, but somehow it's different'. And when you go inside, it is a lot different. It's really cosy. It's very womb-like; you go through the flap of the tent, you know, it's my feminist side coming out. There are anecdotes and side stories, sad things, good things, and you can spend like an hour in there reading it, being very cosy. Now this comes down to the responsibility of an artist. I'm a witness to things, but I try not to exploit friendships or closeness or confidences. And with the tent I thought, yes, just names of everyone I've ever slept with. And of course I'm at the ICA one night and someone comes up to me and says, 'How dare you fucking put my name in your tent?' I said, 'Pardon?' And he said, 'How dare you use my name in your art?' I said, 'Pardon?' He said, 'My name's for my art, it's not for your art'. Which I thought was quite an interesting point; something that I hadn't actually thought about. But of course, he was upset about having his name in there and I did actually say to him, 'Well, you shouldn't have fucked me, then'. He said, 'I didn't know you were going to become a famous artist'.

Anyway, next slide please. There you are, there's a few names. Might recognise a few there. But of course it does look like a cathedral, don't you think? I'd like to make a mock-up with two very tiny people, kind of looking up. It says, 'With myself, always myself, never forgetting'. And of course, the tent isn't only about sex. There are over 102 names. My grandmother's name. I used to go down to Margate. I used to file her nails and pluck her eyebrows and splash her hair; this was when she was ninety-four. And then she couldn't get out of bed so I would just sit in bed with her and hold her hand and fall asleep. You know, it isn't just about sex, it's about the intimacy of sleep. That's what the tent's about. But of course, I'm always with myself, going back. I'm alone. I'm a loner stepping through the world, making this folly to prove that I exist here, to prove to myself, to hold onto something, to anchor me down.

So next slide please. It's my museum. Has anyone been there? Well, we're in the Tate at the moment, but if you haven't been to the Tracey Emin Museum, you haven't lived. It's on 221 Waterloo Road and I financed most of it myself by selling Emin bonds, mini bonds and major bonds. It was an old derelict minicab office. I'd been working on it for three months before it opened in 1995. It's usually open to the public two days a week and I have it open for about six or seven months a year. I have different displays that change. There's also a permanent growing display. When I went into the museum it was completely empty and slowly it's starting to fill up with shelves and different things to look at. A lot of it is just my personal objects or things that I'm working on. I just showed this slide because it's got the tent in, but in the back there's a pink neon sign that says, 'The Tracey Emin Museum'. But now, in the window, it has a curtain, like a muslin curtain, and appliquéd onto it is, 'The Tracey Emin Museum – The Perfect Place to Grow'. And that's because I'm growing. I'll always be growing. So it's like a declaration to myself again.

This is my last slide. Here I am, Monument Valley, with my nan's armchair and with my book, *Exploration of the Soul*. And this work is called *Outside of Myself*. That's because with this whole trip across America, all I wanted back from America was this image of myself in the desert with my grandmother's armchair. That's what I wanted. That's the image that I thought I would come home with. And that's the one, the only piece of work I've actually got to show for the whole trip. And it's an example of just how fantastic art can be: the places it can send you, how it can change your life. I'm really proud of this piece of work and I'm really proud of my nan telling me there's a lot of money in chairs, because she was fucking right. So, that's it.

On intention

CRAIGIE HORSFIELD

Artist

It is probable that, when we're looking at intention in this context, it can be read as a kind of educational add-on, something that you screw on to the artist, after the event, as a justification for what is made. Or, conversely, we may be looking for a formula to assess quality or value when it is slippery and difficult to pin down.

Art, as has been said this morning, is frequently various, lacking in specificity, and in this country so much of it is without ideology or faith, but interestingly, the two speakers who preceded me, Michael Baldwin and Tracey Emin, engaged with both.

My purpose is at first to indicate a very general position vis-à-vis intention and then to look at some specific, one might almost say, strategic, examples. As a marker – as a statement of position – I would be inclined to see the world as being utterly indifferent to intention: things or events or facts cannot be understood, only recorded or described. By themselves they do not speak to us; neither do they pursue purposes. Nor do they act, occur, exist, come to be and pass away. We understand things in terms of what they are intended for. We understand events in the intention of the actors: those who shaped and participated in those events or, indeed, were acted upon by them.

However, rather than pursue this vein (it's very much a marker), I want to look at the specific applications of our need to understand intention. I mean by that, that we fall here into three very specific groups. Michael, Tracey, Cornelia Parker and myself appear to be the body, the material. The body is to be dissected by Patricia Bickers, Sylvia Wicks and Gray Watson. The entrails, finally, are to be looked over, and the runes read by a philosopher, historian, or possibly, more appropriately in this case, the oracle. It's a role that is quite familiar to each of us. It's to some extent uncomfortable. I, along with several others in the audience, no doubt, have attempted on occasion to arrange discussions, conversations, sometimes in public, concerning art and philosophy, or art and economy, art and sociology, and so forth. The experts in each field, full of good will, full of good intention whilst sharing a joke over coffee, appear to share very little in terms of language when they come to the platform. Exchanges are non-existent, excepting, as I say, the exchange of goodwill.

I'll attempt to illustrate some of the problems that flow from this lack of exchange. I speak very, very rarely in this country and part of the reason, as I have said, is that there tends to be a discomfort – and I realise that this audience is not necessarily the one to whom I should aim these observations – with any development of a discussion on art in terms of either ideology or faith. There is a sense that ideas are uncomfortable; they are something with which the work is clothed. Artists retreat from a justification or explanation of their work into performance, into the creation of spectacle, in which the meaning is developed by the critics, by the historians. As illustration of this, here is a recent piece of criticism from a national newspaper. It's Adrian Searle writing in the *Guardian* about Tony Cragg's sculptures, and it very appositely deals with this point. He says, 'Finally freed from the artist's ideas and fantasies of intention, all the conceits that made its existence possible, including the fundamental act of making, the work floats freely, emerging from a kind of blindness'. It couldn't be more succinctly put: all the 'fantasies of intention', the dream of 'making', a 'kind of blindness' – a blindness, a darkness, which is going to be suffused with light by the critics, by the historians and to some extent by the audience who have been guided, hands held, by those intermediaries. My slight unease with the interpretation of historians or philosophers is that it cements, it embeds, more necessarily, their intervention. The audience are only going to get to the surface of the experience. They're going to need this special understanding of intention, which only the philosopher, only the interpreter, only the intermediary, only the acolyte, can bring to the subject.

I will now give three examples as illustration. Michael and I are both currently exhibiting in a show at the Pompidou Centre in Paris called *Face à l'histoire*, concerning the artist and history in the twentieth century. It was intended originally to deal with concern about the connection of history with ideology but became instead, as the title says, the modern artist in the face of the events of history: two notable conditional clauses. I have to say that I think that Michael is in the more vulnerable position in this particular show, in that he is close to the three pictures by Richard Hamilton, which he had borrowed from the Tate Gallery; three execrable pictures of the dirty protest – a manipulative and opportunist group of pictures that represents very much the structure of the whole show.

In attempting to trace the connection of artists with history since 1933 to the present, the exhibition faces what it seems to regard as considerable problems. Much of the art is abstract; it is not representational. And so they rely, to a very great extent, on the titles attached to the work. This can lead to interesting consequences. The intentions of the artists are translated through the titles and then by the rather larger subtitles of the curators, and then of course by the text of the exhibition organisers. They're terrified to take into account the fact that, even within the area of the events of history since 1933, which of course is a succession of catastrophes and disasters, all artists were unfortunately not good. I don't mean not good artists: they were not good people. They were not, in other words, in agreement with ourselves. They weren't liberal, they weren't decent, they didn't accord with the present orthodoxy. Some of them supported Hitlerite Germany. Some of them supported the governments of Mussolini and of Franco. This is very quickly skated over, apologetically, right at the beginning. But throughout there is a kind of complicity – not necessarily by the artists, who are simply the material with intentions open to deflection, to interpretation, to development. It is of course being shown in France, where the greater part of the population, whether complicit or otherwise, were in collaboration with the occupying power. This again is skated over very comfortably. The exhibition, having set up a brave face, collapses in on its own cowardice.

The second example is a group show closer to hand. *Belladonna*, currently at the ICA, goes, in a sense, a step further, in that the material is, or the intentions of the artist are, largely redundant. The intention of the curator is absolutely paramount; or in a sense, the meaning that curator intends for the artists' work is a kind of retrospective intentionality enforced on the artist.

Finally, a small third example. I see that some of my work is to be shown at the Tate Gallery – an institution of great perception – alongside Hannah Collins and Susan Hiller, no doubt artists of considerable merit, in a group of works dealing with memory and remembrance. This is an original interpretation. And once again the intention of the art is virtually invisible. It's absorbed into a general sense of what the meaning of the art may be. Unfortunately, with the addition here that, quite by chance, all three artists make large or largish photographs. In other words, the form, the ease of the form, determines the subject and absorbs all other meaning into it.

Three examples, three perhaps somewhat slanted, weighted examples, but I think that one of the very great problems with *Face à l'histoire* is – and I thought Tracey's Emin's presentation was very telling in this respect – is that we live every part of our lives, if I may return to my introductory remarks, in confrontation with intention. That's the way we survive in the world, the way we move through it, the way we understand both things and others. We attempt to understand the intentions. I attempt to understand your intentions in being here, though I probably embrace them only in very small part. This is something that is at the very core – to attempt to, as is very often done, give a sort of *a priori* justification through intention for the artwork, whether it's a student's work or whether it's an artist who's been working for many years. It seems to me entirely invidious that we come to be through that intention. We should first look at intention. We shouldn't attempt to teach it. We shouldn't attempt to use it as a means for assessing value, so that we can judge. We should first of all address why we make art, why we exist as political beings, how we move through the world; all of these seem to be absolutely the base. If this is the seventh of a series of such seminars, I think it is unfortunate that intention should be the last. I'm inclined to believe that it might have been preferable to see it as the first.

Avoiding the object

CORNELIA PARKER

Artist

My theme is 'Avoiding the Object' – on purpose rather than by accident. I want to show a few slides. When I first thought about making art, a long time ago, I thought I was going to be a painter. The thing that put me off sculpture was that when you're at school, you think sculpture is all about bronze or the lump of stone, about the mass, and for me it seemed almost too dogmatic, too fixed, too solid, and I couldn't absorb it. I started making sculpture when I realised it could be an ephemeral thing; it could be something that's really porous, like Yves Klein's work. He was selling pieces of the void, and this was a very exciting idea to me; that this thing called 'art' could be a sort of molecular thing.

This is a piece I made about ten years ago called *Fleeting Monument*. Before I made this series of works, which uses famous monuments as the starting point, I'd always made works that were quite abstract, without any sort of recognisable element; everything was there to be evocative of other things, but nothing specific. So I used a souvenir of a monument, which is already a kind of cliché, something people only need the smallest clue to be able to recognise. I use these cheap souvenirs that you can buy in any sort of shop, which are very often the only kind of sculpture you have in the home. For a lot of people, the only sculptural thing is a souvenir on the mantelpiece.

This is Big Ben. I made a very simple mould of the little souvenir and cast it many, many times, so the process almost wore away the image. The casts started to become more and more broken up towards the edges. One of the desires for *Fleeting Monument* was to break down this thing that was so monumental, and to make it into something that was understandable, something that you can breathe in. I did a whole series of monuments, occupying different kinds of spaces. This was in a gutter outside my house – nobody saw this work; it was just a very private thing. This is my bath water. I like the idea of these famous monuments being drowned by my intimate bath water, something that I'd been immersed in myself. It was called *Drowned Monuments*.

This is from a few years later, in 1990. It's a derelict schoolhouse in Glasgow. There's nothing inside the schoolhouse except boxes of chalk. I decided I was going to use the chalk to make a monumental piece of work. The whole of the building is completely covered in tiny chalk marks, so it's a kind of drawing. I called it *Exhaled Schoolhouse* and it was almost like trying to break down this red brick institution. To do this piece of work, I had to completely touch every part of the building, so it was almost like the whole building had passed through my hands, and by touching every bit of it, it was almost as if I could digest it or I could understand it; I could inhale it and exhale it. It's like trying to digest something that is indigestible. What I liked about this was that it would get washed away gradually by the rain, and the building would re-emerge.

This was in 1991 at Chisenhale Gallery. The idea of the monument or the institution had become all kinds of things for me: a cliché, a sort of silver object, something that's very familiar, that has almost lost its meaning. This is a garden shed, which is, I think, a British institution, and it is full of all the kinds of things you normally find in a garden shed. There's a light on inside the shed. This was a photograph I took in the gallery before the exhibition started. Then I asked another British institution, the army, to blow it up for me, because I wanted to kind of exhale it and then inhale it again. The resultant fragments were collected and put in the gallery and suspended around the original light bulb. So now, because the walls were porous, the light could spill out and almost recreate the explosion through the shadows. The piece was very formal: the small fragments were around the light bulb, the medium fragments were a bit further away, the large fragments were a little bit further away again, and then the wood was on the outside. And it was called *Cold Dark Matter: An Exploded View*. 'Cold dark matter' and 'exploded view' are two technical terms. The first is taken from science: cold dark matter is the unquantifiable matter in the universe that you can't measure. It's material in the universe that's there but you can't see it. This term, which is very often encased in scientific texts, sounds very poetic, like a psychological state or murder, or something to do with emotion rather than science. I love the idea of it being unquantifiable, yet they had to find a term to describe this unquantifiable thing. Exploded view is a technical term as well. This comes from mechanical manuals, like car manuals, or bike manuals, where they lay out all the elements of the object and label them and tell you how you can put them back together again. So I quite like this sort of limbo between the two states – between something you can't quantify and something you can measure. This work and all my work is about that: trying to measure the immeasurable, by using clichés and monuments, and trying to find the inverse of them. I'm trying to find the most unknown thing.

This piece was at the Serpentine Gallery. It was a collaboration with Tilda Swinton, who was, before this exhibition, famous for being a sort of art-house movie star in Derek Jarman's films and in Sally Potter's *Orlando* and on TV as well. By the time the exhibition was over, she was more famous for being an art object than she was for being a film star. She lay in the Serpentine Gallery asleep for eight hours a day over seven days, as herself. The installation in which she slept was a collection of relics that belonged to famous people from history, a bit like the famous monuments that I was dealing with earlier. They were almost like splinters from the True Cross. These objects surrounded her, so she was the only living thing. All the other objects were already consigned to history. They belonged to famous people who were almost like icons. This is Freud's pillow and the blanket from his couch. All these objects would look just like ordinary objects until you read the captions. Somehow, together they almost added up to a kind of a composite person, a space to be in for somebody living and breathing. This was the pen with which Charles Dickens wrote his last novel – just a scruffy old feather, but when you read the caption, this thing becomes an incredibly loaded object. This is Florence Nightingale's slate. She wrote in her child's handwriting on it before she became famous. This is her handwriting before she was ever known to a greater public.

These last few slides are of works done in Cardiff. It's a series I've been working on since last year called *Avoided Object*. Actually, all the work I've ever done could be called

'Avoided Object' because really it's about trying to get inside the lump, as it were.

These are embryo guns – Colt 45 weapons in the early stage of production. At the point at which I took these from the factory, they were not technically guns, but you can still see what their future is going to be. So instead of killing something off and resur-recting it, I was taking something before it became something, before it had a function; but it still has the blueprint for the future.

This is a man's suit that has been shot by the pearls from a necklace – so the holes are made by pearls, not by bullets. I like this idea of this clichéd object like the pearl neck-lace, which has its own status and place in society, a sort of benign thing, becoming malign when the appropriate force is put behind it.

This is a dress shot by small change from a man's pocket; money makes bigger holes than pearls.

This is a meteorite landing in Epping Forest. The light you're seeing is meteorite light. This is a firework made from iron from a meteorite. So the meteorite is re-land-ing, except this time, through my intention, through my choosing the place and the time. Normally meteorites just land out of the blue and you might be hit on the head by one. At the moment, I'm trying to send a meteorite back into space. I really like the idea of this because it's a very calculated thing that might take months of negotiation, hope-fully with astronauts and people like that, to get this thing sent back, whereas when it first landed, it was a very random thing. You never know when one is going to land. It's a kind of alien. We're trying to send things up into space all the time, from this world, as it were, but I like the idea of sending something back that's fallen here of its own voli-tion.

This is a shirt burnt by a meteorite. The burn on the back of the shirt was made by heating up the meteorite on the stove and applying it to the back of the shirt. This is a very calculated thing, but people looking at it and the caption, might think the meteorite fell out of the skies and hit someone in the back when they were walking down the street.

This is a projection of a piece of dust that was trapped in a glass slide before light was passed through it. This is a close-up of the dust. It is a piece of dust from Freud's blan-ket, from his couch. I asked the museum if I could beat the dust out of the blanket and take it. There's a piece of skin going across diagonally. I don't know if that skin belongs to me, to one of Freud's patients, or to a visitor to the museum, but it almost looks like the exploded shed. By looking at this piece of dust, one doesn't know if it tells you any-thing about Freud, or anything about the human condition, or even what the intention of the artist is, but it's a world to lose yourself in.

This is a feather from Freud's pillow, which has again been projected. I've projected it anamorphically along the wall as I did with the dust. This little benign feather, when you just project it straight on the wall, is very twee and sort of sweet, but when you move it to an angle, it suddenly becomes like a missile; it starts to look like an arrow shot from a bow, or a dart from a gun. I quite like this idea of this very lethal reading of something that signals subconscious and quiet.

This is a close-up of a record that belonged to Hitler. What you're looking at is a kind of microscopic focus on something that's quite innocent – a piece of music, which is cov-ered in scratches. It's a bit like Freud's feather in a way: it looks benign, but when you attach it to someone like Hitler, who's obviously got this huge history filled with horror, you start to look at it in a quite different way.

This is called *Twenty Years of Tarnish (Wedding Presents)*. What I was asking people to look at was the tarnish, collected from famous people's belongings, not necessarily the object at all; so the tarnish itself is the thing I'm interested in rather than the object.

These are bed sheets that have been starched with chalk from the White Cliffs of Dover. And this is an object that was thrown off the White Cliffs of Dover a few years before. The day I threw it off, I polished it, and now it has built up tarnish over a period of about four years.

This is a *Pornographic Drawing*, which was made with ferric oxide from pornographic video tape given to me by Customs & Excise. I dissolved it to make an ink, and then made a Rorschach blot with it. I called it *Pornographic Drawing* as you would if it were a pencil drawing. The medium, the material, is pornography. And I quite like this because Customs & Excise censor things, they take things out of circulation and say we can't inhale them, we can't look at them, we can't drink them, and I think I was wanting people to look again at this material. It is completely random, as Rorschach blots always are. And whatever the intention behind it, the pornographic shapes are completely, so-called subconscious. It was a very calculated thing for me to get the pornography, make it into an ink, and create this blot.

My definition of art has always been to do with how much space there is in something for you, the viewer. What is the available space within an object for projection? And the Customs & Excise people were talking about the available space within the object for concealment. They were talking about objects in terms of where you could hide something. It was almost like the inverse of what I was trying to do with my work. There's a little saying, I think it's a Buddhist saying: 'How do you describe a hole?' If it's a hole in a piece of wood, you describe it in terms of the wood that surrounds the hole, but the substance of the hole is itself really hard to fathom. How can you describe the substance of the hole? I think that's what art is all about for me.

With intent: the burden of proof

PATRICIA BICKERS

Editor, Art Monthly

A driver was stopped by the police for questioning. During a routine search of his car, the policeman found a short, cylindrical piece of wood underneath the driver's seat. The policeman accused the driver of carrying an offensive weapon. The driver denied that it was a weapon, maintaining that the pole was used to support a processional banner and that he had merely forgotten to return it to its rightful place. When it came to court, the case hinged upon the driver's intention in placing the pole/weapon underneath his seat: had it merely rolled there where it had been forgotten, as the driver insisted, or was it, in fact, a concealed weapon?

In 1961, when Piero Manzoni created the first *Living Sculpture* by signing the naked bodies of living people – or potentially became a living sculpture himself by notionally standing on his own plinth for *Socle du Monde*, made for the purpose of transforming any object or person supported by it into a work of art – how did his intention differ from that of Gilbert and George when they became living (singing) sculptures in *Underneath the Arches, Living (Singing) Sculpture* in 1969?[1]

What did Carl Andre intend by using a copy of the Periodic Table of Elements, unaltered, as a poster for his sculpture exhibition at the Wide White Space Gallery in Antwerp in 1968? Or Simon Patterson, when he adapted it in an exercise in free association in *I Quattro Formaggi*, in 1992 and in several works since, notably the '24 hrs' series of paintings that suggests a modern Book of Hours?[2]

What intention lay behind Bruce Nauman's solid concrete, *Cast of the Space Under My Hotel Chair in Düsseldorf* of 1966–8, as compared with Rachel Whiteread's, *Untitled (One Hundred Spaces)* – resin sculptures, cast from the space underneath a chair, of 1995?[3]

What differentiates Bruce Nauman's four-video monitor piece, *Violent Incident* of 1986, from Sam Taylor-Wood's double-projection video, *A Travesty of a Mockery* of 1996, in both of which what the police refer to as a 'domestic' appears to be taking place between a man and a woman?[4] Or again, what is the difference between Bruce Nauman's *Clown Torture* video series of 1987 and Damien Hirst and Angus Fairhurst's collaborative video, *A couple of cannibals eating a clown (I should coco)*, of 1993?

What distinguishes *Breathing in – Breathing Out*, the collaborative performance video by Abramovic and Ulay made in 1977, from Smith/Stewart's videos, *Sustain* and *Mouth to Mouth*, both of 1995, which raise the stakes by immersing one of the protagonists, Edward Stewart, in water?[5]

What is the connection between Lawrence Weiner's tattoo and Douglas Gordon's (and, for that matter, Sean Connery's)? And what about the relationship between Douglas Gordon's *List of Names*, begun in 1991, and On Kawara's ongoing *I Met* project?

How does William Wegman's short 'twiddling thumbs' video differ from Ceal Floyer's *Unfinished (Venice)* video (of twiddling thumbs) first seen in *General Release* during the Venice Biennale of 1995?[6]

Or Vito Acconci's action in which he engaged a professional removal firm to pack up the contents of his apartment and deliver them to the gallery, where they remained for the duration of his exhibition, from Freddy Contreras' similar action during his exhibition at The Showroom gallery in 1995?[7]

What motivated Gordon Matta Clark to set up Food, a co-operative restaurant in New York's SoHo district in the 1970s or Tom Marioni to distribute free beer at the Museum of Contemporary Art, Los Angeles – a continuation of a project of 1970 entitled: *The Act Of Drinking Beer With Friends Is The Highest Form Of Art*, 1970. And how do these initiatives differ from Rirkrit Tiravanija's 'food events' in which he prepares food – Pot Noodles at the 1993 Venice Aperto, for instance – for visitors to consume freely?[8]

What distinguishes Ed Ruscha's *Chocolate Room*, 360 silk-screened paper sheets with which he decorated the walls of the American Pavillion for the Venice Biennale of 1970 (boycotted by several other artists including Robert Rauschenberg, in protest at America's involvement in the Vietnam war, and appropriately, perhaps, later destroyed by ants), from Anya Gallaccio's chocolate room, *Stroke*, of 1994, first installed at the Karsten Schubert Gallery in London ?[9]

Or Allen Ruppersberg's *The Picture of Dorian Gray* of 1974, in which he transcribed the entire text of Oscar Wilde's novel about a painting, freehand, using a Pentel marker, onto twenty unprimed canvas panels, from Fiona Banner's, *The Hunt for Red October* of 1994, in which part of the work comprises her handwritten blow-by-blow account, in pencil, of the action of the film on a long, horizontal roll of paper?[10]

Howard Singerman, writing of an earlier transcription piece by the same artist, *Henry David Thoreau's Walden by Allen Ruppersberg* of 1973, in which he transcribed Thoreau's book by hand onto sheets of paper, pointed out that it rewrote not only Thoreau, but also Borges' *Pierre Menard, Author of Quixote* and commented: 'Despite their different methods, Ruppersberg and Menard and their texts bear the same relationship to their originals: they are different.'[11]

That is exactly the relationship I would claim between the examples of apparently similar works that I have just cited. It may seem obvious, even redundant to emphasise this point, but it is the crux of the matter: they *are* different. Like the defendant in the example at the beginning of this paper, the case hinges upon the artists' intentions.

But how can the critic, historian or teacher, prove such a case?

Postmodernist critiques of the concepts of originality and authorship have apparently relieved the critic of one burden of proof: it is no longer regarded as productive, or even legitimate, to search for the Ur-text, the pristine original from which other works may be descended. This moratorium presumably extends to the artist, too, although the controversy that arose following the publicity provoked by the *Found Painting* show at Adam Dant's Gallerette, in London, suggests that the issues of originality and authorship are still very much alive. For those who do not recall the details, the headline: 'I found a Damien Hirst in a skip' referred to a spin painting that Dant found discarded in the aforementioned skip. It turned out not to be by Hirst but by one Andy Shaw who, it transpired, had experimented with spin painting some time before Hirst took up the lucrative practice. In fact, back in 1994, he had been selected by Hirst's own dealer, Jay Jopling, for inclusion in *The Curator's Egg*, a group exhibition of individual works chosen by various invited selectors, held at the Anthony Reynolds Gallery. And before either of them began their experiments, Alfons Schilling, one of the less well-known members of the Vienna Aktionists, had painted on circular 'rotating discs' way back in 1962 ...[12]

The issue of authorship, if not originality, remains central to connoisseurship that seeks to establish and authenticate an artist's oeuvre. To distinguish, for instance, Gerrit Dou's work from that of his master, Rembrandt, through a study of its provenance, documentation and by means of chemical and stylistic analysis. This is the object of the *Codex Rembrandtiana* project; an enterprise directed as much by economics as scholarship, though criticism, and to a lesser extent, teaching, play a part in this matrix. What critics and teachers concerned with contemporary art must attempt is the even more hazardous task of establishing the artist's intention in making a work.

To re-pose the question, how can an artist's intention be established in order to 'prove' the claim that the differences between apparently similar objects are critical – that the work in question is, as John Baldessari might say, 'This not that'?[13]

The arena of contemporary art is not a court of law, yet in some ways, establishing intention with a view to understanding the outcome – in this case, the work – is a not dissimilar process. Without labouring the point, one can refer to precedents as a way of establishing how this work relates to that, whether by the same artist or another. There is both material and forensic evidence from which to draw, as well as artists' statements and interviews that the critic, historian or teacher, like the lawyer, cannot take at face value; the evidence from primary sources of this kind must be scrutinised as carefully as any other evidence.

In 'An Anatomy of the Interview', published in the special 200th edition of *Art Monthly*, Iwona Blazwick analysed the powerful appeal of the interview: 'The notion of revelation through verbal exchange has emerged from psychoanalysis; the interview can be a process of stripping away layers to reveal an unconscious motive or concept. Maybe it is the promise of true confession that makes it so seductive.'[14] The interview is a relatively new resource that compensates the modern scholar and critic, perhaps, for the loss of traditional forms of art-historical evidence such as artists' contracts, iconographic programmes agreed between artist and patron and so on. All these methods would have to be brought to bear to prove my contention, for instance, that the works by younger artists that I have cited alongside those of older artists are *not* concerned with appropriation, a concern that underlay much neo-Duchampian work of the 1980s that was often heavily overlaid with irony – the 'signature' works of Gavin Turk and the paintings of Glenn Brown come to mind.

The question of intention, in connection with the artists to whom I referred earlier, became more pressing as a result of meeting the curator Anne Rorimer, who with Ann Goldstein, was in the course of completing preparations for the exhibition, *Reconsidering the Object of Art: 1965–1975*, which sought partly to re-orientate the history of Conceptualism to include West Coast-based artists who had been left out of previous accounts. When it became clear that the works already cited above by Wegman, Ruscha and Ruppersberg, among others, were to be included, I thought it appropriate to ask Michael Archer, in his review of the show for *Art Monthly*, to consider also the work of contemporary artists that might appear similar but which differed in intention. The article was published to coincide with the opening of the exhibition in October 1995 at the Museum of Contemporary Art, Los Angeles.[15]

Perhaps, since the subject of this conference is 'intention', I should say that I intended a pre-emptive strike against those who might, to use Archer's phrase, 'talk down the worth of today's work'. To do so would, as Archer pointed out, merely mean that they, the detractors, had not absorbed the 'lesson'. Unlike the work of Turk or Brown, both of whom consciously appropriate the work of others (including Manzoni and Duchamp in the case of the former, and the work of other painters – from Rembrandt to Auerbach – in the latter), the work of Banner, Contreras, Floyer, Gallaccio, Gordon, Patterson, Smith & Stewart, and Whiteread goes, in Archer's words, 'Well beyond the neo-Conceptualism of the 80s. It is not a working through of earlier questions. Certain things have become internalised, accepted'.[16] This is the 'lesson' to which Archer referred earlier. Certain things can be taken as 'read'.

Long before Nauman's recent major touring retrospective began, and before Robert Hughes remarked on it in his recent BBC series on American art, many commentators have noted the extraordinary influence his work has apparently had on much contemporary art practice, second only it seems, to that of Marcel Duchamp. However, as Archer suggests, the process is far more complex than this. An artist may suddenly seem 'relevant' – dreadful word – because artists, as well as curators, critics and teachers, working at a particular time may perceive an affinity between his or her practice and that of more recent contemporary artists. But, however close that affinity may be, a work of art is always of its own time and, *pace* theories of the simulacrum, it will always be different from the work of another time in vital ways. This is even true of a deliberate forgery, though it may be harder still to prove.

No amount of postmodern theory will ever distract the art historian, critic or teacher from seeking after who did what first, a desire perfectly encapsulated in Eduardo Costa's 1970 concept, referred to by Lucy Lippard in the catalogue for the Los Angeles exhibition and cited by Archer in his review: 'A piece that is essentially the same as a piece made by any of the first Conceptual artists, dated two years earlier than the original and signed by somebody else.'[17]

Though they may desire to do so, artists do not have a responsibility consciously to place their work in its historical as well as contemporary context, or to pay their respects to past precedent. That is the responsibility of the art historian, the critic and the teacher, though I am bound to say that it is one that critics, in particular, often fail to do, either through ignorance or through a desire to preserve the element of contemporariness in contemporary art at the expense of art history.

However, developments in both contemporary art and theory have revealed the narrowness of the pursuit of mere priority. The real responsibility of the historian, critic or teacher is to use all the evidence available to them to appreciate and to demonstrate the subtleties of intention that distinguish one work from another – a pole from an offensive weapon.

Notes

1. The first event in which Manzoni signed 'living sculptures' took place at Plinio de Martii's Galleria la Tartaruga, Rome, 22 April 1961. *Socle du Monde*, 1961, is made of wood, 80 × 80 × 60 cm, with two footprints in relief on the uppermost surface; see the chronology edited by Germano Celant in, *Piero Manzoni: Paintings, Reliefs and Objects*, exhibition catalogue, Tate Gallery Publications, London, 1974, p.11. Gilbert and George's work began as *Our New Sculpture*, first performed at St Martin's School of Art in 1969, then evolved into *Underneath the Arches*, a piece performed in art colleges in London and then in different venues, including the Marquee Club and the Lyceum in London, when it became *Singing Sculpture*, and *A Living Sculpture* when it was included in *When Attitudes Become Form* at the ICA, London the same year; see *The Words of Gilbert & George: Portraits of the Artists from 1968 to 1997*, Thames & Hudson, London, 1997, p.305.

2. The original version of *I Quattro Formaggi* was first shown in *Doubletake: Collective Memory and Current Art*, at the Hayward Gallery in February 1992. The second version, in ceramic tiles, was included in the exhibition when it travelled to the Kunsthalle Wien in January 1993. Carl Andre's poster was recently shown alongside two paintings from the '24 hrs' series by Simon Patterson in the exhibition, *Magie der Zahl in der Kunst des 20. Jahrhunderts*, at the Staatsgalerie Stuttgart, in February 1997.

3. Bruce Nauman's *Cast of the Space Under My Hotel Chair in Düsseldorf* (second copy; private collection on loan to the Rijksmuseum Kröller-Müller, Otterlo), was last seen in this country in his show at the Whitechapel Art Gallery, organised by the Whitechapel and the Kunsthalle Basel in January 1987. *Untitled (One Hundred Spaces)* was included in the

'Five Rooms' at the Anthony d'Offay Gallery; *Untitled (Twenty Five Spaces)* was shown the same year at Karsten Schubert Ltd, London.

4. Bruce Nauman's *Violent Incident*, was included in the 1987 Whitechapel Art Gallery show, see note 3 above. Sam Taylor-Wood's video, *Travesty of a Mockery* was first shown at White Cube in 1996.

5. *Mouth to Mouth* is discussed by Catherine Elwes in, 'Videoscan', *Art Monthly*, May 1996, No.196, pp.8–11; *Sustain* is discussed by Melissa Feldman in 'Profile: Love Hurts' in the same issue, pp.24–25.

6. The 'twiddling thumbs' sequence occurs in the video series *Reel 1–6* made between 1970 and 1976. The series was included in the exhibition, *Reconsidering the Object of Art: 1965–1975*, curated by Ann Goldstein and Anne Rorrimer at the Museum of Contemporary Art, Los Angeles, October 1995; the catalogue was published by MoCA, Los Angeles, and The MIT Press, Cambridge, Mass. and London, 1995.

7. The untitled installation was shown, with a work by Ceal Floyer, at the gallery from 26 April to 4 June 1995.

8. Tom Marioni recreated the piece for the *Reconsidering the Object of Art*, at MoCA, Los Angeles; see note 6 above.

9. Michael Archer, in his discussion of this work by Gallaccio, does not refer to the work by Ruscha but taking his cue from the title, *Stroke*, he discusses it very much in terms of painting, specifically the 'Rothko Room' at the Tate Gallery, London; 'What's in a Prefix?', *Art Monthly*, no.173, February 1994, p.5.

10. Allen Ruppersberg's *The Picture of Dorian Gray* was included in *Reconsidering the Object of Art*. Fiona Banner's *The Hunt for Red October* was first shown in her degree show at Goldsmiths College, London, and then in the *New Contemporaries 94–95* touring exhibition.

11. 'Allen Ruppersberg: Drawn from Life' in *Allen Ruppersberg*, p.22, cited by Ann Goldstein, *Reconsidering the Object of Art*, exhibition catalogue published by MoCA, Los Angeles and MIT, 1995, p.204.

12. Adam Dant's *Found Painting* show opened at the Gallerette, London, on 14 April 1996. The original printed invitation proclaimed 'I found a Damien Hirst in a Skip', but this had to be withdrawn in subsequent invitations when it was established that the spin painting was not by Hirst. Unlike Hirst's spin paintings, the 'found' painting was rectangular, rather than circular, in format. On Alfons Schilling, see Veit Loers, 'The Aesthetics of Early Viennese Actionism' in, *From Action Painting to Actionism: Vienna 1960–1965*, Klagenfurt,

1988, p.16. The paintings were attached to a wall and executed vertically; for illustrations see ibid., pp.78–9.

13. *This not that* was the title of John Baldessari's touring exhibition and catalogue, published by Cornerhouse, Manchester, in May 1995. The exhibition was shown in two British venues: Cornerhouse, Manchester, 6 May–25 June, and the Serpentine Gallery, London, 12 July–28 August 1995.

14. *Art Monthly*, October 1996, no.200, pp.15–16.

15. See note 6 above.

16. 'Reconsidering Conceptual Art', *Art Monthly*, no.193, February 1996, pp.12–16.

17. Lucy Lippard, 'Escape Attempts', *Reconsidering the Art Object*, op. cit., pp.17–39, p.29.

Students' intentions, achievement and evaluation

Sylvia Wicks

Assistant Director, Quality Assurance Group,
Higher Education Quality Council

My question for this afternoon is, how important to teaching and evaluation are students' intentions? I'm going to suggest that, in teaching and learning in art and design, the answer is on a sliding scale from important to crucial. I'm going to link intention to evaluation by looking at the contribution of students and teachers. I want to claim support for this view from Arthur Marwick of the Open University who, in his letter to the *Times Higher Education Supplement* of 31 January 1997, writes 'Slick readings from what painters painted, without any analysis of their intentions, predilections and the constraints upon them, merely reproduce weary old platitudes'.

Areas for Discussion

My focus for this paper is teaching and learning. I shall touch very briefly upon inter-institutional comparability and on professional comparability. I will give constructed examples. If something sounds familiar, it is purely coincidental.

I shall also assume that evaluation refers to a pause for reflection on achievement. The reflection may or may not be subsequently associated with a symbol – a red card, the mark 70 per cent, the term 'good', a 5. For teachers, I would submit, any pause for reflection supports students' learning.

Students' Intentions

The staff in this room represent as wide a range of courses as it would be possible to find in any subject area. The extent to which students' intentions are defined by the programme of study, or define the programme, varies between programmes, between institutions and, I believe, between levels of study.

Students' intentions are likely to be defined by the programme in the early stages of study and within programmes operating particular learning strategies. For example, a project brief might specify that by the end of this section of the course students will be able to use a saw, a drill, files and a rule and they will be able to produce, by hand, a straight edge of 5 cm long on a piece of metal 1 mm thick. A student who demonstrates competence with the specified tools and produces the straight edge is judged to be successful. Students match their intentions to those of the course. However perfect or aesthetically appealing a curved edge may be, in the terms of the learning objectives for this exercise, the curve would be judged to be a failure. Students are advised that their intentions should be to achieve a straight edge. Success is a straight edge.

A similar example of matching intention to expectation in order to achieve success might be the commercial competition offered to your department. A drugs company has just developed a new anti-stress drug that will be available over the counter. The company offers a prize of £10,000 to the department that submits a suite of ten images that represent peace and calm to the general public and use mainly the livery colour of the company, which is red. The prize will only be awarded after market-testing the submissions. Matching intentions to the brief will lead to the best chance of winning £10,000. Whatever the evaluation of a suite of, say, blue images, they cannot be readily seen to provide a good match between intentions and specification (or expectation). The criteria for success include a suite of ten images that say peace and calm to the general public, and are mainly red.

Probably more common in art and design, especially as students progress through programmes, is the match of the programme to the students' intentions. Programme aims might state that, by the end of the programme, a student, using appropriate visual techniques will be able to communicate a personal view to a lay audience. Students submit a proposal of their intentions and can expect confirmation that their proposal fits with course aims, or they can expect help from teachers if it doesn't. The result of students' work could be considered solely in terms of the reactions of a lay audience. But I would suggest that an evaluation of the end result that is independent of students' intentions may or may not support the progressive learning of students. Learning might have occurred, but such an independent evaluation process does not readily reveal what the learning has been to either the teacher or to the student. Failing to understand the learning that occurs risks continually reinforcing the same learning and the same achievement.

A teacher managing a programme of learning for such a student needs to know what the student wanted to communicate, and what visual techniques the student considered appropriate. The criteria for success are necessarily discussed in detail with the student. Criteria would take into account the student's view, the argument presented for the appropriateness of the techniques, probably expertise with the technique, the extent to which the end result communicates to the lay audience as well as the aesthetic qualities of the work.

So, to gauge progress in learning, intentions matter. Evaluation that is independent of intentions might present a view of the work, and this might be significant in inter-institutional comparisons or professional comparisons, but linking evaluation to intentions, whether intentions are programme or student defined, helps teachers to plan, and reinforce, learning.

When intentions are programme-defined, it is important that teachers and students are clear about this. When intentions are student-defined, it is crucial for teachers supporting a planned programme of learning, in the first instance, to judge the outcome in terms of students' intentions. As I have suggested, a parallel evaluation against an external professional benchmark might also be appropriate, particularly as learning progresses.

Teachers normally plan a range of learning experiences so that students' learning is sequenced in some way. Students generally respond with two types of questions: how much have I progressed?, and have I reached professional standards? The 'how much have I progressed?' question is the one that is most significant for the planning of learning. In other words, 'what do I now know?' and 'what have I still got to learn?' In planned learning, achievement builds on achievement. The one notion that all learning theorists agree on is that learning depends on what is already known.

Standards

A consideration of students' achievement leads us straight into the current national debate on standards. Standards are social constructs. They are negotiated by and between the whole community of academics, they generally derive from expert practice possessed by academics in the scholarly community and by their professional associates, and standards are not static. Degree-awarding institutions are formally responsible for the standards of their awards. There is no outside body, nor in my view should there be, that dictates to the full community of academics what standards are appropriate for the award of degrees. Each degree-awarding institution specifies ways of checking that its own standards are satisfactory. Checking could be through external examiners, through advisory bodies, through professional and statutory bodies, through research networks, through professional practice or through consultancy.

Definitions of Standards

In higher education, the current definitions of standards locate around three aspects: input standards (what students can do before starting a programme of study), process standards (what happens to students as they proceed through a programme of study) and output standards (what they can do as a result of satisfactorily completing a programme).

Research by Dr Alan Crispin[1] with around forty professional and statutory bodies showed that they were generally concerned with all three aspects of standards, although there was usually an emphasis on one. Professional and statutory bodies were interested in evidence of achievement prior to admission, perhaps in school or professionally. They were concerned about curriculum content, staff expertise, and examination practice. And they were interested in levels of award, statements of competence and records of achievement that gave evidence of minimum professional competence or safety to practice.

The Higher Education Quality Council (HEQC), on the other hand, adopted a definition of standards that concentrates on academic 'output'. We defined standards as: 'Explicit levels of academic attainment that are used to describe and measure academic requirements and achievements of individual students and groups of students'. In other words, statements of standards describe what individual students can achieve within programmes of study.

So in higher education, we have different emphases on aspects of academic standards existing concurrently. Higher education should always encompass such debate. It seems to me that there are three considerations for art and design teachers: which aspect, or aspects, of academic standards are most relevant for student learning in art and design? How should standards be described? How does one demonstrate to students and others that target standards have been achieved?

What do we actually know about standards? It is worth looking further at the operation, in practice, of these definitions of standards. The researchers for the HEQC Graduate Standards Programme interviewed some 2,000 people involved in higher education: they consulted students, academics, employers, managers and administrators.[2] One finding of the research is that 'with certain exceptions, academic standards are generally implicit rather than explicit' (paragraph 18). They add that teachers cannot facilitate students' learning without knowing about aims and required outcome (paragraph 28).

From what I've seen of course documents, I would submit that art and design teachers are further ahead in achieving explicitness than teachers in many other subject areas. Being explicit about standards is not easy, and is probably the next big task facing all academics. In the days of smaller classes and frequent opportunities for discussions with teachers, it was easier, through challenge, debate and example, for students to build up an understanding of standards. Now, time is differently apportioned and there are explicit expectations of teachers in terms of research and teaching, and possibly of administration. Courses are differently constructed. For example, there are modular schemes, credit accumulation schemes and work-based learning programmes. And more students, with a wider range of needs and demands, challenge teachers to be flexible and explicit. The Graduate Standards Programme research found that academics in higher education now generally agree that finding ways of articulating, in explicit and publicly accessible terms, the basis, standards and criteria for judgement of programmes of study is for the benefit of students, employers and society at large (paragraph 18).

May I present some of my evidence for my comment about explicitness in art and design? Many art and design staff have chosen to express standards in terms of outcomes. The following terms will be familiar to most teachers: by the end of the programme a student will have certain skills, specific knowledge and defined understandings. These are expressions of academic outcomes.

For this form of planned learning, it is relatively easy to make explicit what students are expected to achieve and relatively easy for students to match their own intentions to the expectations. But achievement and judgements about standards, in other words knowledge of what success looks like, are not intuitive. As I have said, standards are social constructs. Knowledge about standards has to be learnt, and here I am implying that it has to be taught. I have already argued that, for teachers, planned learning is dependent on a link between students' intentions and evaluation. I would submit that for students, progressive achievement cannot be separated from a knowledge of what standards are expected and what success looks like.

The further into a programme of study a student progresses, the harder it is to develop expressions that have meaning to students. Expressions become more like: by the end of the programme a student will be able to construct an analytical framework afresh for each problem; consider the implications of alternative solutions; determine when a solution is satisfactory; work towards a solution without predetermining an answer. These are expressions of academic outcomes, and I acknowledge that it is not easy to be explicit about what 'success' looks like.

With this approach to learning, I would suggest that each student's ability to understand such ideas is revealed to teachers when they take students' intentions into account in evaluation. Otherwise, from finished work, how do teachers know anything about the analytical framework, the testing of the implications of alternative solutions or the extent to which an idea was derivative.

Let us add more elements to this argument. It seems to me that to plan learning and check that it has taken place, teachers require a knowledge of students' intentions, an ability to judge students' achievements, an ability to define standards, an ability to teach students how to evaluate their own achievements against the taught standards and, finally, the matching of students' evaluations with teachers' evaluations. Isn't this what art and design teaching has always been about? Perhaps we have not been as explicit about it as this. Success – students' learning as demonstrated by academic achievements – depends on the existence of, and connection of, all parts of this chain. If you accept this argument, then being explicit about standards is crucial for students' success. In this model, I think it is easier to see the place for, and role of, external and professional benchmarking. I would suggest that it comes at the point of the teaching of standards and not just at the point of evaluation. However, we do have a difficulty here.

Comparability of Standards

Another finding of the Graduate Standards Programme was that 'the notion of comparability of standards, as hitherto understood, no longer commands general support' (paragraph 18). The findings cast doubts on the effectiveness of mechanisms that were formerly believed to ensure comparability of standards. Indeed comparability in a diverse system of higher education might be implausible when there are no agreed or widely understood parameters with which to chart similarity or dissimilarity (paragraph 24).

More support for this view was presented by Professor Keith Chapman of the University of Aberdeen who researched patterns of degree results between subjects, over time and within subjects.[3] Art and design was not one of the subjects studied. Subjects were: accountancy, biology, civil engineering, French, history, mathematics, physics, politics. His conclusions have challenged our prejudices. He found that:

a) variability in degree results cannot be regarded as proof of differences in standards

b) there tended to be patterns of good degrees for some universities, irrespective of students' qualifications on admission, teaching or resources

c) viewed over time, degree standards are relative not absolute; standards change with advancing knowledge, shifting discipline boundaries and changing views about the balance between subject-specific knowledge and more general transferable skills

d) the external examiner system is designed to ensure that a degree in a subject awarded at one university is comparable in standard with a contemporaneous degree in the same subject at another university. Systematic and persistent variations in the patterns of degrees awarded for each subject between universities represents a direct challenge to this fundamental premise of the UK university system. (paragraph 2.2)

Goodness! We all thought that having external examiners meant that we were working to national standards. In fairness, I do have to emphasise that there is a national view amongst academics that the external-examiner system is a valuable form of exchange and should be supported and there are currently proposals for doing this in work by Andrea Kupferman-Hall.[4] After all, the external-examiner system has been operating in the UK for over 150 years.

However, I think there is something for us to take into account if we are linking intention to evaluation. Comparability is difficult. As professionals and academics you have expertise and information that enable you to compare your students' work with that of students in other institutions or with that of practising professionals. If such comparisons are not easy for experienced academics, how much more difficult will they be for learners? I suggest that this reinforces the need for explicitness of expression of standards inside institutions that, after all, have been approved by act of parliament as capable of awarding their own degrees.

For improvement in students' learning I have established a chain for both teacher and learner that links from intention to achievement, to knowledge of standards, to evaluation of achievement against standards by students, to matching of students' evaluation with expert evaluation. I have just raised difficulties with the meaning of cross-institutional standards in other subjects. We don't have results for art and design, but should similar circumstances exist in art and design, it would seem to me to point to the need for each institution to be explicit with its students about its standards and to teach its students to make judgements against those standards.

Improving Learning

In presenting an argument for the traceability of intention through to evaluation I would not want to imply that such traceability alone improves students' learning. Dai Hounsell at the University of Edinburgh, and Graham Gibbs at Oxford Brooks have both worked for some time on the characteristics of learning and therefore on what might be done to improve learning. Recently Alan Davies of Worcester College of Higher Education has been applying some of the concepts to teaching and learning in art and design. In his paper, *Learning for Living in Art and Design*, he identifies four 'key elements' for improving students' learning. The key elements are: a well-structured knowledge base that allows students to make sense of new concepts by relating them to existing knowledge; motivated students who are keen to increase their knowledge; personalised learning (probably by learner activity) that helps students to make sense of new ideas; interaction with others that enables students to negotiate meaning and manipulate ideas.

May I summarise, and in doing so, offer you one word that I hope might emphasise my point. The word is 'traceability'. It is currently fashionable in higher education to attach new words to common practices. When you go back to your institutions and you have to 'cascade' what you have heard today, let me help you. Just say someone in the afternoon talked about traceability. Traceability is currently a common word in the food-production industry. It means what you would guess it might. People want to know what standards they can expect in food, and this includes knowing where food comes from. In teaching and learning in art and design, both students and teachers want to know what standards they can expect in achievement and this includes knowing where achievement comes from.

A Higher Education in Art and Design

I don't want to leave this paper located within the tight confines of the ideas I've suggested. I've presented no argument for the value of improving learning, although I'm sure that improving learning is a good idea. I do think there is a vision for art and design higher education.

Professor Ronald Barnett has written about the idea of a higher education and what it means to be an educated person. He is about to publish a book entitled *Towards a Higher Education for a New Century*. I was pleased to read in the *Times Higher Education Supplement* that Professor Barnett is interested in how higher education can contribute towards preparing people who can cope with, and indeed create, completely new situations. He is interested in raising questions about what kind of higher education would give people a positive orientation towards uncertainty, complexity and change, and a disposition to openness. I think this is precisely what a higher education in art and design does. Art and design, please take the lead. Be explicit about what you achieve. You have so much to offer other subjects in higher education.

References

1. Dr Alan Crispin, *Quality, Standards and Professional Accreditation: A Mapping Exercise*, HEQC, London, 1996.
2. *The Graduate Standards Programme: Interim Report*, HEQC, London, 1995.
3. Professor Keith Chapman, *Inter-institutional Variability of Degree Results: an Analysis in Selected Subjects*, HEQC, London, 1996.
4. Andrea Kupferman-Hall, *Strengthening External Examining*, HEQC, London, 1996.

The value of vision

GRAY WATSON

Lecturer, History of Art and Contextual Studies, Wimbledon School of Art

I too want to talk about art education but I don't think it's possible to do so without first saying quite a bit about what, for me at least, constitutes the value of art itself.

In speaking of what I see as the value of art, and hence of art education, I shall be directly addressing the question that gives this symposium its primary title: what do you think you are doing? I think that's a great question; and in a way I rather wish it had been left at that. The symposium's subtitle about 'intention', which is presumably intended as a clarification of the original question, but which in fact shifts the focus quite considerably, seems to me to have taken over to too large an extent. Of course, many interesting things can be said – and have been said, including during this symposium – about intention in general and the part it plays in both the creative and the educational process. Nor is it likely that one could speak in any real depth about one's own intentions without at least implicitly alluding to some of these more general considerations. I shall certainly be doing so to some extent myself. Nevertheless, there is the very real danger – and one that has not been entirely avoided – that this more generalised, third-person approach can lead to excessive concentration on issues that, though they may be theoretically intriguing, are of rather minor importance in reality. At the very least, it brings up a whole lot of questions that lead away from the original and more inspiringly provocative second-person question.

So, in saying what I think I'm doing, I shall just be speaking for myself, about *my* intentions. I certainly don't feel qualified to talk about artists' intentions. Indeed, in one sense, I'm not particularly interested in artists' intentions anyhow. I'm far more interested in what they produce at the end of the day, and in how this communicates with their audience. I'm interested, that is to say, in their art and in the meanings that may validly be inferred from it, whether or not these were intended by the artist. However, it is important here to make the absolutely fundamental distinction between conscious and unconscious intentions. When I say I'm not particularly interested in artists' intentions, I'm referring essentially to their conscious intentions. Above all, an artist's explicit, verbalised intentions – whilst clearly being of documentary interest and deserving in any case to be taken into account – are always of, at most, secondary importance in relation to their art, and may sometimes be downright misleading as to the art's deeper significance. But if one accepts that it is meaningful to stretch the concept of intention to include unconscious intention, then in effect one is coming closer to speaking about a an artist's whole way of looking at, relating to and acting in, the world. In that sense, I am of course exceedingly interested in an artist's intentions. One could even say that bringing out these deeper, unconscious intentions is part – only a part, certainly, but an important part – of my own, conscious intentions as a critic, historian and art-history teacher.

The reason I'm so attracted to art, despite not being an artist myself, has something to do, no doubt, with the sheer pleasure it has to offer. But if that were all it was about, it would amount to little more than a hobby. What justifies the very central role that art has assumed in my working life is the fact that, behind and beyond its pleasurable properties, there is what I see as art's promise: that is to say, the potential value it has, not just for artists themselves, or even for those, like myself, who get personal enjoyment from it, but for everyone, for the whole world. I know this is a massive claim; and I had better immediately make two things clear. First, I'm not making it as a blanket claim for all the art that is produced: the potential value of which I speak is extremely unevenly distributed, and probably only a fairly small proportion, quantitatively speaking, of the art produced possesses it to any significant extent. Secondly, I'm well aware that this potential has hardly begun to be fulfilled as yet. Nevertheless – and here, of course, what I'm saying stands in direct opposition to what I take to be the prevalent mood of postmodernist cynicism – I strongly believe that the potential is there.

Now, for art to be of value, in the doubtless highly idealistic sense that I'm proposing, one precondition is absolutely essential: it must spring from a genuine vision. By this I don't necessarily mean a highly original vision, which can only reasonably be expected in a very few instances. But a genuine vision does, I would submit, involve the whole of the artist's being. Every part of them – their intellectual, their emotional, their intuitive and their sensuous faculties – all have to be involved. The vision may well not be overtly prophetic, let alone optimistic. Joseph Beuys undoubtedly fits my criteria for an artist whose vision is of massive potential value, but so does Marina Abramovic, who holds out, so she says, no hope for the future of humanity, and so does Andy Warhol. Nor would I wish to preclude, on principle, those artists who deliberately adopt different styles or different personae on different occasions: one should not take the much overrated doctrine of the 'death of the author' too literally, and a splitting of the self may in certain circumstances even be a means – dare I say it? – to greater authenticity. But if art is treated just as a job, or just as a career, or just as an intellectual game, then a genuine vision is lacking; and in that case, the work will not, I contend, be of any particular value – certainly not outside the narrow parish of the art world. And just as, in order to produce valuable work, an artist needs to have a genuine vision, so too does a critic or historian, and so does a teacher. It's clearly not something that can be put on a CV and, equally clearly, it's a pretty tall order. But if an art educator doesn't have a genuine vision – again, I'm not saying necessarily a highly original one, but a genuine one, involving their whole being – then not only is he or she not contributing to the future production of worthwhile art, but they may be actively hindering it.

My belief, therefore, in the potential value of art is based on my belief in the value of vision, and this is why I've called this talk 'The Value of Vision'. The phrase does, I know, sound a bit reminiscent of Samuel Palmer's '*valley* of vision', which some might find off-putting; but actually I rather like that association, and it's certainly one that seems appropriate here in the Tate. I'd better say a bit more, though, about what I mean by 'vision'. The word can be used in a rather literal way, just referring to things to do with seeing, with using the eye – in other words, more or less as a synonym for 'the visual', where it's distinguished from, say, the aural or verbal. That is the way it is used, for example, in supposedly serious books like the collection of essays *Vision and Visuality* edited by Hal Foster (1988). At the other extreme, 'vision' can be assimilated to 'the visionary' or the seeing of 'visions', in the sense that, for example, William Blake could be called visionary. The way I'm using the word 'vision' – and I think this is the one most in keeping with common usage – is intermediate between these two extremes and incorporates elements of both, whilst at the same time being more general than either. It has to do with one's whole way of seeing the world, with what the Germans call *weltanschauung* – which is a visual metaphor of course, but it also implies one's whole way of understanding, and indeed feeling about, the world.

Thus, as well as a visual artist's vision, one can talk about the vision of a writer or a composer. I would argue that Shostakovich, for example, was able to say in his music – and here I'm allowing, again in keeping with common usage, the verbal to join the visual as a metaphor – things that could not have been said publicly by a writer or visual artist working under the same degree of tyranny. He was saying an awful lot about the real world, including the conditions of life under Stalin. I would call that Shostakovich's vision, and it comes through the music. Nor is this confined to the arts: one can also speak of a politician's vision. One of my favourite books when I was an undergraduate was *Politics and Vision* by Sheldon Wolin (1961). It's sad that President Bush should have found it necessary to send up the 'vision thing'. Whilst I accept that practical politicians have to deal with the practical, the here-and-now, and that 'vision' tends to imply some sense of distance, I believe that the ability to see ahead, to see things in the long term, is something crucially needed by our culture. So this is one of the most important things one is looking for if one says that a politician, or someone engaged in any activity, has vision: that he or she has the ability to see, more than most people can, into the future. The visual metaphor seems especially apt here. At the same time, if one says of an artist, in any medium, that they have vision, one also means that they have something important to communicate, to 'say', and here it is the verbal metaphor that seems most apt. That is why it makes sense to say that those artists who have nothing in particular to say, but for whom art is merely a game or a career, do not possess vision.

The fact that this more general sense of the word vision doesn't necessarily imply the visual makes it easier for it to act as a bridge between the aesthetic faculty and the cognitive and ethical faculties. Now of course, Max Weber – and he's followed in this by Jürgen Habermas – said that these were the things the Enlightenment had pulled apart: the cognitive, the ethical and the aesthetic, which became respectively the realms of science, morality and art. The Romantics wanted to put these things together again, I think quite rightly. There is a great need now for interaction between these domains; and it is no coincidence that the Romantics should have placed such stress on the importance of the imagination, a concept I see as closely allied to that of vision.

How, then, is vision manifested in art? And in what ways can we say that it is of value to the world? I should just like to suggest two ways, both of which seem to me fundamental: one is, in a broad sense, cognitive; and the other has to do with healing. These are not mutually exclusive. Often they co-exist directly in the same work of art and, even when this is not the case, the two functions seem to me to be ultimately complementary. Nevertheless, for the sake of clarity I shall speak of them in turn.

I shall begin with the cognitive function, where 'cognitive' is clearly not to be understood in too narrow or straightforward a sense. And I shall begin, specifically, with an example on which I suppose I can expect a fair measure of agreement. Rembrandt's portraits contain such an extraordinary depth of psychological insight that one learns a massive amount about human beings, about what it is to be a human being, through looking at them. But it's not just learning intellectually. There is also an ethical dimension to it: through the humaneness and depth of empathetic feeling, and notably the dignity he accords his sitters, one is gaining something on the ethical front as well. This is why one can legitimately say that Rembrandt is a greater artist than Frans Hals, which is tantamount to saying that he has a more profound vision than Hals – one from which we have more to learn.

As for modern and contemporary art, there are two types of ways in which it can be of cognitive value to us that particularly excite me. The first of these has to do with telling – I hope this will be a useful shorthand – the 'tale of the tribe'. Much of the contemporary art that interests me most does so because it sheds light on important unconscious elements in public and historical life. If you take seriously at all the idea that the unconscious is a powerful motivation in life, then it seems to me it is not just a matter of one's domestic arrangements, one's love life, one's relationship with one's family and friends, it is also a matter of how one behaves in a public domain, whether in teaching or in politics or in business or in anything else. The unconscious shapes us, not only in our individual lives but collectively, to a much greater extent than any political or cultural theory I know of – though I may be out of date on this – has fully taken on board. Certainly, for example, Frederic Jameson's book *The Political Unconscious* (1983) entirely fails to live up to the promise in its title and has very little to contribute here. However, quite a few artists I can think of have a lot to contribute – not directly, but by hints that have yet to be properly taken up. And they do so, paradoxically, by delving directly into their own most personal and intimate obsessions. That is the deepest sense in which the personal is the political.

I shall give just one example; unfortunately there is not the time to elaborate on it sufficiently to demonstrate convincingly the point I'm trying to make, but hopefully it will at least give an indication of what I'm referring to. That example is Gilbert and George's series of photo pieces, made in 1977, collectively entitled *Dirty Words*, because they incorporated photographs of graffiti with words such as 'shit', 'cunt' and 'queer'. These pictures suggest, it seems to me, remarkable insights into the unconscious dynamic at the root of political activity, up till now an almost exclusively male domain, but one for which the blanket term 'patriarchy' is inadequate insofar as it underestimates the importance of the role taken by the sons, the brothers, in their Oedipal revolt against the father, especially in revolutionary but also in all modern, as opposed to ultra-traditionalist, societies. And the reason, I would submit, that Gilbert and George's work is able to suggest such fresh insights, not as yet to my knowledge incorporated into feminist or any other political theory, is directly connected to their personal interest in young men, especially delinquent or semi-delinquent young men. It's important, furthermore, that Gilbert and George aren't conscious of the insights of which I'm speaking – which have nothing to do with their overt, amusing but rather simplistic political stand – since this very lack of conscious intention on their part seems to me to act as a guarantee of genuineness, unlike most deliberately political art, which merely illustrates already existing political positions.

We should perhaps not be surprised at this connection between the personal and the political, since it relates to the fact that very often people feel that art is most relevant to them when it is most deeply personal to the artist. That's why Van Gogh is so popular. And to the extent that Tracey Emin is really bearing her soul in her work, it makes sense that she too should be popular. The fact is that the deeper and more honestly artists go into themselves, the more they have something to say that – precisely because it gets below the socially accepted surface – is of real, long-term collective relevance. It is through insights derived in this way that, I believe, we shall be able to re-write more accurately what I have called the 'tale of the tribe' or, to put it another way, see more clearly how we've got to where we are.

The other way in which contemporary art can be of cognitive value to us, which I find particularly exciting, is a little more complex. To give an account of it, I must first make reference to what Paul Ricoeur, in his book *Freud and Philosophy* (1977) and elsewhere, has referred to as the 'conflict of interpretations'. For those not familiar with Ricoeur's work, what he means by this is the fundamental divide that exists between two wholly opposed approaches towards interpreting the symbolic systems that have been available to our culture during the twentieth century. 'Symbolic systems' needs to be understood widely, so as to include, for example, dreams, myths and works of creative art, as well as religious, legal and social systems.

One of these approaches is demystification, which Ricoeur calls a 'hermeneutics of suspicion'. For him, the three great enterprises of demystification to which we are heir are those of Marx, Nietzsche and Freud. Each of these great thinkers asks what is the guilty secret behind the symbolic systems they are looking at. Put very crudely, the answer for Marx is class interest, for Nietzsche the will to power, and for Freud, incestuous desire. Since Ricoeur conceived these theories, the fashion for demystification has largely been replaced by that for deconstruction; and although it is true that deconstruction does not presume, as the great demystifiers did, to identify what exactly the one basic guilty secret consists of, it nevertheless essentially continues this tradition of suspicion. The other, fundamentally opposed, tradition of interpretation available to us in the twentieth century, according to Ricoeur, aims at what he calls the 'restoration of meaning'. On this side of the divide he cites various theologians, like Van de Leeuw, and the historian of religions, Mircea Eliade. (I think he should also have cited Jung, but for a number of reasons that don't seem to me sufficiently convincing, he regards Jung as not being worthy of serious attention.) From the restorative point of view, when you look at a symbolic system it's not a matter of asking 'What is it trying to hide?' It's a matter of trying to open oneself up to it by asking 'What can I learn from this?' It is a radically different approach; one that is based in 'listening' to symbols and trying to attune oneself to their 'truth'.

Now, it is clear that these two approaches identified by Ricoeur are so radically opposed that, at a philosophical level, any reconciliation between them is exceedingly difficult and it has certainly not, to the best of my knowledge, been achieved. Nevertheless, a transcendence of this opposition seems an essential task at this historical juncture; and it's one with which art is uniquely equipped to help. Quite a lot of contemporary art – an instance that comes to mind being the blood-soaked actions of Hermann Nitsch, with their provocative references to what Nitsch calls the 'archaeology of religions' – is not only open to both forms of interpretation, but in a sense demands both of them simultaneously. No doubt this is one of the reasons that it is so little understood. But what largely excites me about such art is not only that it provides a *challenge* to transcend the opposition identified by Ricoeur. It also – principally by opening us up emotionally, as well as intellectually to the full force of certain deeply disquieting ambivalences – takes us some way towards understanding how that challenge might be met.

I said that I was going to talk about two fundamental ways in which vision is manifested in art, and how this can be of value to the world. So far, I've talked at some length about the cognitive function; now it's time to talk, much more briefly, about the relationship of art with healing. Matisse famously spoke, of course, about the healing function he hoped his paintings would perform. For me, landscape painting – and I'm not sure if this is because I personally can be made to feel so much better by being in a really beautiful landscape – has always seemed a form of art especially well suited to exercise a healing influence. I would particularly like to cite, even more than that of the great European masters, the landscape painting of the Sung Dynasty in China. That painting is of course rooted in a philosophical vision that deliberately banishes not only pain and violence but all forms of over-excitement, and brings about instead a state of total tranquillity, calm and peace. One could say that it's a typically Oriental conception, shared by Indian as well as Chinese art. By contrast, Joseph Beuys' injunction to 'show your wound' is more typically Western, but it too constitutes a valid approach to healing. And it's important to an understanding of Beuys' art – something made still more explicit in the work of an artist I deeply admire, Alastair MacLennan – that the healing of an individual psyche is actually a political thing, in that rifts in society are largely the product of psychic rifts within the individuals who compose it, so that in overcoming our internal woundings we are more able to contribute to the building of a peaceable world.

It is clear that this showing of individual and collective wounds comes very close to the darker side of the 'tale of the tribe' I was talking about earlier, and this is a perfect illustration of how art's cognitive and healing functions are in fact complementary. What I want to talk about now is how differently pain and darkness are explored in what, for want of a better word, we may call modern art, from how it was in the art of previous epochs.

There has always been an exploration of pain and darkness – Hieronymous Bosch is an obvious example – but ever since the Enlightenment dismantled a certain type of unified world view, the type of exploration became radically different. The crucial turning point was Goya's late, 'Black' paintings. André Malraux saw this, which is why he rightly says that, with these works, 'modern painting begins'. What Goya began to explore there, or more particularly the way he explored it, couldn't have happened in an age of universal faith. Since Goya's time, those artists – I'm thinking, for example, of Max Beckmann, Francis Bacon or Gina Pane – who have explored the darker side of human nature, have done so with a very important new kind of freedom. Sexual desire, too, has been explored in a radically different way in the last 200 years from how it could have been previously. It was certainly explored before: Cranach and Titian come to mind. But if you think of how Edvard Munch or Egon Schiele explored neurosis in relation to sexual desire, or if you think of Hans Bellmer and his evidently perverse desires, or if you think of Carolee Schneemann or Louise Bourgeois exploring the hardly recognised domain of female sexuality, obviously this is something that would not have been possible before. And generally, I think, the exploration of the inner psychic world can take place now in a quite different way from how it could have done before, because there is a new freedom, made possible ultimately by the Enlightenment. This sort of thing would still be totally unacceptable in a fundamentalist or totalitarian society. I think we've got to keep defending ourselves against attacks on this freedom. And we've got to *use* this freedom – not to abuse it, but to use it quite bravely. At the same time, this means that we need to give explanations of why perverse-seeming art, exploring what to most people are morally shocking areas, is actually valuable and can be of enormous help to the world.

I'm sure that had we the freedom to explore our psyches more freely earlier, this would have been of great benefit; but it is certainly more important than ever now, mainly because of the massively greater power that we human beings have achieved over nature, including the power to destroy ourselves completely and to take an awful lot else with us. With the advance of technology, and with the inadvertent side-effects of technological progress, we have come to a point where knowing ourselves better has become an absolute necessity. Looking into ourselves in radically new ways, and at the same time trying to come to terms with the inadvertent side-effects of technological progress, has indeed been a large part of the role of the artistic avant-garde. So has a questioning of the social rationalisation and bureaucratisation that have accompanied the advance of technology. This is particularly evident in that stream within modern art that runs from Romanticism through Expressionism, Dada and Surrealism.

Another crucial aspect of the present situation – which again is linked with technological advance – is the sense that we have entered some sort of spiritual wasteland or desert. Obviously T.S. Eliot's poem *The Waste Land* put down an important marker here. In German poetry, Hölderlin and Rilke explored deep into this territory, as Heidegger brought out in his extraordinary essay 'What Are Poets For?' And, in a very different spirit, Samuel Beckett created an extraordinary beauty out of spiritual desolation: I am particularly haunted by his melancholy title *Imagination Dead – Imagine*. If my belief in the value of vision sounds irrelevant and anachronistic in a world in which vision is sensed as dead, or smashed up, or totally obscured, I would argue that the ability to deal with the crap of everyday life and make some sort of beauty out of it – to create a vision that encompasses the absence of vision, if you like – is of the utmost importance. In a sense, Warhol was doing that, and perhaps in a different way Tracey Emin is doing that – I don't know if she'd agree? In any case, it is a crucial task for art at this time.

It is because art can be of such value to the world that it is so wasteful when it becomes the preserve of snobbery, when it is fenced around by people whose principal motivation is to exhibit their own wealth and taste or their own cleverness, rather than using that wealth or that cleverness, if indeed it is there, to share the art, and the insights it contains, with everybody. It is like the hoarding by a few of the spiritual wealth that by right belongs to the world. The image of Joseph Beuys' *Honey Pump* (1977) comes to mind: art is a form of wealth that needs to be put to use, and snobbery is just no good in this context. Unfortunately, it is well known that the art world is riddled with snobbery: sometimes even a quite old-fashioned class snobbery; sometimes a more trendy version of snobbery based on being part of a particular in-crowd. And a lot of contemporary criticism, especially that which derives from and is respected in academic circles, is guilty of snobbery too. I'm not just making the familiar point that most academic – which essentially means post-structuralist – criticism is couched in terms that are inaccessible to those who are not specifically initiated into it. I'm also complaining about the fact that so often it is blind to what is exciting about the art it tries to claim as its own.

I shall give two quick examples. For a long time, Cindy Sherman's work was used to illustrate the prevalent theory that there is no such thing as a real 'self', that the 'self' is always 'constructed'. Again and again, her early work was reduced to that. She protested that her work was far more complex than that; and she has now been demonstrably vindicated. My other example is Benjamin Buchloh's hilarious interview with Gerhard Richter, re-published in *Art in Theory 1900–1990*, the anthology of critical writings edited by Charles Harrison and Peter Wood. Buchloh repeatedly tries to impose his dreary, unimaginative and visionless theoretical position onto Richter's work, while Richter repeatedly protests that it's not about that at all, and attempts to point to a dimension in his work that totally eludes Buchloh's understanding.

The real problem is that a good deal of these theories are so inferior to the art that there's no way they can be validly used to criticise it. The art goes miles beyond the categories being imposed on it. We should be learning from this art, not trying to reduce it to an illustration of positions that have already been understood. I think too that a lot of academic post-structuralism has inherited some of the worst features of its predecessor in philosophical favour – at least in Anglo-Saxon academe – logical positivism, despite its overt rejection of it. There is the same tendency – no doubt it is an occupational hazard – to nit-picking over details, rather than dealing with what is crucial and actually makes a difference to life. Because so much criticism is infected with this nit-picking attitude, which is really a type of formalism, it inevitably fails to bring out the real ways in which the art it is dealing with can be of relevance to the world. The result is that when the question of how art relates to the world does arise, it is left to those with a predictably reductivist position – which in practice, of course, usually means Marxist or, more often nowadays, disillusioned Marxist – to answer.

René Girard has written brilliantly about this in the Introduction to his collection of essays *To Double Business Bound* (1988). He is writing about literature, but what he says applies to visual art every bit as well. He distinguishes two schools of critics, which he calls the 'aesthetes' and the 'reductivists'. He uses the term 'aesthete' almost exactly as I would use the term 'formalist'; but it is important in either case not to restrict the term to the obsession with the sensuous – i.e. insofar as we are talking about visual art, the visual – but to stretch it to include the post-Duchampian obsession with 'context', meaning, for the most part, the micropolitics of the art world. On the face of it, he says, the two schools exhibit entirely different, almost contrary, approaches. In practice, however, both are linked, if not by an out-and-out inimical attitude towards art, at least by an implicit dismissal of what I have called art's cognitive potential.

Behind the opposition of the two schools lies a common belief in the ultimately inconsequential nature of all works of art as far as real knowledge is concerned. The worshippers of beauty have tacitly surrendered to their adversaries a major part of their inheritance, the treatment of human relations.

For 'worshippers of beauty', we should read 'believers in art for art's sake in whatever form, including contextualist'. Given that little amendment, I can think of no more succinct formulation of what has been wrong with most art criticism, especially academic criticism, for some time now. A little later, Girard goes on:

> In Europe at least, contemporary criticism has come to resemble a funeral
> procession more and more. The reductionists and the antireductionists are now
> marching together behind the hearse, and they confirm by their structuralist and
> poststructuralist association the vanity of their former opposition. Their common
> bond lies in the concepts of the inability of language to deal with anything but
> itself and the absolute irrelevance of all literary works.

For 'literary works', of course, read 'works of art'; and 'language' should be understood to include more than just verbal language. Girard calls both types of critics 'men of little faith'. I would call them 'people of little vision'; and it should come as no surprise that they should engage in intellectual snobbery as a way to try and cover up this lack.

I find it deeply depressing that these un-life-enhancing ideas have found such a welcome place in so many educational establishments and – this is of course a particular concern to me personally – in theory departments especially. One has only to look at the book lists students are given in a number of institutions to see how all-pervasive a certain canon has become – a canon that is for the most part uninspired, uninspiring and positively off-putting. There are far too many stories of students, who naturally tend to lack intellectual self-confidence, being made to feel dumb and being too frightened to say what they really think. And if this partly reflects an ego trip on the part of certain tutors, it goes without saying what a paltry little victory they are scoring – though doubtless this sort of pedagogical malpractice has been going on under different guises since time immemorial. It is not all that much better when the signals that tutors send out are that they too find the theories incomprehensible but that it is a good idea to pretend to understand them for the sake of furthering one's artistic career.

The best and most valuable teaching occurs, it seems to me, when there is a real contact between the visions of the tutors and the visions of the students. And it is extremely important too, of course, that a teacher should be open to visions other than their own, to be able to foster the visions that students have, to be able to bring them on, to encourage them, to see the sparks, even if they're only initial sparks, and help them forward. Theory should be used as a way of helping students to articulate their own visions; doubtless also as a way to extend them and open them up to new things but, above all, never as a way of putting them down. Now I must say, I do not think that reliance on academic structures or formal arrangements of the type we've heard a certain amount about during this conference are particularly helpful in this respect. I think it's nonsense that if you set up a decent structure, it doesn't make much difference who fills the actual posts provided they're academically qualified. It makes all the difference. Everything in the end depends on individuals. Teaching is about the contact between real human beings; otherwise you might as well get the whole thing through a CD-ROM. What is important is that there's a real spark between teachers and students, and generally between all the people involved in the institution. I'm not even sure if it matters if we turn out professionals or not. I've never been too certain about the extreme value that Wimbledon has placed on the notion of the 'professional' artist. Art is not just a profession, though it may be that as well. I think many people gain tremendously from the breadth that an art education can have. I would love to think that some politicians of the future had been exposed to some of the exciting ideas that one can get in art education.

Art has a very important, privileged position in our society. Precisely because, as Oscar Wilde put it, it is 'quite useless', in a straightforward utilitarian sense, it is actually profoundly valuable in a deeper, more long-term sense. It provides an area of freedom in which we can explore things that really need to be explored, including some quite dangerous things, in a relatively safe and supportive environment. And similarly, as a corollary of this, art schools and art departments of universities are very privileged places. I think we're exceedingly lucky to be teaching in them. But with that privilege goes a certain obligation: we must use the situation of creative and intellectual freedom in which we find ourselves, if not directly, then at least ultimately for the good of the world as a whole. And I think it's really important that we do not hide behind formal academic structures. I know one has got to render unto Caesar the things that are Caesar's – I know that we don't get funding if we don't put in certain types of report and go through certain bureaucratic hoops – but these things must not be allowed to become our principal preoccupation. They must not overshadow what education is really about; because if they do, we are not only betraying our students, which would be bad enough, but we are also wasting the very rare and special opportunity we've been given to be of real help to the world.

Beginning with intention

FRED ORTON

Reader in Art History and Theory, University of Leeds

'Intention' has been a controversial concept in literary theory and criticism at least since the publication in 1946 of 'The Intentional Fallacy', an essay by W.M. Wimsatt and M.C. Beardsley. Even now, 'The Intentional Fallacy' offers much food for thought, but it requires more careful reading than it perhaps received when it was first published. Wimsatt and Beardsley wrote in opposition to the legacy of Romantic aesthetics, which, they claimed, privileged intention when it came to judging poetry, particularly lyric poetry. While granting that a poem is an intentional act, they argued that its author's intention should not be used as a standard by which to value it. Wimsatt and Beardsley also wrote in opposition to the emphasis on subjectivity that criticism had inherited from the Romantics. The procedures of literary criticism had to be dissociated from those of literary biography. As far as they were concerned, once a poem had been published, it was public property. On publication, the poem came before the critics, whose job was to judge it, as far as possible, without reference to what they knew about its author's life, psychology, and historical context: 'The evaluation of the work of art remains public: the work is measured against something outside the author.'

Rereading 'The Intentional Fallacy' prior to working on this lecture, I was struck by how much theirs is an argument about evaluation as opposed to meaning. At one point in the fourth section of the essay, where they puzzle over the idea that 'there is a difference between internal and external evidence for the meaning of a poem', they have interesting things to say about how poems might be interpreted but their main concern is with evaluation, not interpretation. The idea – almost a conventional wisdom now – that interpretation should be concerned with only what can be read (or, in its extension to the visual arts, seen) to be the case without reference to the author's purpose, came later. This was either, at worst, a careless reading of 'The Intentional Fallacy', or, at best, associated with American New Criticism, an extension of its concern with value judgement to new ways of understanding balance, contrast, rhetorical structure and so on.

Whatever you might think about 'The Intentional Fallacy' and the arguments it provoked regarding the irrelevance or relevance of intention in the valuation and interpretation of literary texts, for over fifty years intention has been a more-or-less big issue in literary theory and criticism in a way that it rarely has been in art theory and criticism. Indeed, it seems that intention hasn't been much of an issue for art theory and criticism at all. Which is not to say that art theorists and critics have not been aware of the 'intentional fallacy' or some extension of it, or that intention hasn't had its moments in art theory and criticism. But those moments have been few and far between. One such moment was in 1985 when, during the debate in *Art Forum* about the *Primitivism* show at the Museum of Modern Art, New York, Thomas McEvilley took Kirk Varnedoe back to school for a lesson on the 'intentional fallacy', intentionality and intention. Another moment, a much more productive and memorable one, also in 1985, was the publication of Michael Baxandall's book *Patterns of Intention: On the Historical Explanation of Pictures*, a work of high scholarship as remarkable for its seeming avoidance of saying anything about intention as it was disingenuous about the degree to which it was saying something about it. Since then, with the exception of some passages in Richard Wollheim's *Painting as an Art* of 1987, which argues, contrary to the extended idea of the 'intentional fallacy', that the meaning of a work of art is to be properly identified with the intention of its author, there has been little or nothing of value on this issue. In other words, though intention seems never to have been the vexed and vivid topic for art theory and criticism that it has been for literary theory and criticism, it has occasionally been brought onto the agenda only to be evacuated from it almost immediately.

As I understand it, 'intention' is the determining desire or force and structuring process that makes an object what it is and gives it meaning. My interest, of course, is with the work of art. This is not to say that intention and meaning are the same thing. I don't think they are: 'I am not merely saying this, I mean something by it.' Intention is the emotions and desires, thoughts and beliefs that initiate an action to make, structure and form an object that will affect an experience and effect a meaning or meanings in its beholder. Intention is always directed towards meaning. Meaning is always intentional.

As we have seen, 'The Intentional Fallacy' was intended as a contribution to aesthetics. Wollheim's *Painting as an Art* is surely that. Philosophy is unavoidable in a talk about intention, and philosophy has always been concerned with it. But I am no philosopher. I went to college in the early 1960s with the intention of becoming an artist. I became an art historian in the late 1970s. So much for intention. I know very little philosophy, and when my art history has needed it, I have usually appropriated it from Wollheim's work, either *Art and Its Objects* or the essay, first published in *Studio International* in December 1970, 'The Work of Art as Object'. That said, since my art student days when I first read it, I have also, on occasion, turned to the philosophy of Wittgenstein: to the *Tractatus Logico-Philosophicus* (1922) or, more often, to the *Philosophical Investigations* (1953). Fragments of the latter and the *Lectures on Aesthetics* have their place in this talk. But it is Wollheim, not Wittgenstein whom I would want to advert to now. The beginning of his essay 'The Work of Art as Object' serves me very well in so far as it suggests a route to follow or a structure for what I want to say. Here it is:

> If we wanted to say something about art that we could be quite certain was true we might settle for the assertion that art is intentional. And by this we would mean that art is something we do, that works of art are things that human beings make. And the truth of this assertion is in no way challenged by such discoveries, some long known, others freshly brought to light, as that we cannot produce a work of art to order, that improvisation has its place in the making of a work of art, that the artist is not necessarily the best interpreter of his work, that the spectator has a legitimate role to play in the organisation of what he perceives.

If occasionally I have turned to Wollheim's writing for philosophical resources for my art history, I have more often turned to the work of Jasper Johns for my objects of study. As far as I'm concerned, several of Johns' works are amongst the canonical works of twentieth-century art. None more so than *Flag* (1954–6), a work that effects a knowledge about the self and the world that is difficult to accept and impossible to transcend. I believe it has an extraordinary sensual and cognitive value. Over the last twenty years, *Flag* has marked the progress of my art history almost in the manner that it has marked the progress of Johns' art practice. I'm not going to break with my habit of returning to *Flag*. It, and Johns' story of how he came to make it, are such exemplary objects with which to examine, illustrate and explain intention that I would be foolish if I ignored them.

To those people who asked him why he made *Flag*, or how he came to make it, or what it meant, Johns first replied that he 'intuitively' liked to paint flags. Afterwards, he would reply, and thereafter always reply along the same lines, that he 'dreamed one night of painting a large flag' or that he 'had a dream, in which [he] painted a picture of a big Stars and Stripes'. It seems that he told one or two close friends about the dream, and one or the other of them or both of them thought that it presented him with a good idea for a painting. After that, he went out and bought the materials with which to begin. And began. 'Beginning' is important. In several additions to the story of the dream, Johns has said that 'using the design of the American flag took care of a great deal' for him because he didn't have to design it; that 'it had a clearly defined area, which could be measured and transferred to canvas'; and that it was something he could do that would be his.

'If we wanted to say something about art that we could be quite certain was true, we might settle for the assertion that art is intentional. And by this we would mean that art is something we do, that works of art are things that human beings make.' (Wollheim, *The Work of Art as Object*) This makes a distinction between an intentional object and a natural object. Whereas poems, literary texts, paintings and sculptures, music, etc., are made of imagined and invented time, place and form, natural objects have not been invented; their formal, spatial and temporal characters are, as it were, given. Though, according to the 'intentional fallacy', poems and works of art might be judged as natural objects, they could only be so judged as meaningful by ignoring their intentional character. Paul de Man, discussing the relation between form and intent in American New Criticism, put the matter like this:

> Certain entities exist the full meaning of which can be said to equal the totality of their sensory appearances. For an ideal perception, entirely devoid of complications resulting from the interference of the imagination, the 'meaning' of 'stone' could only refer to a totality of sensory appearances. The same applies to all natural objects. But even the most purely intuitive consciousness could never conceive of the significance of an object such as, for instance, a chair, without including in the description an allusion to the use to which it is put; the most rigorous description of the perceptions of the object 'chair' would remain meaningless if one does not organise them in function of the potential act that defines the object; namely, that it is destined to be sat on. The potential act of sitting down is a constitutive part of the object. If it were absent, the object could not be conceived in its totality. The difference between the stone and the chair

distinguishes a natural object from an intentional object. The intentional object requires a reference to a specific act as constitutive of its mode of being.

By asserting … that, in literary language, the meaning is equal to the sum of the sensory appearances, one postulates in fact that the language of literature is of the same order, ontologically speaking, as a natural object. The intentional factor has been bypassed.

What de Man says about the way a literary text and the language of literature are valued and understood according to the 'intentional fallacy' accords with the way paintings and sculptures are valued and understood by those art theorists and critics who hold to the dominant theory of the expressive quality of the work of art. These theorists and critics see themselves as disinterested and evaluate the work of art by its effects as they feel them. This is Clement Greenberg, who, in a common variation on the belief in the expressive quality of the work, holds also to the ineffability of affect and effect: 'Whatever Dante or Tolstoy, Bach or Mozart, Giotto or David intended his art to be about, or said it was about, the works of his go beyond anything specifiable in their effect. That is what art, regardless of the intention of artists, *has* to do, even the worst art'. The dominant theory of the expressive quality of the work of art is, like the 'intentional fallacy', doubly fallacious because it holds not only that the expressive quality of a work of art can be sensed and valued independent of any consideration of the artist's intention but also that what is expressed is a natural expression, is in and of itself expressed naturally – directly and immediately – regardless of any intention.

Chairs and literary texts or, as Baxandall would have it, bridges and paintings, are different kinds of intentional objects, each with its own relation to intention, and to what Wollheim, in 'The Work of Art as Object', referred to as a 'concept' or 'description'. Because works of art are things that human beings make, they must be made according to a concept, or according to various descriptions of the qualities, features, characteristics, etc. that make the work of art – the painting or sculpture – what it is. There will be a hierarchy among these concepts or descriptions that regulates the production of the work of art. At different periods and under different conditions, the relations that hold within the concept will be felt or thought to change. Modern works of art are somewhat different from pre-modern works of art. According to the dominant theory of modern art, as Wollheim understood it in 1970, the material character of the work has to be emphasised. With regard to painting, the concept or description requires that the surface has to be asserted or insisted on – the dominant theory insists on the fact that a painting has a surface – and, if only with regard to the kind of paintings that Wollheim took as his examples, Matisse's *The Open Window* (1913), Rothko's *Red on Maroon* (1959), and Morris Louis' *Alpha Phi* (1962), used as if – Wollheim would not use that 'as if' – to effect in the beholder a sense and cognition of what and how the painter felt and knew, or, for Wollheim, an expressive quality and a kind of beauty.

Works of art, especially works of modern art, are different from other things that human beings make. The act of making a work of art, especially the modern act of making a modern work of art, involves an intention and a concept different from that of, to stay with Baxandall's 'Patterns of Intention', making a bridge where everything, including the designer's sense of expression and beauty, etc. has to be subordinated to the intention of spanning and facilitating movement across a gap. Another example, direct-ly relevant to Johns' *Flag*, is provided by the Stars and Stripes, an intentional object whose manufacture is controlled by a 'description' of its size, proportions, situation of its elements, and colours that can only be altered or amended by law and that is subor-dinated to the legally controlled intention of facilitating the demonstration, affirmation and celebration of citizenship, loyalty and patriotism. Art is both an intentional act and an intentional object, but it is not, as it is with designing and making the Stars and Stripes or a bridge, subordinated to another act that exists beyond the intention of mak-ing it and trying to make it according to that intention. Here I come in line with those who have argued that the modern artist makes a work of art with no intention other than that of making it, where making it constitutes a closed structure, autonomous of what-ever use might be made of it after it has been made; for example: selling it. The artist might well have the intention of selling the work of art once he or she has done making it but that intention of exchanging the work of art for hard cash must exist beyond the intention of making it. To understand works of art in this way is not to insist, as New Criticism insisted, on the idea of the 'self-sufficiency' or 'self-focusedness' of art. Rather, to insist on the way the artist works the sensuous materials of the work of art according to no other intention but to make it, is to insist that making and understand-ing a work of art enables an acute form of 'self-consciousness'.

Art is an intentional act and object of 'self consciousness'. Making a work of art is a 'self-conscious' operation of a mind that would know itself. 'Self-conscious' then, not 'self-sufficient', where 'self-sufficient' is taken as a metaphor for the belief that the pro-duction and consumption of a work of art is independent or autonomous of reference to the world outside its structure and form. And 'self-conscious' then, not 'self-focused', for the point is that there is no originary, ontologically prior or transcendental self that could be focused on and met with or matched in the making and understanding of a work of art. 'Self-conscious', then, because the intention to make a work of art is an intention to inaugurate a structuring process whereby some degree of self-conscious-ness comes into place, only to be put under erasure, negated – it's not that, it's not that – and gone on with. Seen and understood like this, the work of art appears as but one moment in the continuous process of desiring a self-identity wherein material signs – metaphors, metonyms, the full range of tropes and figures of speech or their visual equivalents – of that identity are simultaneously found and lost, placed and displaced. Whatever the modern artist's intentions and whatever he or she wants to mean, he or she makes a work of art to know a self. The modern work of art comes in place of a self's yearning for knowledge of itself. Suffice it to say now that though the work of art can-not be reduced to the intention that brings it into being, the intention of making and understanding a modern work of art maintains itself as a process of self-consciousness. More on this later.

When, in 1964, Johns turned his dream into published discourse, he did so in ways that show that he may not have been clear about what he was doing in it. Remember, on one occasion, he said that he 'dreamed one night of painting a large flag' and, on anoth-er occasion, that 'he had a dream in which [he] painted a picture of a big Stars and Stripes'. Was he, in his dream, dreaming the intention of painting, or was he at work painting? Was he dreaming about doing something, or was he dreaming doing something? Was he intending to make, or was he making, either a large flag with paint, or painting a picture of one? And was the 'large flag' in the first version of the story the 'Stars and Stripes' in the second version? Was it the same flag in both versions or a different flag in each version? Was the object that he was dreaming of making, or dreaming that he was making, a work of art, something insubordinate and self-conscious, or was it a flag, an object seemingly without self-consciousness and subordinate to another intention? The different stories of the dream are intriguing. They effect an uncertainty, irresolvable either by the analysis of grammar or by an appeal for some kind of secondary revision, about what kind of object it was that was there in the dream and which, subsequently, was taken into the object that became *Flag*.

Awake and in the studio, making *Flag*, Johns blurred the distinction between making an object under the concept 'flag' (and making a large Stars and Stripes with paint) and making an object under the concept 'painting' (and painting a picture of a big Stars and Stripes). From the moment that he hit on the idea of having the Stars and Stripes provide the structure and form for the way he was to assert and use the surface of his painting, making the one congruent with the other, the idea of painting a picture of a big Stars and Stripes was compromised. It was further compromised, bearing in mind how a Stars and Stripes is made, by his decision to follow the usual pattern of making a Stars and Stripes and use three separate panels, one canvas for the canton, one for the short stripes to its right, and one for the long stripes below. This will be important for those who know the Stars and Stripes. What Johns was doing was more like making the Stars and Stripes than painting a picture of one.

'A picture represents its subject from a position outside it. (Its standpoint is its representational form.) That is why a picture represents its subject correctly or incorrectly ... A picture cannot, however, place itself outside its representational form.' (Wittgenstein pointed that out. But he hadn't seen Johns' *Flag*.) The point about Johns' *Flag* is that, as a work of art, it does not represent its subject from a position outside its representational form. It both represents its subject and is the subject presented. In managing to do this, it shifts the conditions of 'outside' and 'inside', flag and work of art. (I have to say, however, that modern art had, perhaps, already shifted the conditions of 'outside' and 'inside' as meant by Wittgenstein.)

The peculiar character of *Flag* is such that wherever one looks, there is both flag and painting. *Flag* is neither flag nor painting but both flag and painting. Neither the Stars and Stripes, nor a painting of the Stars and Stripes, it is simultaneously both the Stars and Stripes and a painting of the Stars and Stripes. The oppositions that organise Flag merge in a constant and provocative undecidable exchange of attributes in a way that causes problems for anyone who is concerned to fix its meaning. Whether Johns intended this undecidability or whether it resulted as an effect of how he recollected what he dreamed and took that recollection for an intention, that is what materialised when he made his work congruent with the structure and form of the Stars and Stripes. Or vice versa. However, whatever it was that he intended to make or saw himself making in his dream, he must have been intending to make, or was making it according to some concept of what painting was as an activity. And, awake and in the studio, in so far as his intention was to make whatever it was that he intended to make or was making in the dream, under the description or concept painting, according to the dominant theory of modern art as it related to painting, that intention was frustrated in practice.

'We cannot produce a work of art to order … improvisation has its place in the making of a work of art'. (Wollheim, *The Work of Art as Object*) The intention that Johns dreamed or was acting on in his dream with paint began in actuality with paint also, but then that medium was abandoned in favour of another medium. Johns began making the object that would become *Flag* at the end of 1954 or in 1955, with what would have been regarded as respectable avant-garde materials: enamel paints on a bed sheet. In the mid 1950s, both de Kooning and Pollock were using enamel to make their paintings. For them, it had a value as a non-artistic material – a travesty or negation of fine art materials. And like them, it was important for Johns that the history of the creative process should be part of the finished object. Its past had to be there in its presented state. Johns wanted to show what had gone before and what had been done after. He wanted the process and history of the making of the painting to be part of its meaning and effect. That was a conventional avant-garde strategy of art making. But when he applied the paint, the second brushstroke smeared the first brushstroke unless he waited until the paint dried; and the paint took too long to dry. He was a skilled draughtsman and collager, and had developed the knack of making plaster casts, but it is possible that he was not, then, as patient or as adept as a painter – as an avant-garde painter – to the degree that his intention demanded that he was either too impatient or not sufficiently skilled in asserting and using the surface with enamel paint to succeed with it. He stopped working with enamel and changed to wax. Hot wax dries very quickly. As soon as one stroke had cooled and hardened, he could add another without altering what had been done before. Splashes, drips and dribbles become round as they dry, like enamel paint does but more so, just as wax dribbles down the side of a candle. He found the medium very easy to control and adapted it to his way with collage where more or less rectangular, more or less regular-sized bits of paper, some printed, some plain, would be stuck down next to each other or slightly overlapping, here and there not quite adhering, standing proud at the corners, slightly curling at the edges. The process Johns used for *Flag* involved dipping cut and torn pieces of paper and cloth into hot coloured wax – blue, white and red – and fixing them to the fabric before the wax cooled. This meant that the various textures, value contrasts and texts would remain visible at the same time that their individualities were subsumed and unified by the structure of the Stars and Stripes and the all-over surface gloss of the wax. In some places wax has dripped and dribbled across the edges of stars and stripes, but those drips and dribbles have not been allowed to disrupt, spoil or break the genuine flagness of *Flag*. Wherever the wax has run from a red stripe across a white stripe or from a white stripe across a red stripe, it has been overpainted with either red or white paint or wax to preserve the integrity and colouration of the Stars and Stripes.

Some areas of *Flag*'s surface also include the use of paint and brush: always a kind of dab, though the brush stays on the surface too long to make a proper dab. The two ways of applying paint, with material dipped into hot coloured wax and with paint and brushes, have equal value and follow no particular sequence. (Everywhere there is something fascinating: some texture and text; some touch and textuality.) In coming to make *Flag* like this, in a way that was not quite painting yet not quite its travesty or negation, something happened to the surface – to the fact that, according to dominant theory of modern art, a painting has a surface, and that that surface has to be both asserted and used – for the process that made it might best be characterised not as a way of asserting and using a surface but, rather, as a way of making a surface. The fact of the canvas as ground or surface, undergoing the action of wax, paint and collage matter, almost disappears as something prior that has been asserted. Here, wax, paint and collage matter make the shapes of the stars and stripes in much the same way that the discrete pieces of fabric that make the flag of the United States of America do not assert a surface but construct the Stars and Stripes.

That was not all that there was to making *Flag*, but the description is sufficient for this discussion of intention. Almost. I need to point to one more aspect of its making. A year or so after Johns had thought that he had finished working on *Flag*, he put it on display on a temporary wall in his studio, which someone, at a party, leaned against and knocked over. *Flag* was damaged and had to be repaired. The repair was made with then current newspapers. Begun at the end of 1954 and worked on in 1955, *Flag* was completed – we can tell this from the date of the newspaper used for the repair – on or after 15 February 1956. The manner of *Flag*'s completion, far removed from the intention that brought it into being, was almost unforeseeable and thoroughly contingent.

It has been claimed that though intention is never inconsistent with method, it may well be in conflict or at variance with method. Johns' story of his dream and what I've been able to theorise about how he made *Flag* seems to point to this being the case. Leaving aside the question of whether, in the dream, Johns was intending to make or was painting a picture of the flag of the United States of America, when he began making the object that became *Flag*, his intention, as it transpired, was at odds with the intention of making it with enamel paint on fabric. The activity of making a work of art – the relationship between intention, method and object – depends not only on the foreseeable but also on a multiplicity of more or less unforeseeable actions and events, affects and effects. If Johns intended to do so, he did not eventually paint a picture of a flag. And though he began making *Flag* with enamel paint on fabric, under a concept or description of 'painting', he eventually made it with wax, paint and collage material and invented a new medium and also a new surface, something that until recently evaded description. Then having been made, *Flag* was subsequently damaged and repaired in a – for some – significantly vivid and affective way. The intentional act that makes a modern work of art, unlike that of making the flag of the United States of America, is not an inner image, conscious or unconscious, that can be exactly externalised, reproduced or re-presented in practice according to a description or a set of instructions in law.

Pictorial meaning is conveyed in sensual experience. The artist makes the work of art to effect an experience and meaning in the work's beholder. *Flag* effects the experience and meaning of both a work of art and the Stars and Stripes. That's part of its undecidability. That experience and meaning must be made to try to 'match' the intention that motivated the artist to make the work of art. The artist, of course, is his or her work's first beholder. As the artist makes the work he must continually 'match' his experience and interpretation of what he is doing and bringing into being against the intention that motivated him to begin making what he is making. He sees, feels, smells, hears and explains what he is doing to himself and tries to make sure that the experience – especially the visual and tactile experience – he has and the interpretation that he makes of the work while he is making it is attuned to the intention that was acted on when he began making it. Sense-perception or experience and cognition are in a reciprocal relationship with intention in the process of making a work of art that is one of continuous adjustment and readjustment between the intention that motivated it and what is brought into being, between what was desired and what is achieved. Here is Johns telling the critic David Sylvester something of what happens when an artist makes a work of art:

> JJ: ... You do something in painting and you see it. Now the idea of 'thing' or 'it' can be subjected to great alterations, so that we look in a certain direction and we see one thing, we look in another way and we see another thing. So that what we call 'thing' becomes very elusive and very flexible, and it involves the arrangement of our senses at the time of encountering this thing. It involves the way we focus, what we are willing to accept as being there. In the process of making the painting, all of these things interest me ...
> DS: Obviously each new move is determined by what is already on the canvas; what else is it determined by?
> JJ: By what is not on the canvas.
> DS: But there are a great number of possibilities of what might go on the canvas.
> JJ: That is true, but one's thinking, just the process of thinking, excludes many possibilities. And the process of looking excludes many possibilities, because from moment to moment as we look we see what we see, at another moment in looking we might see differently. At any moment one can't see all the possibilities. And one proceeds as one proceeds, one does something and then one does something else.

In the process of making *Flag*, each added piece of collage matter, each brushstroke, drip and dribble of wax, each text and touch, would have modified what was already in place and partly determined what had to be put in place. Once in place, some matter would have been left there, other matter would have been removed. Or amended. And so on. Though the process that made *Flag* was to a certain extent serendipitous and contingent – I'm thinking of the drips and dribbles of wax and its being damaged – accidents did not make *Flag*. With each addition and subtraction and so on *Flag* would have been a different thing and Johns would have been in a different situation or relationship with it. In other words, the intention that made the object that became *Flag*, effected a train of developing sensual and cognitive moments of intention. The intention that makes the work of modern art is, in this sense, always an intention-in-progress until the moment when the artist decides, for whatever reasons, that the work is finished – when, according to Johns, the artist has 'no other suggestions to make in the painting; no more energy to rearrange things, no more energy to see it differently'.

Although the artist's intention is not thoroughly assured actualisation in the work of art, nevertheless, as the structuring force, it will end up, in it, but somewhat modified. Johns and Wittgenstein can exchange words at this juncture. Johns:

> The energy, the logic, everything which you do takes form in working; the energy tends to run, the form tends to be accomplished or finalised. Then either it is what one intended (or what one is willing to settle for) or one has been involved in a process which has gone in a way that perhaps one did not intend, but has been done so thoroughly that there is no recovery from that situation. You have to leave that situation as itself, and then proceed with something else, begin again, begin a new work.

Wittgenstein: 'And didn't the intention lie also in what I did?' To which I add: (a) without intention the work would have no form, and the fact that it has the form it has – that it is the work – is to some extent the result of the intention that brought it to its mode of being, and (b) yes, the intention is there – does 'lie' – in the work of art, not dominating it but, for sure, to some extent, dependent on it, just as the work of art is, to some extent, dependent on the intention that brought it to its mode of being. And occasionally, as it was with *Flag*, that may well be an uncertain, equivocating and undecidable intention.

Would it help if we asked the artist what the work of art means or what his or her intention was when he or she made it? Probably not. The artist is unlikely to provide a reassuring answer to either question. The most explicit expression of intention is by itself insufficient evidence of intention. If, for example, the artist had said, 'My intention was so and so', would he necessarily have meant that quite seriously? Would he necessarily have meant it at all? (Think of the way that Johns said that he intuitively liked to paint flags.) Would he necessarily know? The work of art might resist his efforts to know it or the intention that was acted on to bring it to its mode of being. Sometimes, given the character of the move from intention to the work of art, the artist may be more or less nonplussed by what he has made. In which case a spectator other than the artist may well reach an understanding of the work and its intention that the artist may want to accept. This way of a modern artist coming to an understanding of his or her intention and its meaning may well be more often the case than we have hitherto realised; indeed, far from being exceptional, it might be the norm. Wollheim is surely right when he says that the 'spectator has a legitimate role to play in the organisation of what he sees' – but his 'he' is ambiguous: it might refer both to the artist and to the spectator who is other than the artist.

There are artists and authors; there are intentions; there are conscious and unconscious purposes. Artists and authors can and do sometimes speak or write their intentions but, as I said, such statements are unlikely to be reassuring or sufficient for coming to terms with the work. Sometimes artists and authors do not let us know their intention. Whether they do or not, close attention to the material substance of the work will enable a glimpse of the intention that brought it to its mode of being. And that glimpsed intention can, must, be placed in relation with whatever the artist or author has said concerning his intention. In a sense, both intentions, the intention that is put into words, as if that is the intention that brought the work to its mode of being, and the intention that ends up inscribed in the work, are intentions after the fact.

It is here that I want to resume what I began to say about the self-consciousness of the modern work of art. If we theorise the 'self' as a product of situated language, and take Johns' *Flag* as if it is equivalent to, for example, a literary text – all representations are, after all, kinds of statements – then we will be able to glimpse something of how the modern artist is involved in a process of moving towards self-consciousness. Here the 'self' of self-consciousness is recognised as one of those totalising metaphors that always claims more authority than it has or can ever achieve. Consciousness, of course, must always be consciousness of something, and the consciousness that a self must always have is consciousness of its self. But as I started to say at the beginning of this paper, that self-consciousness will, however, always be only a partial consciousness of its self because the self is never in place, integral, whole, but always in the process of becoming, of being made, and unmade, erased, abandoned or lost, and made again, and so on. The intention to make a work of art is a self-conscious intention to mean something. When one means something, it is oneself meaning. And if you say: 'How am I to know what he means, when I see nothing but the signs he gives?', then I say: 'How is he to know what he means, when he has nothing but the signs either?'

So, when the artist, making a work of art, experiences and interprets what he or she is making, compares and contrasts it with his or her intention, he or she is also engaged in a process of making, experiencing and interpreting signs of his or her 'self'. A self experiences and interprets and judges the work of art as it brings that work of art into being. As it does so, and because it does so, a self comes to know itself, if only partially and temporarily. The structuring process of making a work of art is, as it were, a relation-in-process between the self of the artist and a modification of that self as it comes to be inscribed in the work of art and effects a new self that demands further work and inscription, and so on. The process of making a work of art, and the process of making a self in the process of making a work of art, is an oscillating process that, as Johns put it with regard to how the artist knows or decides that the work of art is finished, only comes to an end – and then only provisionally – when the artist has no further suggestions to make or energy to expend.

The interpretation of an intentional act or an intentional object implies understanding the intention that brought it to its mode of being by attending to the relations that are there in and as the work's material substantiality, which exist not in themselves, as if the work of art is a natural object, but for the artist and (because of and after him) for us. Coming across Johns' *Flag*, for example, we try to understand how it accords with the description 'flag' and 'painting', and realise that it fits neither and both; we read and understand its texts, and make a kind of sense out of their nonsense; we feel and understand its magnitude of texture and touch by imagining Johns' hand moving and making the surface, matching our sense of his touch to similar forms that we've experienced and understood inside and outside of painting. And so on. The epistemological character of interpretation, by no means disinterested, implies and effects a need to understand the intention that brought the work of art into being, not by adding sets of relations to the work but always with regard to what has actually been brought into being by and for the artist and for us. The process of interpretation is fraught with difficulties and is open to

great abuse. To my mind, it should worry us that so much interpretation goes on by seeing and experiencing relationships that are not actually there in the work; that is, it
should worry us that works of art are all too often made subject to various intentionali-
ties that are not related to the intentions that brought them into being as they are
inscribed on the surface for us to see and understand. Publicly a work becomes not just
intention, but the way it is used. That should trouble us: the way a work of art is 'used'.
It should not trouble us that our interpretation will never accord with the complexity of
the work of art. A work of art, especially a work of modern art, is one of the most complex objects that human beings make: an almost infinite richness of signs. It will always
resist our efforts to give as complete as possible an interpretation of it and its self-
consciousness. And not only of its self-consciousness but of ours.

If we beholders and interpreters who are other than the artist who made it are going
to come to terms with the self-conscious intentional meaning of the work of art, as one
commentator put it with Mark Rothko's work in mind, 'we are going to have to put it in
some kind of narrative sequence between the desire that motivated it (the intention) and
the contingencies it encountered (the experiential and interpretive process of its making), and the affect it effected (its sensual and epistemological character), as it is very
likely that the artist positioned it while he was making it – and it positioned him while
making him into the artist who made it'. The beholder who is other than the artist who
made it is engaged in a complementary process of self-understanding. For him and her,
as was the case for the artist, every development in the interpretation of the work occasions a development in his and her introspective observing and 'observed' self. The
oscillating process of self-consciousness in making and interpreting art cannot be
brought to a conclusion, and, indeed, can only be terminated by that which is beyond
both interpretation and self-consciousness and which, as one commentator put it, is, for
that very reason, something of a 'linguistic predicament'.

I am now approaching the moment when I'll have no more suggestions to make, no
more energy to rearrange things. I commented near the beginning of this presentation
that 'beginning' is important. There is a relationship between *Flag* and Johns' beginning as an artist that makes it appropriate to conclude with some remarks about intention and beginning. You might think that beginning is easy. But it's the start that's
difficult. You can start from anything. But you have to decide. Sometime in 1954, Johns
'decided to stop becoming and to be an artist'. At that moment, perhaps it was just
before or just after he had made *Flag*, he deliberately and methodically destroyed whatever work he had in his possession that he had produced before. As far as Johns was concerned, and thereafter art criticism and history also, 'Jasper Johns' began as an artist
with *Flag*. Johns provides us with a good example of an artist who was especially concerned with beginning, by which I mean that he was very aware of the need to establish
the material and ideological point at which his art would depart from all other practices
and establish relations of difference and continuity with them in such a way that what
he produced would provide the main entry for what he (as an artist) and his art would
be. Continuity and difference. Continuity, because a work of art must be made under a
concept or according to a description of art for it to be recognised and used as art; there
must be some degree of continuity. Difference, because the artist must distinguish his

work of art from all other works of art and to do this he must rethink and practically amend the concept or description with which he is working. Indeed, it seems that this is something that all self-consciously 'modern' artists must do to be 'modern' artists. If I had not (almost) begun with Johns and *Flag* and did not want to conclude with them, I could have begun with other beginnings established by other 'modern' artists. For example: Picasso's *Demoiselles d'Avignon*; Barnett Newman's *Onement*; Helen Frankenthaler's *Mountains and Sea*; Larry Rivers' *Washington Crossing the Delaware*; Frank Stella's series of *Black Paintings*; Anthony Caro's *Twenty-four Hours*; or Roy Lichtenstein's *Look Mickey. I've Hooked a Big One!!* Establishing a beginning involves designating a consequent intent that follows from an object. It establishes an intention-to-be-continued. Even before the method has been decided on and tried, there must be at the beginning a belief that it will go on, that it will be sustainable in practice. As Baxandall put it, intention is the forward-leaning look of things.

There are beginnings and beginnings. The beginning that I'm interested in here, and have been talking about, is what Edward Said in his book *Beginnings: Intention and Method* (1998) has called the 'transitive' beginning. 'Transitive', because it is an action that passes over into an object. The 'transitive' beginning – unlike the 'intransitive' beginning – involves intention. And for the artist, a 'transitive' beginning establishes a practice; a self-conscious practice. You could think of Johns' *Flag* as an almost chance event whose value he was able to understand only after he had decided on the intention to locate a beginning. A beginning is a project always already underway. It has begun before you've noticed it. Because of the close relation of beginning and intention, it might be the case that intention is always similarly in transit before it is identified and acted on. This seems to be something that Johns' story of his dream is telling us. In the dream, he is intending to paint a large flag or is painting a picture of a big Stars and Stripes. He is intending to make, or is making, the object that he will take as his beginning as an artist. The intention to begin is, in the dream, already in mind, or has already been acted on and passed to its object. From the residue of a life and a day, some raw material was taken into the dream that might have been Johns' motive for dreaming it in the first place. In other words, an intention was present in the dream that gave the dream meaning for Johns. The intention to paint a large flag or the act of painting a picture of a big Stars and Stripes must have been present with Johns as raw material before it passed into the dream. It might well be that the raw matter of an intention is always already there to be made over into an intentional act. The complexity here, with regard to Johns' dream, if we follow Freud's theory of interpreting dreams, is that the dreamed intention to paint a large flag or the dreamed act of painting a picture of a big Stars and Stripes would be neither about the intention of painting a large flag, nor about painting a picture of a big Stars and Stripes. This might tell us another thing about intention. I think it does.

All artists worth their salt have been concerned with beginning and intention. They've had to be. It's difficult, but what's required is something of that 'cheerful confidence in things to come' that we read about at the beginning of Wordsworth's *The Prelude*, albeit in the knowledge that inevitably, what will come will not be what was intended. Not exactly. One always does other.

Three mistakes about intention

RICHARD WOLLHEIM

Chairman of the Department of Philosophy,
University of California, Berkley

I didn't prepare any notes when I came today, thinking that I would listen to what people said and see where that left me. Where does it? Well, I shall give you some thoughts and in the course of it I shall refer to some of today's speakers. And when I do so, of necessity of course, I shall garble what they said, I shall condense it so as to fit it into my point. So I hope they won't take offence, though of course I suspect they will!

Let me, first of all, confess to you two prejudices in the light of which I shall speak. The first is that I personally prefer it when art is complex and when what is said about it is simple. That is to say, as simple as it can be, given the other things one aims at. One aims at the truth and one aims at being helpful.

The other prejudice I have is that I think that understanding art is a more basic activity, a far more basic activity, than evaluating art, and I believe that this is the attitude that should be adopted towards art from the very beginning. It is the attitude that should be adopted in teaching art and it is the attitude that we should adopt when we go to museums and see the Old Masters.

I think both these prejudices have been amply confirmed by what I've heard today.

I called this talk 'Three Mistakes About Intention', so you might have thought that I was well-prepared in what I was going to say. Not at all. Of course there are an indefinite number of mistakes that one can make about intention, but what I thought I would do is to try to pick up on three that have played some role in today's discussion, either because people have shown great skill in avoiding them, or perhaps even because they've made them. You can decide.

The first mistake, I think, is this: it's one that has to be historically understood and it's one to which other speakers have drawn attention. In the 1920s or so, there came from a number of different directions the feeling that works of art of all kinds were not to be understood in terms of the psychological factors that brought them about. We were told this by T.S. Eliot, by Paul Valery, and such a view was also institutionalised, not for the better, in the new criticism that swept the universities of America and, to some degree, the UK.

When the reaction came against that and it was thought that psychological factors should – indeed, how could they not – be introduced into a proper understanding of works of art, the banner under which that reaction took place was that intention must be given its proper place in the understanding of art, taking that phrase over from those who had wished to ban intention from consideration and from criticism.

So 'intention' in this discussion is really a kind of shorthand word for the psychological fact, the general psychological fact, of desires, emotions, wishes, hopes, fears, dreads, etc. And I think that if the discussion about intention is to make any sense, then a broad understanding of it has to be preserved. In other words, we do wrong if we think of intention exclusively as something rather like a decision, moreover an explicit decision, that could be put into words. As I understood him, I think Michael Baldwin talked largely about intention in that narrow sense. It seems to me that what is wrong is to understand intention exclusively in that sense because that seems not so interesting, except, of course, to those who are interested in it.

So that I think is the first error of which we have to purge ourselves. To take a broad view of what intention means, we are talking about the psychology – not necessarily the biography, that's a totally different issue – but the psychology of the artist.

The second error, it seems to me, is this: once we realise that intentions have to play a part in the understanding of art, we might go on to think that the meaning of a work of art is given by the intentions of the artist. And that is, of course, when we reflect upon it, completely untrue. The meaning of art – and meaning is, of course, not the whole of what art is – the meaning of a work of art is given only by fulfilled intentions, those intentions that have been realised in the work of art.

Now, what is this notion of realisation? It is a vast subject and any of us who are interested in works of art have given plenty of thought to the issue. What is it in visual art for an intention to find its visual counterpart? What is it for something in a visual work of art to match the psychological factors that motivated it?

You may have asked yourselves this question when Cornelia Parker showed a slide of a suit with, seemingly, moth-holes in it but, actually, holes that were made by shooting, she assured us, pearls into it. She said that she associated this idea with the way in which something that was culturally or socially somewhat trivial could be turned to another more malign purpose. Well, it's one matter, of course, that she associated what she did with that idea. The further question, an open question as far as we're concerned, is whether that idea actually did find fulfilment when it was realised in that work; whether something in that work visually, if that's the right area in which to look, matched that intention.

Patricia Bickers gave us most interesting examples of pairs of objects that appeared to be, visually or in some other way, more or less identical. And then she suggested that these works nevertheless were distinguished by their intention. Now, of course, if there had not been different intentions behind them, they would not have been differentiated, but it seems to me that the mere fact that there were different intentions behind them is not the whole of the matter. The question is whether these different intentions actually found expression in the different works. Those of you who are familiar with the very amusing, the genius story by Borges, cited by Patricia, of Pierre Menard (in which he copies out two chapters from Cevantes' *Don Quixote* and in the process makes a different work of art) may ask the question whether he really did so. Intention alone would not have sufficed, but was there something more that surrounded this intention, some way in which the intention gets realised, which justified such a claim on his part? That's the big question.

Now, one little error I don't want to appear to encourage is the notion that intention is, by itself, enough. I don't think it is ever quite enough. A very optimistic view, and optimism always delights me, was put forward by Tracey Emin when she said that the crucial thing is whether the student, the artist, has something to say. Of course that is a crucial element. But the further question is, of course, whether they succeed in saying it. However, do not let me be taken to support the terrible mistake, the truly terrible mistake, which wreaks havoc in education, that failure is the worst thing that can happen. It isn't. Any system of education that thinks people have done nothing because they've failed is totally wrong. They couldn't, of course, have failed unless they had done something. And I think it is a very foolish idea to think that the one thing students have to avoid at all costs is failure. I think one of the major elements in the educational system is that students should be taught how to survive failure.

The third mistake I want to mention, and on which I'll end, is this: it's sometimes assumed – although a number of speakers today have talked against it – that if we believe that intention, that psychological factors, are the crucial thing, or *a* crucial thing, in determining the meaning of a work of art, then this has two consequences. First of all, the assumption is that the artist knows best, and secondly, that others don't know at all. Both those views have really absolutely nothing to be said for them. The whole experience of our lives tells us so. Our entire everyday life with other people, all our dealings with them, constantly tell us that, at any rate in the short run, people are not the best judges of what they intended to do. And at the same time, thank God, we have considerable insight into the intentions of others. How would we even survive for more than two or three minutes if we actually believed, in our everyday lives, those dangerous myths that are brought into our understanding of art?

There is an odd view sometimes put forward that though it is possible to grasp the intentions of others whom we meet, the intentions of artists, the psychological factors that motivate them, have a peculiar kind of elusiveness. I wonder why we should think that, given that art is, in a sense that I have, alas, no time to elaborate, essentially a social activity. People have no hesitation in writing military history, in which they talk about the intentions of generals, when of course generals, by their very nature, are totally committed to concealment of their intentions. But nevertheless, the idea persists about artists. And, of course, it isn't true. It doesn't follow from this that works of art are particularly easy to understand. Some are, some aren't. Or what I should say is that for any given person, some will be so and some won't be so. I say, 'for any given person', because of course how easy a work of art is to understand depends upon where we start from, how much we know, how much we're in sympathy with the artist. A current myth, which I think certain things today have implicitly encouraged and which many, many institutions in our society are designed to encourage, is the idea that the art of our own day is peculiarly accessible to us. When we start going through the mists of history to get to things like the nineteenth century or the eighteenth century, the Renaissance or antiquity, there, of course, fog descends, and who can say what people were up to? That, I think, is a ridiculous idea. The great philosopher David Hume really appreciated this. By and large the understanding of art is something that can be expected to unfold over long periods of time. And therefore we would expect great works of art of our own day perhaps to elude us. Only very careful thought like, for instance, that which Fred Orton put into the understanding of Jasper Johns' *Flag* will gradually make the present, the art of the present, accessible to us. But as I say, a great deal of the basis from which a lot of art education starts and a great deal of the ideas that surround the institutions and museums of contemporary art, encourage us in the false view that we only have to go into a gallery of contemporary art and see something done in 1996 or, even better still, in 1997, and it's all clear. It isn't.

Chair's summing up

CHRISTOPHER FRAYLING

Pro-Rector, Royal College of Art, London

It is now time for me to try and summarise, which is particularly difficult because several people have attempted to summarise already in the course of the day.

I tried, in the introduction, to draw a distinction, which we came back to throughout the day, between the intention in doing something and the intention to do something. The intention in doing it is all about the process itself, the intention to do something is something you declare in advance.

Michael Baldwin's session took us through some text-works, which he referred to variously as, 'promissory notes', 'quasi contracts', 'planning applications', 'agendas for paintings' and showed how radically impossible it is to establish a connection between that promissory note in words before the fact and the work of art itself: it is implausible and impossible in relation to the multivalence of the artefact . He referred to his talk as 'a bit of grit in the oyster'. The concept of intention, he suggested, is old fashioned but still valuable.

Tracey Emin took a radically different tack by talking about art as autobiography. Here are a series of phrases she used: 'the whole person is in the art', 'my art is so much about myself', 'everything comes from my own experience in my own life', 'I am a witness to things'. She finished off by saying that she wasn't using intention in an intellectual sense, but that she externalises her life. Clearly, in terms of the issue of intention, that has fairly radical implications because one has to know an awful lot about Tracy Emin to understand the result.

Craigie Horsfield started off by talking about the dangers of using intention as an educational add-on, after the event, or in some kind of formula to access quality, which actually relates very much to the debate. He then talked about the dangers of the different languages of discourses used by artists, critics and philosophers and he projected on to the structure of the day that tripartite division, which he referred to as the 'body', the 'dissectors' and the 'entrails'. He talked of the dangers, particularly in an era that lacks ideological commitment or faith, in describing intention. Where does intention come from if it isn't grounded in some sort of system? He used examples of curators projecting false intentions onto artists in the name of group shows. However, he finished on the thought that when we attempt to understand each other, intention, why we do things, is at the core of that understanding.

Cornelia Parker talked about a kind of art that deliberately avoids the object; a kind of art that is about a void or absence. So how do you describe an absence, in scientific terms, 'cold dark matter', material in the universe you can't see?

The ensuing discussion raised the issue of the left-hand and right-hand side of the brain, and the role of the spectator in the creation of meaning. The spectator had had rather a rough ride up to that point. The radical relativism of seeing intention as utterly different in every single work of art, which was Andrew's position, shows how difficult it is to generalise at all about this issue, given the self-absorption of the artist (not used in a pejorative sense) and the relationship of this process to what happens outside.

On the burden of proof, Patricia Bickers gave us an extremely interesting comparison of the importance of intention described, not from the point of view of before the fact, but during the fact, in establishing whether something was a criminal act on the one hand and in differentiating between apparently similar materials and practices in art, on the other. The subtleties of intention she argued, very plausibly, are the way of distinguishing between them, and we must not talk down today's work because it is too close to us and we have difficulty with that. I thought that was a good ending.

Sylvia Wicks gave three reasons why intention in the teaching and learning experience is of key importance. First, she said, it can reveal what learning has been to the teacher and the student. Secondly, it can reveal what the student wants to communicate and how successful he or she has been in that communication, and the whole issue of competence. Thirdly it can let the student know how much he or she has progressed. Otherwise, where do you find a benchmark? She went on with two thoughts, and I was quite surprised about the first of them, which was how standards in our system are social constructs: they don't come from anywhere except the social worlds we inhabit, i.e. the professional art world, the networks we belong to, and the critics who write about us. I thought that was interesting because we tend to believe that standards are projected on to us from somewhere else. Another interesting thought was that maybe our kind of education is a possible model for the university of the future, preparing students for a world of uncertainty and radical paradigm shifts, which we take for granted, but which in other disciplines happen very rarely.

Gray Watson preferred the title 'What Do You Think You Are Doing?' to the subtitle about 'intention' and really talked to us about what that phrase might mean. He talked about how art has enormous value to our culture, which we sometimes downgrade, and how artists can sometimes see the world more clearly, deeply, without, as he put it, conformist fear, and about how the whole being of the artist is involved in that process. Therefore it is impossible, at some level, to redescribe. He then talked about vision, and I was reminded, because he got very impassioned about this, of the biblical reference in Ecclesiastes 'where there is no vision, people perish'. An artist with a vision, he said, is an artist with something to say. He finished on the distinction, which was new to me and very interesting, between the hermeneutics of suspicion, a slightly paranoid look at what is going on behind the scenes – deconstruction, structuralism – and on the other hand, the hermeneutics of the restoration of meaning – making sense out of the component parts of what is around us – and how art uniquely brings those two together.

The discussion then focused on the student as distinct from the professional artist. For example, the diagnostic function of the foundation, and how in terms of education it is anathema to talk about intention in a nailed-down sort of way because the whole point is to try and fly without a net. We also talked about hyper-accountability with its excessive stress on intention, and about the need to be articulate, although we don't want to be forced to be. There was a kind of consensus, or at least I thought there was until it fell apart later, that at a very deep level, intention was fundamental to what artists want to say.

Fred Orton, who talked about beginning and intention for art students, said that intention is relevant and especially important that it is taught to art students. He took as his case-study a very detailed look at Jasper Johns' *Flag*, the product of a dream, a ready-made, something Johns could make his own, a concept, a process involving conversations with others, all of which resulted in what he called an intentional object. He found this case study very valuable in introducing art students to the concept, because it was a beginning, and he drew various parallels with other beginnings. Art, he concluded, is an intentional act; the act is not subordinated to any other act beyond the intention of making it. It is a self-focused activity as distinct, for example, from design.

Finally Richard Wollheim declared two prejudices at the outset: he preferred his art to be complex and what is said about it to be simple, and he thought that understanding art was a far more basic achievement than explaining it. Then he talked about three mistakes in intention; firstly, the idea that the work of art cannot be understood with reference to psychology – the T.S. Eliot position and the 1920s view – with which he radically disagreed. But he interpreted psychology loosely, as I understand it, as the vocabulary of everyday life. The second mistake he identified was the notion that the meaning of the work of art can be understood with reference to intention, whereas really, the meaning can be understood only with reference to the realisation of intention. In other words, to have something to say is not the same as saying it successfully. The third error, he claimed, is that if we believe the intention is the crucial component then the artist knows best and the others know nothing at all, with which Wollheim radically disagreed. This sparked a discussion about contemporary art not being as easy to understand as art over periods of time. There was a fairly radical disagreement, I think between Craigie and Richard on this issue of others knowing a great deal more about the art than the artist might.

Finally, in our discussion, we talked about the issues of the person and the work, of understanding the present and the past, of projecting theory onto art, known now as the 'Sarah Kent Effect', and the issue of integrity and intention. So in short, we haven't come up with any answers, and we've made the questions extremely complicated. But I think what we have done – and this is quite unusual for these conferences – is we have stuck to the point throughout the day and what results is a portfolio of different perspectives on this central question of 'is intention important?' But whether you interpret intention loosely, as a vision, or more tightly as 'what do you intend?', what you have got are philosophical, practical, critical, historical and educational perspectives on that central issue, which has amounted to a very interesting day.

From Varying Positions

Introductory address

ANDREW BRIGHTON

Head of Public Events, Tate Gallery, London

The Tate Gallery organises a number of conferences with various institutions, educational institutions included. For example, we recently staged a two-day conference on museums of modern art and their spectators, with Warwick University. We've been collaborating with Wimbledon School of Art on these conferences for longer that any other institution, however. This is because they've brought a generosity of mind and a willingness to organise the work involved that is very difficult to match. So I was very pleased to hear from Rod Bugg that he wanted to continue that tradition when he took over from Colin Painter as Principal. It is with great pleasure then, that, at the beginning of this new epoch, I ask Rod to say a few words.

Welcome

ROD BUGG

Principal, Wimbledon School of Art

I've been to this conference as a delegate on a number of occasions over the last seven years. I'm now very conscious of the fact that I'm standing in the very big shoes left by Colin, who set up this project with the Tate. It has been a very important project in terms of the staff development and research profile of the School. It also provides an opportunity to bring all the colleagues from around the country together to discuss issues that are central to the whole business of the teaching and practice of fine arts.

I feel confident that we're going to have an extremely stimulating discussion today. I'm sure there will be aspects of controversy. Those of you who have read the *Independent* will realise that some very interesting debates are going to take place today. [This is a reference to Brian Sedgemore's article in the *Independent*, 6 February 1998 attacking New Labour for its misappropriation of culture.]

Chair's introduction

MARJORIE ALLTHORPE-GUYTON

Director of Visual Arts, Arts Council of England

This is a very timely occasion. We are in the middle of one of the biggest reviews of higher education ever – the Deering Report – when issues to do with professionalism and practice are acute. With the growing number of students and simultaneous reductions in resources, the issue of how artists are placed in society and how they are educated and trained is a dominant question for our time. I want to say something about those issues, which in a sense is flying a red rag to those present. Very briefly, the two points I want to make are to do with issues about professionalism and about the research culture that is growing fast in the art school environment.

The Arts Council tends to deal with the visual arts culture post fine art education, but everything in that culture is integrated. I have spent the last two or three days ploughing through a number of recent research reports, which we commissioned, on artists' career paths, fees, payments, earnings, taxation and Social Security issues, and the money available in terms of grants, bursaries, fellowships in this country and internationally, in order to try and get a pitch of the whole visual-arts economy and culture for artists, and how that reflects on the place of artists in our culture and society as a whole.

A colleague of mine, Dr Jane O'Brien has written a very important unpublished working paper called 'Professional Status as a Means of Improving Visual Artists' Incomes'. It draws on all the research to which I have just referred in order to ascertain whether a strategy seeking professional status for visual artists, plus changes to the tax and Social Security systems, would be able to increase their low incomes in light of their working patterns, the labour market, and a balance of artistic aspiration over income maximisation. This is very much the speak of policy analysts but nonetheless, the paper is extremely rigorous. It examines whether there can be such a thing as a professional ethos, and indeed a professional association or group of visual artists, because of the culture of visual practice, the diversity of positions and philosophy of visual arts. The concluding two lines sum up the thrust of the paper: 'It is unusual to find an occupation at which so many people want to make a living but so few are capable of doing so.' That is quite a devastating comment to make.

The success of the much-vaunted Young British Artists (or YBAs) is certainly not representative. The recent qualitative research and analysis to which I've referred indicates certain common traits and problems: multiple job holding, imbalance between artistic and non-artistic work, relatively low levels of income from artistic practice, a paucity of commissions, awards, bursaries and residencies. At the same time – and this is the bit I find interesting in terms of a wider political perspective on artistic practice – artists' high level of drive, their ingenuity, strategies for survival and complex career matrix offer creative lessons in what is increasingly becoming a contract-culture. Indeed, I hope one of our four speakers, Sara Selwood, who has recently produced a publication called *Art, Craft and Design in the National Economy*, a handbook for the Policies Studies Institute, will look at those issues in more depth. There is no question that the practice of being an artist is the fastest growing cultural occupational group. The census of 1991 shows a 71 per cent increase over a decade of individuals who regard themselves as artists. Now, the complex thing is that within this group are artists, commercial artists and graphic designers. Clearly there is a great division between certain kinds of practice and what we regard as fine art practice. Of that, a total figure of 93,000 individuals, it is estimated that 34,000 are visual artists and probably somewhere near half of those live in London.

The average income for the visual artists surveyed is £7,936. Now that is quite a shocking level of income. The average income for manual workers in Britain in 1995 was £17,000. Teaching and work related to artistic practice are the most important sources of income for most artists. Against that, in terms of income from their work, 72 per cent have never received a fee from a publicly funded space. The average gross income from an exhibition in a public space was £140, and for a commercial space £250. This is compounded by the inequitable practices of the Inland Revenue. There are none of the special arrangements that Equity, for example, achieved for its membership. The Job Seeker Allowance and availability for work criteria impacts very severely on visual artists, as it does in other art forms. So it is clear that many artists are not driven by commercial motives; they are more concerned with the quality of their work and with peer-group approbation. Contrary to accepted labour theory, artists are an occupational group who derive satisfaction from their work and lifestyle. This satisfaction is very quaintly described in the major piece of research on career paths by the Institute for Employment Studies who conducted the research, as 'psychic income'. So the conclusion is – and this is where it is politically very tricky – many artists leave art school with poor negotiation skills and no business acumen, and this leaves them ill-equipped to achieve not only reasonable fees and payments but the networking knowledge to grasp opportunities.

Now this all seems very gloomy, but actually I believe there is a shift. Not only are more artists getting work, the National Lottery has had a considerable impact, and this research was done over the last two years and does not analyse this impact. Over £120 million has gone to capital visual arts projects: new buildings and refurbishment of spaces; £25 million has gone to public art projects. Some of those projects are really quite interesting and are not all stand-alone monuments to heritage. Some of them are working with new media – they are temporary works, so it is a very interesting force for change in art-form practice. About £12 million has gone to projects through a new stream of lottery money, some of which has gone to artist-run spaces and artists' groups and not to curators or promoters. So there is a shift, and I think there's a greater entre-preneurism among artists; their appetites have been whetted to try and change this sort of culture of poverty, which really hasn't shifted, according to this recent research, since the Gulbenkian Report of 1985, which after all is fifteen years ago. So I pose here the question of professionalism: what it means, how should an artist practice after art school and what does this imply for training within art schools?

The Deering Report makes reference to developing a research culture within the

Humanities and I understand that there is new money to develop research within the art school sector. But there is not as much as Deering recommended, and part of the issue is to maintain the diversity and the quality of teaching practice across art schools. The erosion of part-time teaching does mean that students have been exposed to fewer practising artists over the last few years.

It has been a concern of the Arts Council that artists outside art schools should somehow have a relationship with the institutions in their region. In order to push that forward, we have been working with the National Association for Fine Art Education to try and devise a national scheme for artists to have access to art school facilities and resources, and this is based on a pilot scheme that worked extremely well in different ways in three institutions. There is a major Lottery application going through to this effect. Of course, we are not fully able to guarantee that at this stage it will go through. But if it does, over twenty colleges throughout the country will be subsidised to give resources and facilities to practising artists who are not on the teaching staff on those institutions. That is some way of engendering both a wider diversity of practices for students, and of developing a kind of research culture further within the art school environment. Clearly, there is a growing research culture in the art school environment, but the healthiness of having an open art school system is keyed to taking that forward.

New Labour, Tony Blair and
the future of fine art

Brian Sedgemore

MP for Hackney South and Shoreditch

I used to believe that the main role of a fine artist was to mediate between the world as it is and the world as it should be. But that was before Fukuyama proclaimed the end of history and Tony Blair decreed the end of politics. Clearly, any fine art institution must take these momentous declarations into account when considering its future and those of its members or students.

Fine art decorates, illuminates, inspires, challenges, initiates aesthetic research and visual literacy, and makes us want to weep on those occasions when it expresses the impotence of mankind in the face of nature and of its own soul. Hence at the Tate Gallery Picasso's *Weeping Woman* is perhaps my favourite painting outside of the Rothko Room. It would be nice if fine art institutions churned out modern-day Picassos, Duchamps and Rothkos – the people, not the paintings – but it may be that the continuous creation of genius is not in their gift, and in any event, I understand that many in the art world doubt the concept of genius and that feminism is one factor in crystallising and negating that concept. Yet fine art institutions that produce fine artists who can make paintings, sculptures and illustrations, or design things that keep them out of the Welfare to Work programme and make money, preferably foreign money, preferably US dollars, are clearly institutions of which Tony Blair would approve and which politicians will be pleased to fund. Let's not sneer at this part of the Blair project: art as the innovator for an engine of cultural industries, art as the creator of transferable thoughts and skills. Producing artists who can survive, not just as eccentrics in local villages working out their existential angst in garrets, but as big commercial players on the global stage, are people we should value. The problem, however, comes when their art is seen more as a backcloth to life as false as Muzak, and, more ominously, as a backcloth to conspicuous wealth, than as a vibrant, buzzing, essential part of life itself. Fine art institutions have to produce artists who play to the soul and not just to Mammon. To say, as someone once did, that the drip of Jackson Pollock's brush is as American as the Ritz cracker or the Ford motor car was in my view to denigrate the meaning of the Abstract Expressionism of Jackson Pollock and at the same time to elevate the Ritz cracker to a status and taste it scarcely deserves.

To whom should fine art institutions be accountable? Obviously, in part to the fine artists and students themselves. So perhaps the question should be, to whom is the fine artist accountable? Ever since the Enlightenment, and subsequently the Romantic movement, in which artists rather than God provided the hope of the world, artists have in the main seen their accountability as being to themselves. That will not do any more, since neither the public at large – certainly in this philistine island – nor the politicians who represent them, worship beneath the paintings and sculptures of artists. Perhaps it is no bad thing that fine artists and fine art institutions should account for their actions to the community and the public purse through and in public art, architecture, private but accessible spaces and buildings, schools, hospitals and town halls, etc. Maybe fine art could operate more directly in these spheres. Yet even as I speak, I can hear my good friend Andrew Brighton, saying that these are the tired old nostrums of the 1980s. However, I'm old-fashioned enough to believe that there have to be building blocks in art and elsewhere that enable people, myself included, to improve themselves. I come from Hackney, where there are more artists per square metre than anywhere else in the world. But not nearly enough of their art is physically accessible and available, although there are more open studio shows then there used to be. Maybe more people would turn up if more of the art were intellectually accessible.

Fine art institutions have to make their work and that of their students intellectually and physically accessible. More than ever, with cash restraints, they will either have to get sponsorship, some of which may demand that the art itself is constrained by commercial considerations, or they will have to engage in Darwinian struggles to convince the doubting Arts Correspondent of the *Sun* that their endeavours are worthy. I hope I am not dealing in oxymorons and contradictions here. In future, students will need the ability to negotiate different sorts of constraints from a variety of sources. It is important, however, that fine art institutions are funded; they should not become slaves to New Labour focus groups or of public and commercial opinion. We do not want fine artists or fine art institutions that pander to the lowest common denominator. A few years ago, I remember an occasion on which Norman Tebitt declared that he could not see the difference between a page-three girl in the *Sun* and the nude portraits that hang in the world's great art galleries. Does Norman really believe that there is no difference between Mariella's breasts sloshing into the cornflakes over breakfast and a lingering look at Botticelli's *The Birth of Venus*? I sometimes believe that a little elitism does not go amiss, if only because value-free art is empty art. Maybe though, Norman could get some support for his views from John Berger's *Ways of Seeing* (1972); even Berger, however, risked the value judgement when he identified the differences between Rembrandt's touching portraits of his wife and what he called 'normative traditions'.

For what it's worth, I want fine art colleges that produce individualists and idiosyncratic students so diverse so as to include subversives; institutions that encourage visual literacy, aesthetic research, history, philosophy and the ability to make judgements. Unfortunately, I don't rule the world. Tony Blair does. New Labour, New Britain, New World, New Art. Okay? Tony Blair's political beliefs often appear as an enigma hidden in a riddle, apart from one thing: he really does believe that you can have politics without conflict. As such, the notion of subversive art becomes not merely offensive but meaningless. What is there to subvert? Dare I answer my own question by saying that New Labour cries out to have its piety and authoritarianism subverted. New Labour wants art that is as pungent as processed cheese, as soul-searching as a conversation between the Teletubbies, as original as Dolly the sheep. As part of the politics of contentment, New Labour wants colours that do not clash, textures that do not distort and shapes that Cubists would not understand. 'Turner in: Conceptual art out' should now be the slogan that hangs outside the Tate.

Of course, Tony Blair's belief that you can have politics without conflict and art to match, is a fantasy born perhaps out of Rousseau's concept of the existence of the general will, or possibly from the later idea of wish-fulfilment dreams. Basically, politics is about mediating between competing claims in a world of scarce resources. In that sense, conflict is the bedrock of politics. The threat to fine art institutions is that deep down, New Labour, not withstanding its sensitive, cultured Secretary of State, Chris Smith, is every bit as philistine as old Toryism. New Labour wants the people's art: art, that is, that keeps the people amused, contented and quiet but doesn't want to pay for it. It doesn't want *Sensation*, or palm-print portraits of Myra Hindley. I expect you read about the trouble recently when New Labour announced that most lessons in art and music in primary schools will be dropped. This will ensure that children's imaginations do not wander beyond the basics. But who has kicked up a fuss? Fine-art institutions surely ought to be among the first to challenge the New Labour philistines and the new Puritanism that says that life is work and school a preparation for that work even at the age of five. Simon Rattle has complained on behalf of music, why not you? Is it too much to hope that students and lecturers in fine art colleges should see it as part of their remit to offer more than cowardly silence when these things happen? What is the point of teaching students cultural theories if they can't use it to locate themselves in the political world and speak out against cultural and philosophical horrors? Art students and lecturers must realise that the new Cartesian dualism is not, I think therefore I am, but, I speak out therefore I am. To mediate they must engage and be heard.

Are we – are *you* – prepared to accept New Labour's assertion that the perfect way to sum up 2,000 years of culture is through the Millennium Dome, which at a staggering cost of £850 million will give the country the secret policeman's politically correct vision of the future? Think for a moment just how many museums and galleries could be kept open, and for how many years, without an entrance fee, at a fraction of the cost of £850 million. Ask yourself just how much art education could be improved between now and the millennium if that sum of money were available. In a world of scarce resources, Blair and Peter Mandelson, without the support of the Cabinet, are about to waste resources on the Dome on a scale never before seen in Britain. Already I can sense that there is a new Gibbon poised to write about the Dome as the ultimate symbol of the decline and fall of Britain. Of course, we're talking Lottery money here. Soon I fear fine art institutions and the Arts Council may find themselves talking about little else. It's only a matter of time before the Lottery pays for core art funding as the Government withdraws altogether from funding for the arts. I give it from ten to fifteen years before the Government frees itself from paying for what New Labour and old Toryism regard as a dispensable burden. I'm in favour of the Lottery. I'm glad that the Tate Gallery and even the Royal Opera House have benefited, but I look into the future and I don't like it. In the end, even Lottery funds for the arts may dry up, and the notion of subsiding the arts could become but a fading memory.

'I do it because I want to': fine artists, self-sufficiency and the arts economy

SARA SELWOOD

*Quinn Hogg Research Fellow, School of Communication,
Design and Media, University of Westminster*

At a time when the 'creative industries' are officially promoted as a major contributor to the economy, and Brit Art and Cool Britannia hit the headlines with unerring regularity, a recent assertion made by the *Guardian* is far from uncommon. This was that the arts 'are example of the mixed economy … a big success story employing hundreds and thousands of people. Unlike the motor industry, the arts earn a strong trade surplus'.[1] Since the mid-1980s, it has been common for the arts to be described as economically important.[2] But statements like these blur the distinctions between the arts and the creative industries, fine art and design, and commercial and subsidised practices. Fine art itself is also persistently presented as economically important. Artists are credited with spearheading the gentrification of urban areas, and are cast in the role of catalysts in urban regeneration. In a recent article, Marjorie Allthorpe-Guyton emphasised the importance of artists' contribution to cultural tourism, in particular, the assumed benefits that their presence in exhibitions brought to hotels, restaurants and the travel trade in Munster, Kassel, Venice and the north of England.[3]

But calculating the precise economic impact of such events is enormously complex and the claims made cannot always be substantiated.[4] What can be said, however, with absolute certainty is that while the presence of such events might contribute to the wider local or regional economy, it does not necessarily mean that the arts economy itself is buoyant. Nor does it mean that the majority of artists can bathe in the reflected financial glory. How well do fine artists do? More specifically, what are we doing to ensure that the graduates of our arts schools are able to earn a living in their chosen field of activity?

The following paper approaches these questions in various ways. It considers the information produced by art schools, official statistics, ad hoc surveys, and it examines what artists themselves expect.

Information Produced by Art Schools

Art schools in the UK have produced very little systematic data about the careers of art students. According to the Higher Education Statistics Agency (1996) 2,845 students graduated in fine art in the UK at the end of the 1994/95 academic year. We have no idea how many of them will end up as artists. Nearly ten years ago, the CNAA (Council for National Academic Awards, 1989) found that art and design students were less satisfied than graduates from any other fields with the courses they had taken. More recent research has found that they regard the preparation for economic survival they received as inadequate: 'There should be much more emphasis on the actual big bad world out there and the way it works, instead of this cosy atmosphere of education. It is just assumed that if you learn all the things you go to learn, you will be successful as a result.'[5] Among observations made by students were the following: 'I was so ill prepared for the realities'; 'I was not prepared for the shock of leaving college'; 'Learning by trial and error takes so much longer than being shown how'; 'The last year has been a huge struggle'.[6]

Various reports have described the need for more and better integrated career advice in courses: 'Respondents emphasised that these should become an integral part of the course curriculum provided not only by careers advisers, but also tutors, visiting lecturers and professionals from ... art, design and media'.[7]

It may well be that it makes little sense to consider the effects of art school education much before say twenty years after graduation – when most ex-students are either at, or reaching, the height of their careers and their optimal earning capacity. But recent national data produced by the Higher Education Statistics Agency (1996) considered students' destinations only six months after graduation. The Institute of Employment Studies' research for the London Institute considered students who had completed HND and first degree courses up to four years previously.[8]

Some higher-education institutions have, however, recently taken steps to find out about graduates' careers five years on. The Royal College of Art's intention in doing so is to defend itself against threats to its funding and justify the costs of preparing students for entry into particular professions.[9] Like the London Institute, Birmingham Institute of Art & Design has been researching students' careers in order to improve the contents of its courses and thereby contribute to graduates' future success.[10]

Research Findings

According to the Arts Council of England, in 1995 there were about 34,000 visual artists in Great Britain.[11] Unfortunately, official national statistics on employment and earnings are of little, if any, use in assessing how much fine artists earn. Information about fine artists is combined with that about other kinds of practitioners and cannot be disaggregated.[12] So, according to the standard occupational classification used, in 1996, artists, commercial artists and graphic designers in full-time employment earned an average of £20,800. Those who were self-employed and worked full-time earned less than half that (£10,287). However, neither figure describes the specific economic situation of the fine artist accurately.

By comparison with these official statistics, the data produced by ad hoc studies are less accurate. They use much smaller samples, usually focus on artists who have some relationship with the funding system, and often only refer to particular geographical areas. However, they provide rather more focused data. It has to be said that they present a dire picture.

A recent report commissioned by the National Artists Association[13] found that in 1995 the average artist's income was £7,936 – at a time when the average for manual workers in Great Britain was £17,148.[14] While the maximum income recorded for artists was over £500,000, the majority earned considerably less. Around two-thirds earned less than £10,000, and over a third earned less than £5,000. Other research has found that graduates' income levels grow, albeit rather slowly, the longer they are in the labour market.[15] A year and a half after graduation, 33 per cent of graduates earned less than £5,000. For graduates who had left college two and a half and three and a half years previously, only a quarter earned less than £5,000. These sums refer to artists' total earnings, and include income from non-artistic sources.

Most artists are self employed, and finance periods of production themselves.[16] Not only do fewer than half (47 per cent) work full-time at their principal artistic activity, but only around 10 per cent derive all their income from their artistic work. About 60 percent earned less than half their income from it, and nearly 30 per cent earned nothing from it.[17] On average, the amount artists earn from their artistic practice is very low – around £1,746.[18]

The two most important sources of income for artists are teaching and work unrelated to their practice. Although on average the amounts received from private and exhibition sales were £260 and £143 respectively, these were what artists spent most of their time pursuing.[19] Grants and awards only ranked about eighth place in terms of the importance of their contribution to artists' incomes. In many respects, these findings suggest a parallel with actors – many of whom have to generate income from other activities. Economists might describe the situation facing both professions as one in which supply outstrips demand, and might ask whether it meant that there were too few opportunities for the number of artists or actors produced, or too few practitioners of a sufficient standard to develop the opportunities available.

What Artists Themselves Expect

Artists' own descriptions of their careers point to the fact that money is not the driving force behind making work. Nor are the amounts of money earned as a result of artistic practices necessarily seen as signifying success.[20] Success is much more likely to be associated with the perceived quality of work; sustaining its production long enough to develop a reputation; and, being recognised by other artists. Ultimately, many artists profess to work for themselves – 'I do it because I want to'. So, while exhibiting may be necessary to generate sales, for many artists what is more important is that it enables their work to be seen 'unless it's out there, who the hell knows about you?'[21]

Money is, of course, more important than these comments imply. The lack of funds may hinder success since it determines whether artists can afford studio space, where it might be located, what materials they can buy, whether they can be in the right place to meet the right people, and so on. Money is part of a vicious circle. As Honey et al suggest, if artists could earn enough from making art, they would not be obliged to do other jobs, and could spend more time developing work. Such observations show that artists view earning a living as a necessary evil, rather than one of the rewards of pursuing their chosen profession. In fact, according to the National Artists' Association survey:

> a significant proportion of the artists surveyed had a relatively low level of
> interest in or awareness of the business side of their profession. In many ways this
> is compounded by their relative poverty and desperation to have their work

shown, which in turn reduces their bargaining power and self-confidence. Many artists indicated that they are prepared to work 'for little, nothing, or at a loss, to have their work seen'.[22]

Other research presents the situation as rather less about artists' self confidence than about their low levels of competence in particular areas:

> the largest gaps were related to negotiating and networking skills; smaller but still significant gaps emerged in relation to self confidence, self promotion, entrepreneurial skills, time management and the ability to cope with uncertainty; in the other areas (i.e. self-motivation, decision making, problem solving, creativity, communication, team working and craft and technical skills) there were smaller gaps between the level of competence developed during the course and the current importance of these skills.[23]

Observations

Despite all the reports recently produced under the auspices of the National Artists' Association and the Arts Councils of England and Scotland,[24] and for the Department of Education and Employment,[25] there are still gaps in our knowledge about artists and their careers. We know next to nothing about the long-term careers of artists – how many art students go on to be artists, whether they are satisfied with the lives they make for themselves. Nor do reports suggest how artists might best be able to support themselves, or how we as citizens might contribute financially to the production of art that might be considered to contribute to the 'public good'. It is clearly within the realms of policy making and practices – be it by art schools, arts funding bodies or government – to affect these issues.

Conventionally, it could be said that there are two ways in which artists support themselves in the UK. They can rely on private patronage, or public-sector funding – state funding delivered though teaching opportunities, grants, publicly funded commissions, and the welfare system. It has been suggested that an ideal world for all artists would be one that is home to a large proliferation of private patrons and buyers – in other words, one that allows the greatest number of people to accumulate and spend private wealth since a multiplicity of diverse tastes means greater artistic freedom.[26] In many respects, artists in receipt of funding from such private sources as the Paul Hamlyn Foundation's Awards for Artists[27] have fewer conditions to abide by than those in receipt of public funding.

A standard reflex among arts constituencies is to argue for more subsidy for artists. The Arts Council of England recently commissioned an investigation into new and alternative mechanisms for financing the arts and artists,[28] and the London Arts Board, for example, is currently proposing to increase funding to individual artists.[29] But, at base, certain questions continue to inform the culture of public arts funding – not least, how to distribute a finite amount of subsidy among what might conceivably be a growing population of artists. Clearly, the prospect of public subsidy in a system that is highly bureaucratised, prone to employ performance indicators and strapped for cash, inevitably raises a whole host of issues about decision making, entitlement and creativity. Does funding a critical mass of artists improve the quality of what is produced? Which artists do you fund, and at what point in their careers – at the height of their creative abilities, or in periods when they are not doing so well? What criteria do you employ? Do you means test them, or impose other kinds of judgements? How do you avoid creating a hegemony? In many respects, artists who exist outside the arts-funding system succeed in avoiding much of this bureaucratic fall-out. Whatever they themselves might be doing to provide direct support for artists in the future, the Arts Councils of England and Scotland are currently lobbying to protect artists' social security benefits. As one of the most vociferous objectors to Welfare to Work suggests, the New Deal – targeted at people under twenty-five (a group that includes young graduates) – potentially cuts off 'the lifeblood of our creative future':

> If we want the benefits that music brings – the money, the cultural diversity, the result from overseas – we have to allow musicians to eat. I am, not to put too fine a point on it, pissed off with the ill-judged work fare initiative. I urge the Government to take a long hard look at the issue again.[30]

For their part, the Arts Councils are proposing that young artists should be exempted from the New Deal and allowed to participate in a revamped version of the Enterprise Allowance Scheme: 'We need something which would allow our artists and musicians of the future to pursue their careers rather than being forced into inappropriate employment where they would not be able to develop their skills and talents.'[31] One might well ask whether the social security system represents the best mechanism for supporting our young artists. Moreover, one might question whether these proposed alternatives to the benefits system will merely add to the highly bureaucratised and administered system of state subsidies we already have. More importantly, will they succeed in stimulating anything other than mediocre art?

Acknowledgements

I am grateful to Professor Nick Stanley, Birmingham Institute of Art and Design, University of Central England for allowing me to refer to the findings of *Ambitions and Destinations Project*, 1996–7 (see note 10); Professor Roger Breakwell, Camberwell College of Arts; and Tim Estop and Holly Donagh, Arts Council of England.

1. *Guardian*, 15 July 1997, p.14.
2. See, for example, J. Myerscough, *The Economic Importance of the Arts in Britain*, Policy Studies Institute, London, 1988.
3. M. Allthorpe-Guyton, 'Points of View', in 'Culture as Business', *Times Higher Education Supplement*, 7 November 1997.
4. F. van Puffelen, 'Uses and Abuses of Impact Studies in the Arts', *Cultural Policy*, 2, 1996.
5. S. Honey, P. Heron and C. Jackson for the Institute of Employment Studies, *Career Paths of Visual Artists*, Arts Council of England, London, 1997.
6. R. Breakwell, 'Along Cork Street', unpublished presentation for *Crafts 2000: A Future in the Making*, 1997.
7. I. La Valle, S. O'Regan and C. Jackson for the Institute of Employment Studies, *The Art of Getting Started: Graduate Skills in a Fragmented Labour Market*, Institute of Employment Studies for the London Institute, Brighton, 1997.
8. Ibid.
9. K. Patel, 'Painting a Rosy Picture', in 'Culture as Business', *Times Higher Education Supplement*, 7 November 1997; Royal College of Art, *Graduate Destinations 1992–1996*, Royal College of Art, London (undated brochure), [1997].
10. J. Aston, '*Ambitions and Destinations: the Careers and Retrospective Views of Arts and Design Graduates and Postgraduates*', JADE, London [forthcoming at time of presentation].
11. J. O'Brien, 'Professional Status as a Means of Improving Visual Artists' Incomes', working paper, 1997.
12. See S. Selwood and R. Dunlop 'Art, Craft and Design in the National Economy', a handbook for the CHEAD Links Group, Policy Studies Institute, London (unpublished), 1998.
13. P. Shaw and K. Allen, 'Artists Rights Programme: A Review of Artists' Earning for Exhibitions and Commissions', Report commissioned by the National Artists' Association, 1997.
14. Office for National Statistics data cited by O'Brien 1997, op. cit.
15. La Valle et al 1997, op. cit.
16. See Honey et al 1997, op. cit.; Shaw and Allen 1997, op. cit.
17. O'Brien 1997, op. cit.; Scottish Arts Council, 'A Socio-economic Study of Artists in Scotland', Scottish Arts Council, Edinburgh, 1995.
18. O'Brien 1997, op. cit.
19. Ibid.
20. Tilly Baker, *Artists' Rights Programme: Taxation and Employment Status of Visual Artists*, National Artists Association, London 1997; A. Douglas and N. Wegner, *Artists' Stories*, AN Publications, Sunderland 1996; Honey et al 1997, op. cit.; O'Brien 1997, op. cit.; Shaw and Allen 1997, op. cit.
21. Honey et al 1997, op. cit.
22. Shaw and Allen 1997, op. cit.
23. La Valle et al 1997, op. cit.
24. Baker 1997, op. cit.; Honey et al 1997, op. cit; O'Brien 1997, op. cit.; SAC 1995, op. cit.; Shaw and Allen 1997, op. cit.
25. La Valle et al 1997, op. cit.
26. J. Daley, 'Cuts in the Arts Budget? Let's Blame Mrs Thatcher', *Daily Telegraph*, 27 January 1998, p.18.
27. 'Visual Arts to Receive £450,000. The Paul Hamlyn Foundation Announces UK & Ireland's Largest Artists' Awards', Paul Hamlyn Foundation press release, 10 March 1998.
28. 'London Economics: New and Alternative Mechanisms for Financing the Arts', report for the Arts Council of England and the English Regional Arts Board, Arts Council of England, London, 1997.
29. 'Substantial Grant Increases to Many London Arts Organisations', London Arts Board press release, 22 January 1998.
30. Alan McGee, cited by I. Mimeo O'Rorke, 'How the Dole Made Britain Swing ... and How Labour is about to Destroy All That', *Guardian*, 6 January 1998.
31. Arts Council of England spokesperson cited in L. Donegan, 'Artists and Musicians May Win Welfare to Work Opt-out', *Guardian*, 4 March 1998.

Burning questions, fiery answers

GAVIN JANTJES

Artist and Artistic Director of the Henie-Onstad Kunstsenter, Oslo

I would like to narrate a story with roots in both the realm of the continental European art school and that of fantasy. It is about the undoing of a once-renowned artist and academic, whose career as an art school lecturer came to grief in the most unexpected manner. Buried somewhere within this tale lies a moral, but exactly where and what it is, I am unable to pinpoint.

My story begins in a dingy visitation room of a local prison where a young journalist interested in the arts, is interviewing an inmate.

JOURNALIST: [Somewhat bewildered] Could you explain to me just how matters have come to such a terrible pass? Here we are, meeting in a prison of all places. You, a renowned figure in the arts and me, an arts journalist fresh from art school. We should be meeting in your studio or your comfortable office in the art college.

INMATE: Well, yes, that's true, but it's a long story. [Smiles] But let me say right from the outset that I do not intend to shirk responsibility or evade the issue behind your question. I take full responsibility for my actions, and I'm willing to state categorically as I did in court, that I am the one who burnt down the art school. Burnt it to a cinder, reduced it to ashes. [Pause, takes a deep breath] In retrospect, you could say that this fire was either a reckless, even futile act, or a symbolic academic cremation. But let me assure you that in the ideological and mental conflict of the time, it appeared to me, as natural even logical. It was most importantly, the act of my salvation. [Looks the young man straight in the eye] I'd like to smoke one of those Havana cigars you brought me. I Haven't had a smoke in months. [Journalist passes the inmate a lighter, he lights the Havana, and exhales a stream of blue smoke]

Today, I sit here in prison facing a possible lengthy sentence, but I am aware that at the end of it all, I will be free. The day come when I can walk away from here with something concluded. While working at the art school I never could see an end to anything. I felt trapped in the rituals of art school teaching, doomed to spend my time in the cycle of recruitment interviews and degree examinations, trapped in seminars discussing the same student problems masked each year by a fresh face. This fire, this incineration, was a liberation from all of that. [Taps the burning cigar on his prison boot to loosen the ash]

JOURNALIST: But just how did the fire start? What caused it?

INMATE: I would have to go back into history, to say accurately how it all came about, but the fire, as you know, was quite a spectacular event in every sense. Students will be talking about it for many years to come and it will be a subject for debate among academics and artists alike. They may even hold a conference at the Tate Gallery about it.

[Smirks. Then, with agitation:] The whole goddamn building was burnt to the ground! From the roof to the cellar, everything reduced to dust! The flames were so high, one could see them for miles around. It drew a large crowd. It reached so high into the night sky I swear it was the closest any art school ever came to heaven. The fire burnt through all the intermediary floors and particularly vehemently in administration. There was so much bureaucratic fuel in these offices it could sustain a dozen very large bonfires. My fire really took hold there, feeding on the unnecessary stockpile. All those minutes from the Academic Board, the Board of Studies, the Progress Review boards, the reports of the Corporate Management Team, the Academic Planning Committee, the Strategic Review Committee, the Strategic Planning Executive – what the hell that was I still don't know! – The Student Management Council reports, the Staff Review reports, the School's Corporate Image report and, never to be forgotten, the detailed reports from the Health and Safety Committee. They all went up in a puff of smoke. [He continues before the journalist can get in another question] But let me get to the real reason for the inferno. This I'm afraid draws its spark from the friction of a pedagogic conflict. [Shaking index finger at the ceiling] A collision of ideologies so heavy that it caused a spontaneous combustion within me. [Agitated] Having begun my academic career as an artist who taught young citizens to discover their creative ability, I noticed that after many years I had begun to succumb to the encroaching bureaucracy that art school managers built around teaching. My failure to maintain an artistic concept led me to sacrifice everything I believed in, and in order to sustain an academic report with my students, I sought something spectacular, something unavoidable and shocking. [Takes a long draw on the Havana and rolls the cigar between thumb and forefinger] Life really began for me when I recognised I was an artist with a 'cool' artistic concept. Everything nice and tidy. A clean studio and an organised mind. My artistic practice reflected clear thoughts. As an art school teacher, I tried to establish an intellectual position with pristine surroundings. [Brushes the flakes of ash from his prison uniform] Art schools are bloody dirty places. You walk through the front door of any art school in the land and something foreign attaches itself to you. Just like that! [Snaps fingers] If it's not paint smeared on the door handles of toilets, then it's dust from the sanding and scraping in the sculpture studios. It settles everywhere. It gets into your clothes and into your hair. No wonder art school lecturers are always so badly dressed. They wear their worst clothes for protection. But how can one think clearly in such a mess? You can tidy any room in the art school in the morning and I bet you my last puff of this cigar that it's filthy before the day is out. The futility of tidying up reflects a malaise in art schools that sets you on the road to messiness. You fight a losing battle for academic cleanliness. The dirt from the art school destroyed my cool artistic concept. Wiped it out. I was at the end of my tether. The artistic disciplines I strove for, those rock-solid foundations of an academic art upon which I built my vision of a modern world, sunk into the rising swamp of art school garbage. Art was drowning in our modern times … [Quickly correcting himself in mid-sentence] Did I say 'modern'? No! Not modern, postmodern, I mean post … this slippery slimy, wordy talk about artistic practice that has us all believing we are in on it, while we are more confused than ever. [Sticks his outstretched fingers into his thinning grey hair and slowly slides them over the emerging bald patch at the back of his head] When I realised that I had lost, that my cool concept had failed, I tried to salvage my position by taking a totally different view. A new, and some would say radical tack. If the debates in art were about difference, I was going to be different. I decided to be HOT! [Stubs out the cigar on the heel of his boot, rubbing his palms together like a Neanderthal making fire with a stick] I was going to move to a hot concept that nobody could ignore. So I began to bring fire to my studio work. Little burn marks on the canvas was how it all started, but that simply wasn't enough. It needed to be more. I needed a sense of the dramatic and spectacular, something irresponsible and shocking, aligned to the belief that artists have relinquished being an avant-garde, have forsaken responsibility for themselves and their actions. [Leans right back in his chair, tilts his head back, speaks in a whisper] I decided to bring a real fire to the heart of the problem. I would halt the torture I suffered in the art school by bringing a torch of fire to it. I would bring light into the gloom and doom of the art student's life. I would throw a spark into the academy and set ablaze the bureaucracy!

[The young journalist looks at the inmate transfixed. Could art school teaching really do this to someone's sanity? Or was he sitting opposite a man who was expressing some truth too shocking for the logical mind?]

INMATE: [Almost apologetically] What started as a personal problem became one of pedagogy. Fire, I very quickly discovered, was like creative thought and therefore a very difficult thing to control. In all my time as a teacher, I had always wanted my ideas to permeate art education in this manner. A rapid and volatile shift of ideas that cut across all areas of practice, collapsing the walls that divided the studios of painting from those of sculpture, printmaking and those media we would not call art and therefore give the generic name 'alternative' or 'combined'. But before I knew what had happened, before I was able to mould or shape the heat of my ideas into a an intense, blue blowtorch, great tongues of flame took over the little studio I was working in. The fire spread rapidly and in all directions. My fire treated all artistic disciplines equally.

JOURNALIST: In which department did you start your fire?

INMATE: The way you frame that question shows that even you have not been able to ignore the artificial boundaries of the old academy. What does it matter in which department it began? The flames simply consumed everything, proving the radical nature of my idea. Everything except a few chiselled blocks of stone and some bronzes in the sculpture room: good old-fashioned materials that have been in the academy since time immemorial and are able to survive almost anything. But oil paint, I don't have to remind you young man, burns like the devil. So the painting department simply melted. But even though the flames lapped up all those terrible experiments with paint that stand around the corridors of art schools pretending to be works of art, the fire seemed to enjoy itself most in the media area. It crackled, hissed and exploded as if to express its joy at the melting of video screens. With less vehemence than the quarrels that dominated departmental discussions about the ownership of the video equipment, the fire sent the editing suites and digital systems to an ashen grave. And all those little spinning, fiery logos of the virtual world that had transfixed students as they surfed the Internet were no match for the real thing. 'Simulation' the great buzz word of the 1990s, frizzled in the heat of the real.

JOURNALIST: But what did you do to stop the fire once you knew it was becoming dangerous?

INMATE: [Sharp retort] Fire is not benign! It's always dangerous. That's the reason I chose to work with it. To touch something vital and alive again. Fire is elemental and I wanted to return students' attention to the fundamentals, and away from the superficialities nurtured in the discourse of the art press. You know, those glossy art magazines students read like comic books. But when the fire got out of control I ran out into the corridors and studios to raise the alarm. I searched throughout the school to warn people of the imminent danger. It was a normal working day, in the middle of the week, but maybe because there was something of importance taking place in the school, something of real significance to art education, there was not a single student around. Not a lecturer in sight. The school was empty. Not a soul. No one. Even with the constant increases in student numbers, the building was deserted. Those education advisers of the state who assured us that greater student numbers was not about getting the unemployed removed from the national statistics but was necessary to give educational opportunity to the broadest range of students, they would not have believed what I saw that day. I had attended all those training sessions about a multicultural arts education and equal opportunities and now I could not find a student from the ethnic minorities, no one in a wheelchair, not even a dyslexic student who couldn't decipher the instructions of the fire drill. Where were they on this vital day? There was no scheduled student strike about fees or some such urgent matter. No march to parliament to protest about conditions in arts education. In fact there had hardly been any significant student protest since the 1960s. So why were they not there? The art school's lawyers, when questioned by the judge, could not give a reason for this in the court proceedings.

JOURNALIST: But it was fortunate that nobody was hurt.

INMATE: Yes that is true, but I never intended to hurt anyone. My action was pedagogical.

JOURNALIST: Do you think the art school should be rebuilt?

INMATE: That is not a question, young man; it's a challenge to the state and to the artists of the land. There has to be a place where young artists can experiment with their ideas and meet like-minded fellows who also want to communicate something via the visual experience. But if it is to be rebuilt, it must be clean and unbureaucratic; it must be full of students who want to be there all the time and most of all, it must have lots of sprinklers.

Teaching ignorance: a one-step programme

Francis McKee

Head of Programme at the Centre for Contemporary Art, Glasgow.
Tutor at Glasgow School of Art

Since I'm badly dressed, you can see I'm still teaching at Glasgow. I actually feel a bit of an impostor being here, even though I teach one day a week in the Glasgow School of Art on the Master of Fine Arts. The other four days I work as Head of Programme at the CCA in Glasgow. I'm not qualified for either job in the slightest. This time last year, I was in the medical faculty of the University of Glasgow teaching History of Medicine. So, I'm not very sure how I ended up here, but I think maybe I'll come back to that question at the end. When I was contacted and asked, what do I expect from an art school?, very naive answers came to mind. I had two replies. One, to myself, was a 'good time' and the other was 'artists'. They seem increasingly naive the more I go on.

As I said, I teach on the MFA. There are four of us and I have no specific brief on what I teach. I just go in and talk to the students and they talk back and then we go home.

I'm not sure how strange the post is in Britain, but the Head of Programme at CCA is required to curate and programme Visual Art, Performance, Literature, Music, Dance and any other events that happen as well. So the brief is fairly broad. And that's having an increasing impact on what I'm expecting from art schools because when I go to art schools I'm looked at with bafflement in some ways. I also have quite a schizo-phrenic response to this particular question. On the one hand, I have expectations of an art school as a so-called curator, and on the other, I have expectations of the art school as a teacher – what I expect from students or what students expect from me. The two things are completely contradictory at times: thus what I say in the first half of this talk will doubtless be contradicted by the second half.

I guess that mostly what I expect from art schools is healthy suspicion. That would be perfect. Because as a curator, I think that is really what everyone should approach me with. The very first basic thing I would expect from the art school as a curator at CCA – the institutions are within yards of each other – is an audience from the art school. They are my core audience and I would also expect them to be the most critical audi-ence, the audience that actually drives the institution, rather than me sitting there on my own trying to do that. I expect them to turn up, even if there is no free beer, to the openings. I expect them to come to the talks and debates and I expect them to drive the agenda of the CCA as much as the rest of the audience outside of that community. I expect, or I would hope, that the art school will provide the critical audience and the core of thinking for what we do.

On a more frustrated note, I guess I would expect more professional awareness from young artists. This is speaking totally as a sinister curator perhaps, but students should be taught how to make proposals and know what they are doing and what they can expect when they approach an institution. Again, they should operate with a healthy scepticism about the institution, but they should know how to present the work and how to sell themselves, very bluntly, to the institution. I see poor artists going far and I see very good artists not able to sell themselves in the environment that we have created, and I don't see the art schools actually providing much in the way of helping them to address those things. It goes way beyond proposals; it includes a knowledge of finance, which it is increasingly important for artists working with a curator or working within an institution to know – how exactly the institution works in terms of finance and how you finance an exhibition. This is very basic but no one in art schools seems to tell the students.

So the students graduate and expect an institution like the CCA, which is always struggling for funds, to have vast quantities of money. If there is a quantity of money going into an exhibition they expect it to be driven towards them and more often than not, unfortunately, a lot of the money is driven towards invigilation, production costs etc. And that can be an immense disappointment and an immense source of friction between artists and curators. I think that the more knowledge the artist has of how an exhibition is financed and produced, the more possibility there is that they can actually engage with that procedure and get something more positive out of it, rather than maybe coming out of an exhibition feeling that they never really got to do what they wanted within that project. I think that is a major source of frustration. It may appear to be a very banal issue, but I think it is a very important one.

As someone said earlier, we teach artists how to live in a very cosy environment but we don't teach them anything about the outside world. It starts with finance. It extends to the media and publicity where artists just cannot cope most of the time. Very young artists need to know how to use the media or how the media wants to use them in an exhibition. Even on a very simple, local level. If it is the *Glasgow Herald*, for instance, you can end up feeling uncomfortable as they portray you in a very sweet way and try to make your work very sweet too, and it isn't. They're always looking for that 'nice' angle and their photographer will cast a shadow behind you and you'll look like a deep, profound artist and a genius.

I think the broader process of how an institution works, the pace of an institution, the amount of bureaucracy and frustration that comes with an institution, are also important factors. If you're a young artist coming in, and you want to do something, you want to build a soundproof wall, for instance, then you'll be told (a) well, we don't have a ceiling because it's a glass roof and so it can't be sound proofed, (b) we can't afford to build the wall, (c) even if we can, we'll have to talk to the Gallery Manager, the Institution Manager, the Director, Head of Marketing, etc. We have to talk to about ten different departments before we come back to you with an answer and even after that we'll have to go off and get sponsors, and after that we'll have to think about it very hard before we can make any decision.

Those kind of frustrations can create a real depression in artists having to work within an institution. The larger the institution, the more that goes on, even for artists who are furthering their careers. Working with a larger institution, it remains a problem. It would be lovely if artists could come and do placements in galleries at some point, just simply to see how they work. We have a prototype of this at CCA, in that we employ half the artists in Glasgow as invigilators and pay them almost nothing. So at least they begin to see how this works, but it would be nice if they could get up to the next floor and see how the administration works and actually get an insight into how a gallery operates.

Someone mentioned at the start that maybe artists should do work that is more intellectually accessible. That worried me slightly. I know why that was said and the direction it came from but I think that shouldn't be the case. Artists should do whatever work they want to do. It's up to the institution to try and make it more accessible to the audience. It's not for the artist to start with that compromise. It's for the institution to make an effort in its marketing or in its interpretation policy in order to allow that work to exist in the gallery. They should tell people why they think it's worth being there. I don't think we should put that onto the artist.

Younger artists should be shown what a curator is in all his or her glory and they should explore what their expectation of a curator is and what the debate about a curator can focus on. People don't really know what a curator is in an art school. They have no idea. This mythical figure who wears a suit, comes in, and sort of does something, generally financial.

There isn't enough debate around the nature of what a curator can do or what a curator is, or do we actually need curators? That debate needs to start in art schools first and for artists who, when they approach a curator, would have their own ideas of what a curator should be offering them and what they should be expecting from a curator. I think those are vital questions that really aren't being raised. We have more and more curators surfacing now in Britain, and the curators are in some ways becoming as important as the artist, and some of them are becoming as famous as artists, but there's not enough debate yet about what exactly a curator can do. The breadth of the debate we get on artists just isn't there for curators and I don't think we expect enough creativity from them in some ways.

Curators are still seen much in an administrative or financial role and there isn't enough recognition, perhaps, of how curators can be artists in their own right. I think it can be a form of art if it's done well, and I don't think that is recognised, or perhaps it is considered silly within art schools. The curator is there to work off the artist and to collaborate with the artist. Who is the real creative element in that relationship? I believe it's a shared creation, but if that is not understood, it creates a lot of problems.

I think the artist should be taught how to curate as well. It happens anyway, but it happens in a very informal way. I think that would help artists think about how they would do it. Finally, I would hope that art schools would teach artists to think about gallery spaces. Too often, the young artist comes into the space and accepts it as is, without really questioning the kind of space it is or whether or not they want to be there in the first place. They're so driven by the need to get into a space, simply for career needs, that they'll go into a space without giving proper consideration to what that space will do to their work and what they can do to the space. I think a larger debate about the nature of gallery space (particularly at the moment with Lottery capital funding of so much new space) needs to happen more often for young artists from art schools to really know what they're going into.

The other question, which is tangential, is that within the institution of the CCA, we ourselves are now debating charges. We're not likely to introduce them, but we're trying to consider the question because in the entire institution of the CCA, the only person who doesn't get paid is the artist. Everyone else gets paid and that's become more apparent for me as I programme everything from performance through music, dance, etc to visual arts. I pay performers, I pay dancers, I pay writers, I pay invigilators and marketing staff and the only person in the building that doesn't get paid is the artist, and that seems incredible.[1] It raises all sorts of questions that I had never considered, such as why a visual art exhibition is free in the public space but performances aren't? Why do you pay to go and see Forced Entertainment but you don't pay to see Damien Hirst? What's the difference there? Why do we charge for one thing and not for another? I think that artists graduating need to know what they're worth and who is paying them, and why they may not be paying visual artists when they're paying practitioners in every other art form in Britain. They're good questions and it's worth asking how the Government can justify that kind of approach.

As a teacher, everything is completely different. I expect the school to be a refuge from people like me, where artists can get away from all of that, especially on the MFA where we can offer them two years in which they can experiment and fail as much as they want. In the environment of the contemporary gallery you're not meant to fail, you're meant to produce something, produce the goods. The MFA offers people a chance to experiment and do something they can't do anywhere else. They can make a complete mess of things for two years and leave, and it doesn't make any difference. But they don't get that chance anywhere else outside. No one gets subsidised to get the chance to fail anymore, so that would be one of the main functions I see for a school of art – to give people the refuge to experiment, because experiment is the one thing that is vanishing quickly. Today, you have to get it right first time and it had better be good. That doesn't always work in real life.

The basic skeleton of any art school is formed on technical skills: how to paint, or how to make a video, and edit video and how to make something well, even if you don't want to make it well in the end. I'd like to try and take that further. At the moment, we teach very basic visual-art skills and a very narrow range of education, which basically you wouldn't get away with in any other institution. Again, as Head of Programme responsible for all art forms, you notice that visual artists coming out of art schools have an increasing separation from, and lack of knowledge of, the other art forms. There isn't enough collaboration between art forms and there's ignorance about something like performance. Of course, there are one or two people scattered about the art school who will know about it as students with a personal interest, but there really isn't the attempt to combine those interests, to combine a knowledge of contemporary music, of contemporary literature, or performance with fine art. Those things don't seem to exist together. They all exist in their own separate cells and I think the way the funding structures are going, the way the debates are going, those separations are increasing in many ways, particularly if you look at performance and visual arts.

There is so little communication between the two worlds it seems quite incredible. Some suggestion of how these elements could work well together are to be found in the performances of groups such as Goat Island or artists such as Marina Abramovitch. In Anna Teresa de Keersmaker's dance school in Brussels they take the students to a whole series of different environments and put them in different locations, different contexts. It might be anything from taking them to a criminal court case or a railway station, through to a series of philosophy lectures, rather than just concentrating on one discipline. I think this breadth of education needs to be explored much more, to try and increase the breadth of experience for students. I still don't think it's strong enough at the moment and that is reflected in some of the art we're seeing in Britain. It's becoming increasingly insular and increasingly flippant at times as well. I think that's because there's so little breadth that goes into the thinking and education of the art student. You can't really have a thinking, Conceptual artist or painter graduating if they aren't getting that breadth of education that feeds in from every different angle.

Another point I'd like to make about art schools in general is that I'd love to see a different attitude to foreign students, who, at the moment, are used as props for art schools in Britain rather than being used in a much more positive way as a cultural input to the school. I see hundreds of art students wandering around schools looking incredibly lost, lonely and alienated from the rest of the school. It's very clear that they're simply there because they pay overseas fees, which are twice as much as normal fees. These are very basic points, but it just leads to a bad atmosphere and more insularity, a kind of imperialism, that's bad in general. I think this is increasingly surfacing in British art, where British culture is everything, and there's not enough opening up again to the rest of the world. I think it's becoming quite claustrophobic and hard to breathe.

To end, just two things on why I called this paper 'Teaching Ignorance'. In discussing the aim of teaching, we've talked about finance and we've talked about facts and we've talked about careers. But the last thing really is *what* you attempt to teach and what knowledge is. I think what we miss a lot of the time now in art schools is discussion. Wayne Biggs talked about 'wild conversations', rather than academic direction. Academic direction takes over our schools more and more. We have PhDs in art now and we have an academic drive for research in the art schools to achieve funding and all of that misses the point of conversations and dialogue and something less academic. Barbara Johnson, a literary critic in America, talking about teaching said 'to teach ignorance is for Socrates to teach to unknow, to become conscious of the fact that what one thinks is knowledge is really an array of received ideas, prejudices and opinions, a way of not knowing that one does not know'. The question of education is the question not of how to transmit, but of how to suspend, knowledge, how to realise that we don't know anything. To see an artist graduating knowing they know nothing would be a much greater benefit than to see an artist graduating armed with too much knowledge and too many facts and ways to imitate other more successful artists, or career strategies. I think Philip K. Dick in his *Confessions of a Crap Artist* sums it up: 'all the facts that I learned were just so much crap. I realised sitting there that I was a nut. What a thing to realise, all those years wasted. I saw it as clearly as hell. It was just a lot of crap'. I think if an artist got to that point then you would actually be talking about someone who could become a good artist. And I think that will be where I will end.

Note

1. This talk was given just after Francis McKee's arrival at CCA. Shortly afterwards, he made artists' fees a standard practice.

Mighty baby

MATTHEW COLLINGS
Artist, writer and broadcaster

I'm afraid I'm going to read some bits from my book, *Blimey!*, about my experiences as an art student. I was an art student in the 1970s and again in the 1990s at two very different schools and at two very different times. Many people at this conference, including me, probably think of themselves as products of art schools even if they're now in control of art schools or are running departments in art schools. In my case, I virtually didn't go to any other school and my formal education stopped – for one reason or another, some of which you'll hear about in this reading – when I was about thirteen. After spending a few years in various places, I ended up in an art school.

There was some discussion this morning about the typical art student's inability to communicate, or to get across their ideas, which struck me very strongly in that ever since going to art school, I've made a life out of communicating, and communicating about art. It was really due to my art school education that I was able to do that.

I'm sure that no one who works there now will mind if I say that Byam Shaw was an incredibly conservative little art school when I was there in the 1970s. There were right-on, trendy art schools at that time – it's not as if the 1970s were the dark ages. There were many very sophisticated art courses and art schools, but the Byam Shaw wasn't one of them.

The first of these two excerpts from my book is about the 1970s, when I was at art school, and why I happened to have no education or ability to communicate in a formal way, or to think formally, and how that resulted in my going to art school. The second is about returning to art school – to Goldsmiths – in the 1990s, although it isn't about my experiences at Goldsmiths, but about the general Goldsmith's consciousness that's reflected at the moment in British art. In a way, British art is currently in a post-*Freeze* consciousness, and this second extract is about the moment of *Freeze* and what that meant. I'm afraid this is rather an artistic book and some of the stuff I'm going to read will seem sentimental or incoherent or rubbish, but every now and then there will be bits you'll get. All the passages I'm going to read are divided into little sections and sometimes I'll be giving you the titles of the sections. 'Mighty Baby' is the title of the first section.

> Mother Rachel! Mother Rachel! That's the cry I remember going up in the
> middle of the night from the kitchen at 93 Oakley Street, Chelsea. It was the
> Glasgow Poet, Eddie Linden, drunk, with red hair, frightening the unmarried
> mothers. There were always lots of them there. My own mother was one of them.
> We used to sit in a circle of mothers watching the black and white TV. 'The
> Wednesday Play' or 'The Virginian' or 'All Our Yesterdays'.
>   It was a permanently shabby kitchen. The walls were yellow and there was red

lino on the floor. There was a Sellotaped collage of magazine photos from the Sunday papers almost covering one wall. Starving Africans. David Hockney's *Tired Indians*. Over and in between the pictures were pencilled and felt-penned phone numbers, and slogans from the writings of R.D. Laing.

Rachel Pinney, who ran the house, was a psychiatrist and a campaigner for world peace. This was the last of the several homes she used to own. She had made it into a shore for the lost and drifting to wash up on, for £3 and £5 per week rent. Eddie Linden wasn't really her son, any more than I was. He had been one of her patients. He was just drunk and raving and had washed up here briefly. Her real son had been hitch-hiking in Israel, so news reports about the Six Days War was another thing we used to watch. I passed through here every weekend between the ages of six and thirteen, when I lived in a council-run children's home at St Mary's Cray, in Orpington. I came to Chelsea on the train on Fridays and returned to the home on Sunday evenings.

All sorts passed through. Peace campaigners, patients, doctors, shaky people who'd had electric shock treatment. Sometimes Quentin Crisp came round, with blue hair, to play chess. Dust was piled up thickly in his flat across the road in Oakley Gardens.

Later, when it was the end of the 60s, the mothers drifted away and the place filled up with members of rock bands. The Family, who recorded an instrumental named after the house, '93's OK J', and the lesser known Mighty Baby, who had been to India. They sat in their rooms, wearing their afghans and afros and snakeskin boots, and listening to Neil Young's 'Cinnamon Girl' and Frank Zapper's 'Peaches En Regalia', eating lychees.

Rachel, who tolerated the rockers and took their rent – which was now up to £5 and £10 a week – but didn't socialise with them because she didn't understand them and was afraid of their drugs, ate bankrupt soup.

That was her name for it. It was what the kitchen always smelled of. It was an army-sized tureen of old vegetables and slightly off meat that she would just add to now and then, and reheat, until some mother or band member or other couldn't bear the smell any longer and would throw it away. But then, horribly, it would start up again.

The Mounties

For the cause of world peace she didn't talk on Wednesdays. She would just write things down on a piece of paper. 'I'm afraid the answer is No'. Or, 'Where are my glasses?' Once she allowed an autistic child to cut all her hair off with nail scissors and for a few weeks she had a radical ragged grey prison haircut instead of her normal severe lesbian do.

But then she really did go to prison, for six months, in 1970, for kidnapping me when I was fourteen. She gave me some money to run away to Canada. Some detectives arrested me there after a month and when I was brought back to London, by a London detective and a WPC who had come out to get me, it turned out Interpol, the FBI, Scotland Yard and the Mounties had all been in on the search.

[184]

The Bohemians

People who are in the art world get there by all sorts of different springboards. For some of them it is a step up the social ladder, from working class to middle class. But some of course are born into that class. I was born into the Bohemian class, which is a branch of the middle class. My mother went to art school and then later on taught art in secondary schools. Her mother was a dancer and her father distributed films in South America for J. Arthur Rank.

Weeping

After I was kidnapped I was sent to a therapeutic community in Kent, and when I left I did some manual labouring jobs for two years, which were very tiring, like refuse-collecting, cleaning at the British Museum, putting up 'Residents Only' parking signs and mixing concrete.

And then I went to the Byam Shaw School of Painting, where my mother had been when she was fifteen. It was the 1970s. I studied the art magazines in the library and learned to recognise works by contemporary New York artists like Mel Bochner and Lawrence Weiner. They did diagrams of triangles on the floor made of pebbles or lengths of tape, and words on the wall that said things like 'Eight Pints of White Paint'. Then I bought a book called *Six Years*. It documented in awesome detail six years' worth of Conceptual art from 1966 to 1972.

There were the early sayings of Gilbert & George, which went something like 'Art we only wish to serve you'. And the first Conceptual art manifestos by Joseph Kosuth. There were photos of cooling towers and mounds of earth in the dessert, and Robert Smithson's *Spiral Jetty* photographed from the air, and a woman weeping. [Actually some of you may know that it was actually a man: Bas Jan Ader.]

Art & Language

A man came to the school and gave us a lecture about Art & Language. They were an international art group, spread all over the world, in New York, Australia and Oxford. They typed the letter 'A' in the middle of a sheet of paper, and then after that one of them left, because it was only formalism, which was a bit confusing because we'd just got used to the idea that formalism was Minimalism.

One Second

We went to exhibitions in Cork Street and at the ICA, in the Mall. We saw colour field paintings in acrylic by John Hoyland and some suitcases and railway sleepers by a Greek Conceptual artist. At the Tate Gallery we saw a John Latham 'Retrospective'. He burned books and made one-second drawings done with spattered ink. And at the Serpentine Gallery we saw a Howard Hodgkin retrospective. He painted dots and patterns and abstract figures who were always in restaurants.

Space

Also at the art school I learned about space, which we had to paint and draw in life classes. The naked models stood or lay around in set-ups with easels and draped sheets and pieces of coloured paper, to make the space richer, with the daylight streaming in through the big grid-shaped windows.

We had to draw or paint the scenes with a ruthless spatial eye. Not first of all putting the model's eyes, nose, ears and mouth, or nipples, in the middle of the paper or canvas, with a very sharp pencil or tiny sable brush, as we would have very much liked to have done, and as we all certainly did on our first morning's life class when we started at the school. But instead blocking in the big areas first, not caring if it was an arm or an easel or a window or a door or the side of the head of the student in front of us. And then gradually getting all the shapes to relate together, so a convincing space would appear.

We would go on from there, blocking in smaller and smaller shapes and going back and correcting the big ones. And then somewhere in all that blocking, after many hours or days, there would be the naked model rendered at last, all dots and dashes and wobbly squares and rectangles and negative shapes, in rugged thick black charcoal or 6B pencil outlines, looking like a wonky diagram of a human.

Or if it was a painting the lines and shapes would be in thick rich mixed-up oil colours, every contour the result of endless other contours shuffling and colliding, and the model would look like a poor hot and cold coloured paint creature, glowing from a nuclear explosion.

I did have some thoughts this morning. There was a comment about careers and that art school could be good because it enabled you to have an alternative career, a sort of non-mainstream career, and yet a well-paid career, or even formed a sort of alternative springboard to enter into the mainstream. Then there was another thought about the romantic ideal of art school, where you're actively encouraged to express yourself, or to be creative, without any thought of a career, and suddenly you're at the mercy of the cruel Benefits Office system. In a way, although the second picture has faded out of view, or come to be seen as hopelessly romantic or absurd, that's actually my most vivid impression of the art school life, and one that I did sort of live.

Although I've got this television series coming up, which has got this enormous budget, and this splendid book here, which every time you buy a copy I get some money from, these things came after two years of not having any work on the telly. The only reason I wasn't on the dole in that period was that I really couldn't understand the forms for self-employment. I actually tried to get a job at the ICA working on the talks on that day because I couldn't get through these forms, but they wouldn't give me one. I tried to get a job teaching at the RCA by some kind of stream-of-thought process and they wouldn't give me one either. I was really struggling, and then weirdly a hand came from the TV world and said here is £1.5 million, do your series. But it was only because I had a vivid enough inner life, which found the unpleasant realities an amusing and interesting process, and which I'd got from being at art school, that I was able to do those money-making jobs. It wasn't at all through having a good idea about careers and how to communicate in a way that would get you a career. It was simply that I naturally enjoyed communicating and so those monolithic structures where the money resides tend to notice you after a while.

The Goldsmiths MA, I don't know if you know this, is a kind of remedial course. Maybe all MAs are based on the traumas that you suffered during your art school education. So if you go to do an MA, it's because it went wrong the first time around; if it hadn't gone wrong you wouldn't have to go there. For me, it was a fantastic experience – it was an amusing experience. People often think that Goldsmiths is a kind of brainwashing experience, where you're taught to be a coke-sniffing artistic sensation and so on. It's not that I didn't find it a brainwashing experience, but I found it painful in the first year because it was very much a brain-exposing experience, where what is at the back of your brain, and makes you go to the studio every day, is exposed and looked at during a lot of therapy-type talk where you have to say what's at the back of your mind. Normally you don't really say those things; you believe that they're true, and you hope that nobody notices that you think them, and suddenly they're exposed and you talk about them and they take them apart. And that can be very painful, especially if you have some arrogance or confidence and you don't particularly want to be assaulted by people who are outside of that situation. You might even look down upon or believe that they are incoherent and can't put a sentence together and you suddenly realise the clarity of their thinking compared to the rubbish in your own head.

Warehouse Shows

The 1980s saw the rise of Young British Art. The first thing was a series of group shows held in warehouse spaces. These shows were called things like *Freeze*, *Modern Medicine*, *Gambler*, or *East Country Yard Show*. Meaningless titles which have now entered legend. The art wasn't all that different from anything that had been seen before. But the exhibitions were very professionally organised. Even though they were only put on by students, or recently graduated students, they had a bold European *Kunsthalle* look, or a SoHo in New York look, or pages of *Flash Art* or *Art Forum* look.

666 [That's just a jokey title.]

The main personality to come out of the Warehouse Shows was Damien Hirst. In the exhibition called *Gambler*, which was a little bit after *Freeze*, he showed a sculpture that was two six-feet-square glass cases next to each other, connected by a circular hole. Vitrines. They looked like recycled Minimalism, which was quite normal for the time … [I'm going to skip some of this description of *A Hundred Years* by Damien Hirst.]

… A Good Idea

Clearly it was a good idea. The vitrines looked like Minimalism in the sense that they looked like the parodies of 60s Minimalism that were going on a lot in the art of the 80s. But the flies were a twist in a different direction. The idea with the normal Minimalism parodies of the 80s was to re-do 60s Minimalism in a formally impure way, that went against the essence of the original movement, which was to be utterly pure, but retained its handsome look. So the parody Minimalism was supposed to be critical in some way. Critical of art or life or society. Whatever. You went around frowning and saying 'Hmm, yes, that's very interesting, it's critical …

… Silk Cuts

It soon went around that Charles Saatchi had bought that flies sculpture, and after that you would always hear about Damien Hirst in connection with Saatchi. Saatchi had given him an idea for this, and told him to do that, and so on.

One thing he perhaps told him to do, or gave him the idea for, was a vitrine huge enough to have an executive style desk and a chair inside it, with a lot of space round the objects, enough for a person to walk in and sit down, except that the vitrine was completely sealed. On the desk was a packet of Silk Cut cigarettes and an ashtray full of butts. It was handsome and ugly at the same time. It was as good as the flies, but different. They both seemed to be about bringing back the old heavy contents of art but still being smart, clever and emotionally disengaged. Of course nowadays we wonder if we really care for that emotionally disengaged sense as much as we used to.

The Meaning of Vitrines

Unexpected things in vitrines became his style. As well as the big boxes and cubes of 60s Minimalism, vitrines recalled Joseph Beuys. Joseph Beuys, who died in 1986, was the opposite of Minimalism. Minimalism was the *ne plus ultra* of formalism, and the last moment of High Modernism, whereas Joseph Beuys was an anti-formalist and one of the innovators of a far-out branch of Modernism that eventually became Post-Modernism. But by the 80s it was all the same. It could all be used again differently to make new parody art.

Nothing

Without the imposing, Minimal sculpture-like vitrine with its sheet glass sides and heavy steel edges, the Silk Cuts artwork would have looked a bit of nothing. Nowadays, in the 90s, the nothing look would be good. Today someone else might easily do the Silk Cuts and ashtray without the vitrine, and everybody would be able to tell it was still some kind of art. In fact I might do it myself. But in those days there was a different mood.

My time's up. Thank you very much for listening.

Travelling light: a brief analysis of the end of the work and the triumph of the photographic colour transparency

PHYLLIDA BARLOW

Head of Undergraduate Sculpture, The Slade School of Fine Art,
University College London

While I was preparing for a talk recently, I decided to make a slide copy of Tony Smith's *Die*, 1962. The particular image I wanted to document was from the catalogue, *The Art of the Real*, accompanying the exhibition of the same title, which had toured from the Metropolitan in New York to the Tate in 1969. The image of Smith's *Die* shows the infamous black steel cube situated in an ambiguous space, which partly suggests a large urban garden and partly a rural environment. The cube itself is streaked and stained, anything but pristine, and placed awkwardly within the boundaries of the black and white photograph, printed on thin, now slightly yellowing, glossy paper. Wherever the location might be, the photograph clearly states that it is only a record, taken for expedient reasons. As a photographic document it proclaims that to know anything about what this work is really like, you will have to be there with it. The photograph is exactly that – a photograph – and as such makes absolutely no effort whatever to enhance either the appearance of the cube or its less than sophisticated environment.

In comparison, a more recent 1984 catalogue of other work produced in the 1960s and early 1970s, now identified as Minimalism (interestingly nowhere in *The Art of the Real* is this particular word to be found), there is a reversal of priorities. Gone is the semi-domestic garden or rural setting. Instead, the photographs show clean, rectilinear spaces, representing the simplicity of the gallery, where any visual competition with the artwork has been removed, and the space, if it has to be shown, as with the Carl Andre floor pieces, does not interfere with one's reading of the work. In fact, the Sol LeWitts exist in a kind of cyberspace, so important has it been deemed, by this particular catalogue designer, to eradicate any kind of environmental intrusion.

The confidence shown by the 1984 catalogue in how the photographic images represent the work, as well as its overall design, inform us in no uncertain terms of what it believes the Minimalist ideal to be. That is, the cleansed photographs reflect Minimalist didacticism.

This 1984 catalogue heralds the rise of the fundamental importance attached to photographic representation for an understanding the original work. The artwork serves the catalogue, which, in turn, re-presents, or re-offers the work on the conditions of the medium of catalogue production. As we all know, the catalogue has become an artwork in its own right. It is symbiotic with the work, forming a parasite/host relationship, where it can dictate the ideology that is most convenient, stylish, enhancing, sensational, of how it wants the artwork to be projected, and the most effective and successful way of achieving this within the available choices offered through the medium of catalogue production.

Therefore, there is no need to be there with the work; its representative, in the form of the idealised photographic image, presented through the object of the catalogue, can be believed to communicate far more than experiencing the reality of the work itself. But this displacement of the reality of the work by its alter ego, its photographic representation of itself, provides a model that I would question, and in which I feel an increasing lack of confidence, both as an artist and as a lecturer. This is despite the fact that I rely heavily on photography, not only within my own work, but in discussing students' work, or when participating in the selection of applicants to the Slade, and elsewhere. Last week, for example, I looked at over 7,000 slides as part of the submission for the 1998 *New Contemporaries* exhibition.

This model I have referred to, I believe, demonstrates the relationship of the catalogue, and its partner, the photograph (particularly the colour slide), to what identifies and specifies professionalism. It is the absolute necessity of the colour slide that has enabled it to become the representative not only of the work photographed, but also of what creative position the artist is pursuing, so clearly manifested through the all-important choice of the how, the where, the when, and with what of the colour-slide image. And it is through these choices imaged by the colour slide that the professional style of the artist can be identified. A young artist showing an image of their work in the manner of this photograph of Tony Smith's *Die* would be given short shrift because of their severe lack of professionalism. And such criticism could be justified because there would be genuine concern for how best such a student should represent their work as a photographic image.

The holiday brochure, the tourist industry's equivalent to the catalogue, also offers a visual representation of what is supposed to be the actual experience. The holiday can be represented through photographs shot in heavily staged and contrived studio settings, where blue skies and sandy beaches are nothing more than ingenious visual lies. The demand for more and more exotic and challenging forms of travel has to be responded to with the appropriate supply of journeys, tours, treks, outward-bound vacations, culture breaks, adventure holidays, luxury cruises, off-the-beaten-track adventures, scenic-route tours, etc. You name it and a tour operator will come up with the goods. Even climbing Mount Everest has to be booked years in advance to ensure that you have enough room, along with all the other climbers, to stand on its summit. It is still possible to travel as a free spirit without a specific destination, but there are plenty of dangers to be heeded and certainly the tour operators will be following close behind to see if they can exploit your example and turn it into another packaged opportunity.

Similarly, today, artists find themselves confronted by a plethora of choices – a choice of journeys, perhaps – to continue the metaphorical comparison with tourism. But underlying all these choices is the confrontation with the orthodoxy of professionalism. Therefore, if the choice an artist decides upon is to go it alone, shun the art world and all that it involves, in order to make that decision, some kind of knowledge of what the art world is has to be recognised in order to shun it. But clearly, one way of avoiding any contact with the art world is to have absolutely no photographic documentation of your work. This could be the journey without destination.

So hugely important has the evolved form of artwork documentation become, that without doubt, the catalogue, which exemplifies this evolution, has become a superb souvenir of the original artwork. It is the enticement for the reality, but it can also allow the dispensation of the reality. The tourist industry's plethora of brochures entice in the same way, and as long as the bookings roll in, little interest need be paid to the actual experience, undoubtedly longed for, and often wonderful, but possibly nothing like the advertised image. Therefore, whatever choice of journey the young artist decides upon, and whatever choice of journey mature artists have decided upon, the catalogue provides the zenith of professionalism in terms of how it records that journey, and it cannot represent that record without photographic documentation. These photographic images are not enough in themselves, for the catalogue does not only represent the work. The accompanying professions of curator, theorist, historian, plus the catalogue designer are also represented, to provide the information that authenticates the catalogue as the height of professionalism. The greater number of these satellite professions are represented, the greater the level of professionalism attained. It is a clear but highly flawed system. Its clarity, however, does in fact generate choice: the choice of whether you, as an artist, and in this case, young artists at art school, want to, or are able to measure up to the level of professionalism as manifested by these state-of-the-art catalogues.

The contemporary catalogue, with its outstanding photographic representations, is, in the context of a takeaway culture, the takeaway exhibition. Not only does it superbly represent the work, it re-presents the work in compacted, portable book form, where the art objects within, whatever their original form – sculpture, painting, film, or whatever – become reduced to a single idealised portrait of that original work. This idealised portrait becomes the visual resource of information, so often used by art schools in particular, through which an artist's intentions become disseminated. The singular, highly reduced, cleansed, framed photographic image, without scale, without surface, without gravity, without time, without smell, without movement, without the contact between you and it, without so much, becomes the carrier of, and is responsible for, so much.

However, the reality of the package holiday, or the trek across Nepal, or the cultural tour down the Nile, can be a very different experience from the blue-skied, yellow-sanded image offered by the travel brochure. The violent stomach upset is definitely not featured! Nor the screaming child who has developed an uncontrollable aversion to sand. What neither the glowing brochure nor the seamless catalogue ever show is mistakes.

For me, mistakes are intriguing because they reveal something that was not meant to be revealed. On a holiday, or trekking adventure, this can be anything from a bloody nuisance to life-threatening disaster. But within art, it can be the meeting point of possibilities, generating a scheme of choices otherwise not only previously unconsidered, but also not thought possible. The ethos of the accident in art as a potential for a creative process can be a dubious ethos when the art accident becomes a kind of mannerism. Mistakes, I believe, are different, because the intention is one thing and the result is another. Anyway, accidents are part of mistakes in so much as they reveal, change, divert, intervene, confront. Mistakes set up the kind of contention that demands a response, and the contention is that it is an unexpected response that is demanded. A new reality intervenes to question the previous pretence.

Mistakes provide subversion, and reciprocally, professional orthodoxy invites subversion. If the catalogue presents the height of professionalism, then there will be subversion of its orthodoxy. And this is what art schools can initiate. They can provide the critical framework in which young artists can test out their tolerance for the professional orthodoxy of the day. A young artist within art school who produces work that can seriously and effectively challenge and subvert the orthodoxy of professionalism is, I believe, achieving something significant, because he or she will be producing work that will not be dependent on what is already given. However, I am sure that the art machine, like the tour operator trailing the free-spirited traveller, will be quick off the mark to absorb this subversive act.

Essentially, the process within art schools is experimental, and because experiments embrace the mistake, they defy the memorial grandeur of the catalogue, simply because catalogues never show mistakes. The ever-present companion to mistakes is doubt. This is similarly absent from catalogue culture because essentially a catalogue is an advertisement and as such it must be promoting its product. It must offer the product's most successful identity, and because doubt would undermine that proffered conviction, doubt is therefore not a quality used by catalogues. But the process of discussion and critical analysis, as used within art schools, is one of both encouraging doubt and allaying it, and such prevarication between the two is, on the terms of the prevailing professional orthodoxy, unacceptable. However, the orthodoxy of professionalism has irrevocably established that the photograph, in particular the colour slide, is the single most important memento of the art school experience with which students leave.

But what makes art school documentation different, is its accommodation of mistakes, and the understanding and collusion between all concerned for the interest in mistakes, and doubt and enquiry and guesswork. These identities are constantly up for discussion, and critical analysis, but supported by the pleasure derived from the fact that there is the freedom to engage with them. Because the catalogue exemplifies a professional orthodoxy and as such cannot accommodate any hint of mistake or doubt, they become the representatives of failure. And this is the major flaw in the professional orthodoxy: its presumption of what is and what is not failure. For me, the emphasis on the immaculate, the unblemished and the eradication of process has displaced the sensuality of failure with the anaesthesia of success. Success, that is, exemplified by the professional orthodoxy of the catalogue. This is a success not based on discovery through experimentation, but success based on what is already known, and received through the photographic image.

The fact that professionalism, as exemplified through the catalogue, is identified through the perfection of a photographic image, is helpful in making young artists recognise and act on the importance of the production of good slide documentation of their work, but is absolutely no good for disseminating the wealth of innovative experimentation that evolves within art schools.

The catalogue clings to its orthodoxy, and as yet, there is no apparent reason why it should not, because it is so undeniably successful. But there are signs that its influence might be inhibiting the opportunities that art schools can provide for mistakes to be made and experienced. And where this influence is most noticeable is with the annual degree shows.

There does seem to be a dilemma where the degree show, which is the event at the interface between the art school and the professional world, is vulnerable to the rigidity of the professional orthodoxy as manifested by the catalogue, filled as it is with its cleansed images of works, inhabiting their equally cleansed hyper-spaces. The numerous imitations of this ideal make themselves evident every year in the inadequacies of these studio-turned-gallery spaces, not only endorsing the model for the degree show as the ubiquitous white cube, but also endorsing what the white cube represents as a professional ideal.

I hope that art schools can precipitate the challenge to the conventions of professionalism without lapsing into nostalgia for past solutions, or mimicking the ubiquitous white cube. It is a real challenge. So powerful are the instructions from outside art schools as to what constitutes professionalism that the innovation of a new form for what an exhibition could be confronts every young artist today. The fact is that the numerous exhibition spaces now available can make such a confrontation seem like a waste of time and creative energy, especially when the prevailing professional orthodoxy is interpreted as 'exhibit or die'. Therefore, to take the time, and to consider and demand particular conditions for how to exhibit in relation to the work, and how imaginatively to reinvent the exhibition orthodoxy, can seem like professional suicide. Therefore, I'm beginning to feel that the time when the convention of the degree show is changed, or developed, will be the time when the relationship between the experience of the reality of the artwork and its representation as a photographic image will itself be changed, because of a recognition of the need to challenge what the relationship is between the art object and its image as representing a professional orthodoxy. I believe that it is within the relationship between the work and its photographic representation that the contention of professionalism – for what and for whom – will be, and already is being, argued, and out of which a reinvention of professionalism could appear.

In order to generate the confidence that can initiate change, there has to be the recognition of choice. I feel that despite the vast choice on offer in terms of materials, media, form, aesthetics, content and subject, the young artist can believe that they, in fact, have no choice, and therefore no confidence in the imaginative possibilities of how to put these choices back into the world through exhibition. And this is then reciprocated by a pessimism about how young artists perceive their future, as if there is only one route, and that is the idealised success route as represented, and demonstrated through the catalogue.

But as the hardened traveller, without the assistance of the ubiquitous tour operator, will tell you, there are numerous potentially successful routes along which the young artist can travel. The most important advice is probably that the young artist should get to know their temperament, and come to terms with that temperament so that they can travel appropriately, to find the journey that is most rewarding to them, and not feel obliged to travel to where they think everyone else is travelling. Because, like Everest's summit, it could be horribly overcrowded, or it could be an all-to-familiar sight-seeing tour, or an over-organised package holiday. On the other hand, if that is what is needed and wanted temperamentally, then that is where to go.

The fact is that there is choice, and tourism is not the only way in which to experience the world, at the mercy of the tour operator and the travel brochure. And art schools have to throw caution to the wind and not be so controlled by the conventions of tourism, either through totally rejecting it, or by complete submission to it. The current professional orthodoxy is unashamedly ambitious in how it defines success, and in how it manifests that success through the catalogue and its cargo of photographic images. The art school should be able to present equivalent ambitions, through investigating what the choices actually are, so that it can manipulate to its advantage professional orthodoxy, and, without academicising them, initiate how to change and subvert those orthodoxies for the creative benefit of all concerned. Professionalism in the visual arts is there to be evolved, and where better for this to happen than in art schools?

The invisible subject:
views from the missionary position

BRIAN CATLING

Head of Sculpture, The Ruskin School of Art, Oxford

I want to begin by giving you the key to the end and tell you about the origin of clapping, which I'm sure some of you already know. When earlier peoples summoned the gods in magical ceremonies, it was necessary, after the transformational event, to step back into the normal world; to find a way to break the air waves, to change the condition and make it a safe place. This was done by clapping – by physically breaking the airwaves as a way of reducing power. This is why we aren't encouraged to clap in churches, it's a kind of boomerang.

The Invisible Subject

I want to use this moment to carve a notch, to drive a wedge into the asymmetrical structure of art-educational debate and its tight rings of nervy history, to overstate the obvious and celebrate a unique method of teaching. This conference seems the ideal place to applaud ourselves for the success of the unique experiment; to see the 'invisible subject' before it is dismantled or erased. Current financial and political mindsets seem to be trundling in that direction.

Many of the forces controlling and influencing art education are now essentially expedient; over-dressed ignorance making itself appealing in a shimmering mock democracy of student numbers. I recognise that this sounds like ominous mumblings approaching old fartdom, or the perfect glow of a lost golden age illuminating static attitudes and atrophied thinking. I will attempt to deflect such bouts of ostrich cynicism, and sensibly weigh and taste both the baby and the bath water in this tribal ceremony of displacement.

The experiment began after the Coldstream Report in the late 1950s with a radical new approach to the teaching of fine art. This was the first stage in a basic philosophical shift in emphasis from taught craft skills to individual imaginative thinking. It was the beginning of a complex evolution that was seeded in the conflict between the creaking atrophied academy and the isolated but inspired outbreaks of original thought. In the thirty years that followed, potent streams and layers of growth were woven. Fine art departments were queuing and jousting to add different strata of meanings and applications. There had of course been minor outbreaks of formalist fundamentalism and odd regressive lapses to stone carving and compulsory scratching in life rooms. But basically there was an optimistic sweep of invention. This was choke-chained by a brutish change of government demanding a new rationalism in higher education that herded the art schools towards academic shelter inside the universities and polytechnics. Some of the snivelling tactics employed by weak-minded Thatcherites are still in place today. Drastic forms of accountability appeared. Unnatural parallels were dragged before the inquisition. Crippling tools of restrictive bureaucracy were designed. 'Transferable skills' were taken seriously. It was under this cloud of insecurity and threat that the 'invisible subject' became most vulnerable. It simply could not be mentioned, so that the most original foundation stone of the new teaching remained unclaimed, uncelebrated and concealed, almost an embarrassment. It has never really regained its natural status, but remains a basic principle in the growth and quality of contemporary art in this country.

What I grew up with, and continue, with my colleagues, to teach, is not painting, printmaking and sculpture. Nor is it performance, video and text – nor even fine art. These are details of the core. It is the invisible subject – the imagination – particularly the visual imagination, but ultimately, imagination prime. We, at art schools, have the only educational system that deals with the imagination of our students directly. In syllabuses, the student's creative and critical intelligence is filtered through the study of past or accepted forms of the subject, be it in the arts or sciences at undergraduate level. Most of us know that this is an inappropriate scholastic mechanism for an artist, even if at first glance it appears more critically rigorous. We are the only clan in pedagogy that expects its young to practice and exercise its ingenious muscle from day one; to run alongside us rather than be distantly trained through imitation and conoisseurship. I know this ambitious claim for a true democratic optimism seems very grand and perhaps naive, but I believe that its worth and continual function is proven. The true transferable skill we have passed on one to another is the language of imaginative intelligence. The extraordinary breadth of creative flexibility being its key signature. That is what makes all the meagre compromises so distasteful. Many of our community have been so intimidated before various tribunals as to list minor DIY skills as significant academic achievements and even to convince themselves of this spurious validity.

The contrast is glaring and in its light we can see most of the corners, horizons and perspectives that distinguish quality and failure in our system. This open, but layered enmeshing of understanding and exchange is of course open to abuse. The privilege of sharing aspects of each others' imaginative pathways must be conducted with caution, skill and the commitment for the mutual excitement of the venture to continue. I am sure we have all witnessed exhibitions of the subject being conducted by poor minds; the flexing voice of power that designs irrelevant obstacles and problems for students to experience and solve: the hoops-of-fire principal of teaching. Such tactics take us back to training techniques and are obviously the shabby tools of the defeated. Even worse at close range are the amateur Freudians. Barrack-room analysts are desperate to create fresh carrion to enliven their neurosis. Vacant egotists scavenge for disciples among the eager and the trusting. But these blights will always attach themselves to the magnetic field of any positive system. They are minor symptoms of a process that is essentially generous, and driven by a mutual desire to improve and actively shape and evolve knowledge, making it accessible to all its participants. The quintessential mechanism we have for sustained and responsible teaching is reflection. Reflection held in conversation, using our experience like a concave mirror. The surface is pliant and capable of subtle distortion, so that the ideas and dreams conjured between student and tutor always belong to the former. This is the place where language is attached to desire, where structure is grown onto intention, where procedure is twined with ambition. It is the sublime, fragile and vigorous centre of the externalisation of the invisible. A territory where all aspects of humanity may enter by mutual consent, be examined, developed and returned and sometimes ignited. All other aspects of education are slaves or props to this continual moment. Core structure, administrative planning and other forms of necessary support apparatus must remain felt but concealed, shielded from the enigmatic flame of imaginative communion, or they might be consumed – confused into believing they are the same thing. The invisible subject is therefore more process than fact. Its achievement is greater than any simple listing of its component parts could expose. This is why I want you to celebrate its unique form and your part in its creation and operation; to recognise and applaud a very successful experiment. To applaud it in silence and recollection so that nothing escapes, nothing is sealed off, and nothing is lost.

This is tomorrow

UTE META BAUER

Guest Professor and Head of the Institute of Contemporary Art,
Academy of Fine Art, Vienna

I think it's important that speakers talk about their own backgrounds and, like most of you, I have various kinds of professions. As an artist, you somehow have to fulfil many skills and jobs, and I think of it all as my artistic practice.

I called this talk 'This Is Tomorrow' after the exhibition held in 1956 at the Whitechapel Art Gallery. In this venture many people from lots of different kinds of fields accomplished an exhibition in which they imagined the art and culture of their tomorrow. I think one of the jobs we have in the academies today is considering what will be the tomorrow of the people we are training.

First, a brief introduction to what the Institute of Contemporary Art does. Our activities comprise lectures, seminars, the organisation of workshops and symposia as well as exhibitions and excursions. In terms of subject matter, the Institute focuses primarily on the interaction between current artistic practice and theory as well as the social function and relevancy of art and cultural production today. It deals with the constantly changing notion of the meaning of art. Its historical links and anchor points are the focus of our mandate in terms of education and mediation. I use the term 'mediation' because our programme addresses both students and an interested public.

In the Institute at the moment we have a staff of seven permanent lecturers working full time and contracted for three years. That is one of the benefits of the hierarchical system that we have in Austria. I have complete freedom to do whatever I want within our department. So I can invite whoever I think is beneficial for our discourse. When our students first come into the school, they try to go five days a week making drawings – they will hardly leave their studios. So it is very difficult to get them to understand the notion that art theory could be interesting to them. As we do many workshops – about ten a year – and have several guest lecturers for the public, we have a greater number of participants outside the school than inside it.

What follows is a brief description of our postgraduate programme for artists, architects and art historians and whoever is interested in the notion of what art and culture will mean tomorrow. The general objective of the programme is to offer an opportunity to expand and deepen the knowledge and skills that people attending have acquired in their previous training, with special emphasis on the field of current art and cultural theory. The aim is also to develop new forms of disseminating information on art while taking into account the changing understanding of art production. A common postgraduate programme for those who produce and for those who inform the public about art would serve to create a practical, mutual understanding of the diverse tasks of both groups.

In terms of my own education, I somehow see myself as being an autodidact because, mostly, nobody prepares you in art school for what will come later on in your profession. We had studio arts, we even had a progressive art school, but nobody trained us for later on: being our own publicists, curators, fundraisers etc. The objective of this programme is to familiarise students with the structures and mechanisms of the art and cultural world in order to prepare them for a practice-orientated approach to the day-to-day business in art and culture, which has undergone fundamental changes in the thoroughly mediated society in which we live today. This includes new ways of disseminating information on art and the development of adequate ways to impart knowledge of current notions of art and culture. These intensive efforts to address the public, which are fundamental to contemporary artistic practice, require reflection on various concepts of what is public as well as an analysis of the various habits of reception, and aesthetic structures related to reception in the overall social context. These two mainstays of the programme are based on the developments in art that have taken place in the past decades, resulting in major changes in the professional profile of the artist. In contrast to what might be common internationally, no other such postgraduate programme has been offered in Austria so far. As a matter of fact, no such postgraduate programme exists in any of the German-speaking countries, and until now, no curating course existed in any fine art institution.

The traditional typology of 'genius' artists who exclusively consider themselves to be spontaneous, creative individuals has been replaced by a notion of artists whose understanding of themselves is as subjects critical of social processes, engaged in shaping themselves as subjects, and for whom reflection on their own work is a matter of course. These developments must be taken into account to a greater extent. Contemporary art is situated in an interdisciplinary field in which distinguishing between individual media such as sculpture, painting, installation, video, photography, etc. and artistic forms such as visual art, music, literature, film, performance, is of secondary importance. The notion of art is increasingly based on a more natural and flexible approach to these categories. The classic dividing lines between art and non-art, high art, Pop art, sub-culture, are emphatically called into question, and the sites of art are no longer restricted to classic systems of representation such as museums, galleries or other art institutions. These changes are reflected in the current range of subjects and events we offer within our department. One course, for instance, focuses on feminists discourses from the past three decades that have caused artists to engage, to a growing extent, with the construction of gender identity, social definitions of gender and related mechanisms of representation. Another course focuses on engagement with the art world. The structures and mechanisms at work in practical and theoretical issues are fundamental to the work of artists. The clusters of topics strike a balance between theory and practice, thus enabling meaningful exchange and synergy between these two closely related areas. This is supported by the selection of the regular staff as well as our visiting professors who are practitioners of art and culture or come from related fields of interest such as psychoanalysis, the mainstream media and others. A diversity of teaching methods must be foreseen to match the complexity of the subject matter involved. In addition to lectures primarily geared to imparting knowledge, students deepen their understanding with reading and work. The major focus is on projects that enhance the participants' initiative and sense of responsibility. Special project-orientated work is undertaken in various types of presentations designed to link up theory and practice and to develop and test structures that serve to convey information. The group debates and thinks about what our field of tomorrow could be. To quote the title of a recent exhibition by Regina Müller, 'our job does not exist as yet'.

For some of you, perhaps this draft of a proposed graduate programme will seem familiar, even in terms of the more unusual fields it addresses. But I should give you the background from which it all started. The Academy is more than 300 years old – one of the oldest in Europe. It is still linked with what was once a feudal set-up of emperors, painters, sculptors, and architects. Even now, we still have our own state by-laws in Austrian higher education, which are currently under evaluation with the view to integration within the common laws shared by all state universities. Our faculty consists of twenty-six full-time professors for 650 students divided into individual master schools, which means exactly what the name suggests. Each school is represented by one master, and the students stay with that one specific master for the whole time of study, which is between four and five years. Before I started in 1996, there had only been two other women professors in the 300-year history of the Academy: one during the Second World War, who was Professor of Tapestry, and Erica Billiger, who held my position eight years ago. Within the last year, we have increased the number of female full-time professors to six – a revolutionary percentage within Austria, where the outstanding percentage of 3.9 university professors are female! The year I came, 1996, one third of our senior faculty, who had been masters for a quarter of a century, were on the way out, which created a tremendous wave of change within this old, dark bastion. The average age of teachers went down visibly. The classical curricula of paintings and graphics were updated with the inclusion of photography – which previously hadn't been allowed in – new media, context-orientated art and consideration of art in public spaces.

That which the school stood for – the hierarchy of master schools – has stayed firmly in place, however, which has forced tactical categories to occur like mutations: a master school of painting with a focus on public art for example. Our department is one of the biggest within the Academy, but contemporary art is still not on our curricula, which means that none of our courses are accredited for the masters schools of painting and architecture and our staff of seven must still attract students who are simply interested in what we're doing. A number of students on other courses were even forbidden, until recently, by their masters to visit our courses or even to show us their work. I have tried to convince all my various colleagues that a certain knowledge of contemporary art and culture might be beneficial for students of today. The three schools of culture were the first and only who have added us to their curriculum. Keeping in mind that nothing like these changes could occur until 30 per cent of the senior faculty – those in power for more than twenty-five years – were gone, is a clear indication of the reality of 300-year-old structures.

This proposal for a postgraduate programme still meets with incredible resistance within our academy, functioning like a kind of virus within the school. But it may remind you of exactly why we bother with educational programmes, including diverse artistic practices, issues of representation, cultural identity and political structures.

The atelier: mixes, crossovers, displacements

GUADALUPE ECHEVARRIA

Director, Ecole des Beaux Arts, Bordeaux

I want to bring to your attention a series of ideas and practices at the Ecole des Beaux Arts in Bordeaux, which we understand to be a present-day interpretation of the role of the atelier, the studio.

As we approach the turn of the century, we are no longer devoted to specific artistic research. There is no longer the space to define every particular method by creating images and forms. More than ever, the mixes, the influences, the displacements, the multiple events, the new media, cannot be ignored. The many categories of multi-media practices that no longer fit within the traditional approach, not only develop and animate the work, but also create a need to redefine the idea of the studio.

The very idea of the atelier implies a variety of meanings that are inherent to the historical moment to which they apply. The word 'atelier' comes from the Latin meaning 'shaving or cutting', in other words, a place full of fragments. It would seem that what follows in the history of the atelier – during the Medieval period or in the Renaissance – is less the apprenticeship towards a skill, than furtherance of skills within a set idea of art and creativity. It is to be noted that the atelier has always had the double meaning of the workshop where the artist works, and the team with which the artist works. In other words, a sort of amalgam of factory, warehouse, drawing-room, embassy, studio-group, shop, club. The atelier is a sort of machine or building that proposes a programme of representations and an ongoing inventory of images. The atelier is something tied to history, something that permits the meeting of the past and the present so that what disappears and what appears find a link.

The mould of the master's atelier, with its strictly defined traditions, was thrown out by the events of May 1968, when French schools turned their backs on academicism. They espoused a largely unstructured and unacademic approach to what was to be taught. This, in itself, opened up new methods in education. Even though some collective projects took place, on the whole, individualism reigned. The magic word was *la démarche*, which could roughly be translated as 'the gait' or 'the bearing'. Implied in this umbrella, was the idea that the way forward was through the development of individual identity, with a complete indifference to society. Compared to some university courses in the same period, one could imagine that this emphasis on the self corresponded with new practices in the human sciences – such as linguistics, psychoanalysis, philosophy – but this behaviour, even if rebellious, was at the same time profoundly anti-intellectual. Some courses, which were orientated around art history and complementary studies, couldn't agree upon a set body of knowledge, and the separation between the architecture school and the art school that took place after May 1968, has polarised into pro- and anti- approaches to industrial design, media, graphic design, bearing in mind the possibility of engagement with more professionally orientated requirements.

In other words, the teaching of art in the 1970s and 1980s has seen a clean break between what was understood as art history and the learning of technique as a professional function on the one hand, and the act of creation as a symbolic activity in itself on the other. I have been working on a new school project since 1991, and have frequently been overwhelmed by the sheer size of the exercise. Since the beginning, it has raised the issues of both what is taught and how it is taught. We, in Bordeaux, have approached the question in two ways: by asking how we can discern the positive values of unstructured and non-theoretical education in such a way as to provide an association between practice, theory, technique and experience; and by asking how a new relationship could be established between the art school and the social environment.

In order to answer these problems, we've moved through the city and travelled world wide. We've started a reformation, largely based upon a multi-disciplinary approach, and here I will outline the main points. We've injected new blood into the idea of the atelier. We've founded a unit model that meets the experiences of both learning and practice, with teachers and visiting artists, and which acts as an overall watchdog framing a wide range of collective activities. The atelier organises knowledge around themes or subjects with methods that provide the student with skills, techniques and access to specific cultures. In no way, though, does the need for skills and techniques determine the choice and issue of the atelier. We've created a system of interaction between the various ateliers so that there's a constant possibility of exchange, of mutual inspirations between different approaches to the arts and design. As much as possible, the 'town and gown' situation has been dealt with through a rich and varied network of artists, music and drama events, architectural and design institutions, both public and private. The three Bordeaux centres, CAPC (Contemporary Art Centre), FRAC (Contemporary Art Collection), and Arc en Rev (Architecture Centre), have all been constantly involved in these meetings and exchanges. The use of the atelier as a central unit of the art school, and the creation of inter-linked ateliers as the pedagogic system, attempts to provide not only an open, but also a structured, activity. The student project aims to deal with a production that could articulate all inputs together, no matter how strangely constructed. The three core disciplines of Art, Media and Design are presented equally and students are able to identify for themselves between their different choices. For each student, the concept and development of independent projects is considered the mainstay of their qualification; their project draws attention to the relationship between their inventions, viewpoints, works and the real world.

If we follow the definitions and opportunities that we have ourselves put into place and encouraged to a logical conclusion, there remains no absolute distinction between what forms the artist, the designer, the architect, etc. In particular, the notion that can be inserted into a more dynamic and less specific form is that of authorship, which here assigns a central place to the problems of relation, mobility, exchange. Although many of these concepts and much of this work is still at a tentative stage, our approach does offer radically different perspectives towards artistic practice, production and work conditions.

At the end of the day

Mel Gooding
Writer and Critic

I hope you won't mind if, at the end of a long day, I offer a kind of collage of observations and quotations (mostly from myself), plus some propositions.

I do have a certain anger, connected with disappointment, in relation to the subject of our forum. The disappointment is at what has happened, or has not happened, in the months since 1997's glorious 1st of May. This week, I heard the Secretary of State for Education talking of 'creativity' as something that gave (in the dreary language of current educational policy) 'added value' to literacy and numeracy. 'Creativity' enhanced 'employability' in the workforce of the future. I am appalled at the poverty of imagination and vision implicit in this language.

In 1990, when Margaret Thatcher still looked as if she would endure, unrusted by time, forever, I wrote a polemical article on the state of fine art education. This is something of what I said:

> Pure scientists have left the country in droves. Pure research in our universities is in tatters. Philosophers have been sacked or prematurely retired from the philosophy departments that have always been the first for the axe. In art education it has been a field-day for the administrator and the apparatchik, a time of 'rationalisation', and of the reappraisal of initiatives based on absurd definitions and idiotic distinctions: 'broad-based versus specialist'; 'centres of excellence' versus what? – peripheries of mediocrity?

What has changed, what is changing, in the new climate? Does anyone working day-to-day in the art schools, feel that a new dawn is here? Do the college administrators feel that they can now begin to think within different conditions, to operate within a set of different constraints? I doubt it. Artist-teachers continue to hear about credit accumulation, transferable skills, etc. as if they didn't know that most fine art graduates go out into the world as adaptable as most others, if not more so. Most of these graduates, for better or worse, will find ways of making a living outside of the art business. Like most people, they will do it by a combination of applied wit and hard work. Over many of their graduate contemporaries in other disciplines they will have had the advantage of an education that has put a premium on imagination and speculation, encouraged resourcefulness and demanded practical skills, and taught them something about the loneliness of the creative act. If not professional artists themselves, they will be, if they choose, in the first circle of the audience for art. Informed and sympathetic, the best of them will continue to be necessary to the success of that most valuable enterprise in our culture, the project of art.

The disappointment many of us feel goes back a long way in the British politics of education: as far back indeed as to previous Labour administrations. What David Blunkett expresses, without realising it, or rather perhaps, without admitting it, is an impoverished and impoverishing idea of education: one that values the instrumental, utilitarian function above all others. It is a view that does not acknowledge that numeracy and literacy are themselves creative: that writing, reading and mathematics are active components of the creative imagination. That impoverished and impoverishing idea to which Blunkett subscribes (and not without a certain arrogance) implicitly denigrates and belittles the arts, expressing an ignorant and foolish denial of their true place at the centre of civilised life. Disdain for the crucial activities of art, music, dance, drama, has naturally been expressed in the reduction of resources and of the time available in the curriculum for them. What is regarded as inessential to the general good, and as peripheral to educational requirements, is understandably held cheap.

Against that prevailing view, I want to assert that fine art is at once a mode of research and a form of knowledge. At the highest level it is a discipline, together with disinterested science and philosophy, absolutely necessary to the survival of the culture as a whole. 'The origin of the work of art', wrote Heidegger, 'that is, the origin of both the creators and the preservers, which is to say, of a people's historical existence, is art. This is so because art is by nature an origin, a distinctive way in which truth comes into being, that is, becomes historical'. I reflected on this some time ago in an essay on artists' residencies in art schools:

How are young human beings to learn to be artists? I say 'to be', not 'to become': for it is undeniably the case that there exists the creative impulse within us all; it is what defines us as human beings in the first place. *Homo sapiens* became that by way of being *homo ludens, homo faber*: Knowledge and wisdom together are achieved through mental and physical playing and making. We may observe the truth in this in the development of every infant. We are born fully human, our every potentiality genetically inherent. Education is all too often a process by means of which potential is denied and the inborn creative impulse, so visible in every young child, is suppressed.

Within our own culture, at this time, the work of the art schools is crucial to the constant renewal of creative possibilities; to the extent, I may say, that art itself is crucial to the health of a civilised society. This is not a matter of preserving the cultural forms of that society, or of perpetuating particular media and certain procedures on the grounds of the histories of artistic success. Art changes not only in response to social and general cultural changes, including those of science and technology, and of philosophy, but in anticipation of them, and as an agency within them. (It is no coincidence that new forms in art are often attacked by those who are reactionary in politics – whether of the Left or the Right – and conservative in philosophy.) It is a matter of maintaining diversity, of creating conditions within which new forms and media can develop and flourish whilst those that are traditional can continue to be transformed as the means to make new discoveries. What we know is that good work, whether it is innovative in form or of a kind that resorts to established modes, will be received, by and large, with hostility (or, at best by indifference) in the broader contexts of our culture. It is a culture that places greater value upon other kinds of information.

How then, to rephrase my question in terms borrowed from Heidegger, can we bring artists into being, *their* being? As Heidegger points out, in an extension of his simple and profound opposition that the 'artist is the origin of the work/the work is the origin of the artist', both artist and work of art are defined by virtue of that which gives them both their names: 'Art is the origin of the artwork and the artist'. To reduce this to the practical, what are the conditions conducive in a school of art to the making of artists and the production of works of art? The first must be a consciousness within the school of the necessity of artists to society, in the deepest sense of both terms: artists as the origin of works of art; society as the community of humankind in a particular historical manifestation, whose culture is defined by its propensity to the creation of images of the inner life as well as of the external world, and the definition and projection of the forms of felt life, of thought, emotion and dream. I am being severely practical, for what would be the point of setting up an art school unless this first condition were met, and its implications fully realised?'

The second condition must be the creation of a community in which teachers and students are enabled to contribute what skills and knowledge they have, and take from it what they need in order to develop their work. There are many different models for such an academic community – and we have heard of some interesting ones today, from Ute Meta Bauer and Guadalupe Echevarria amongst others – but a vitally interactive fellowship, however it is achieved, is what defines the true academy. This give-and-take is the practical enactment, at the day-to-day level, of the dynamic principle at the centre of any art training worth the name: the recognition that the inherent creativity of the individual is an *energy*, whose realisations – its shaping into the forms of art – are in the nature of a collaboration. No music without ears to hear it; no painting without eyes to see it; no words without a shared language to answer to them. This is to place criticism, understood in Barthes' terms as 'the giving of meaning to the work', at the heart of the academic process.

What we need in fine art education, to be specific now, is a coherent philosophy, and the revival of the concept of the Academy as a disciplined community committed to rigorous procedures of research and learning within the ambit of art and its discourses. The quality of an academic community is defined by the level of the discussion that goes on within it. In the case of the art school, this applies to exchanges that might take place between teachers and students, between teachers and teachers – as teachers and as artists – and between students and students. The vitality of the discourse will be determined by the quality of the cultural and spiritual environment. Such an Academy will not be a seat of orthodoxy; indeed, its greatest strength will lie in the diversity of its teachers and visitors. No collaboration across disciplines – between painters and sculptors, printmakers, film- and video-makers, composers, typographers, dancers, architects, geographers, physicists, mathematicians – would be regarded as inappropriate, but encouraged, rather, as inevitable and natural. There is no discipline that does not fall within the interest of the artist. There is no human activity that art does not touch.

The academy is by definition concerned with the methodologies of creativity and the languages of criticism. Out of differences of approach and diversities of expertise spring new possibilities of expression. This is something Paul Klee, the purest of 'fine artists', valued at the Bauhaus. Writing to Gropius, he said:

I am glad that such differently directed [artistic] powers work so well together at the Bauhaus, as also I welcome the struggle of such powers against each other when their solution achieves something … Because ultimately there is not right or wrong but only development and life in the interplay of powers, as in life good and bad finally may work together for good.

The richness and diversity of environment necessary to good work would be ensured in the academy by attracting the best spirits of the age, creative teachers and brilliant guests, securing a continuous interchange of information and ideas between those within and those without. At the heart of the enterprise would be the absolute principle that continuity is essential to the development of the student-artist, a development that is defined not simply by the achievement of progressive instrumental and intellectual objectives, but upon the nurturing of the faculty of intuition. Developing intuition requires time and practice; it is not inculcated cumulatively, by careful and cautious steps, so much as by imaginative leaps and unpremeditated connections, surprising and unpredictable illuminations. Systematic knowledge and advanced techniques may be necessary to some kinds of artistic work but they are not sufficient for its success.

Here is Klee again, writing for the 'Bauhaus Prospectus' on the subject of intuition:

We construct and construct, and yet, intuition is still an excellent thing. Much can be done without intuition but not everything. For a considerable time one can do all manner of things, but not everything. Where intuition is allied to exact research it accelerates its progress. Sometimes exactitude, inspired by intuition, is superior … Art also has been given space enough for exact research, and the doors have been wide open to this end for some time.

The idea that art is a mode of research is not new: its instituting in academic practice goes back to the foundation of the Bauhaus and to Malevich's Unovis at Vitebsk. Klee and Malevich and their artist-teacher colleagues were deeply concerned with the civilising functions of the art academy, with its centrality to the culture as a whole. In the concluding paragraphs to his seminal essay 'On Modern Art', Klee regrets the cultural isolation of the visual artist: 'We still lack the ultimate power: for the people are not with us. But we seek a people. We began over there in the Bauhaus. We began there with a community to which each of us gave what he had. More we cannot do.'

The humane idealism of those great modernists – Klee, Malevich, Kandinsky, Vordemberge-Gildewart, Albers, Herbert Read, Ad Reinhardt among others – who devoted thought and effort to the concept of the Academy (and to its realisations), must be the inspiration of the artist-teachers and art school administrators of today. The rationalising busybodies, the accountants and assessors, the political philistines of successive administrations and those in the Treasury who determine so much of their policies have shown little appreciation or understanding of the discourses of art, or of its meanings and purposes in the great ambit of human culture. The utilitarian instrumentalists – Ruskin's 'conforming legalists' – must not be allowed to carry the day. What must underpin resistance to them is a coherent philosophy, and there can be no philosophical coherence without forums in which the free exchange and development of ideas does not take place. (Forums such as this.) It is time for the art schools to assert the absolute values of the disciplines they exist to promote. We must challenge the arrogant claims of entrepreneurial man to represent the true nature of humankind. Against *homo economicus*, by necessity morally blind, by definition acting always in the spirit of self-interest, we should oppose the values of the philosopher, the artist, the scientist: *homo ludens*, the imaginative human-being at play, tempering rational intelligence with intuition, reason with feeling.

'What kind of art education takes place in schools without artists of high intelligence?' asked Ad Reinhardt at a conference like this of art school teachers in 1953. He ended his address with two further questions, poignant in their direct relevance to our considerations here today: 'Is it too optimistic to think that perhaps some new activity among artists, possibly towards a true modern academy, could free the circumstances again? Am I being too pessimistic to feel a great doubt about this?'

Some years ago, with Bruce McLean, an artist of whom it can properly be said that his teaching is continuous with his practice, I wrote, optimistically, a 'prospectus' for the Knife Edge Academy, a moveable academy to be created round a portable table and a phone; an academy devoted to what Brian Catling calls the 'invisible subject'. A questioning conversation would be its primary activity. I will conclude by reading that prospectus, which we published in the form of a set of six silk-screen prints, marked and obscured by written and collaged additions.

A DREAM OF ART
A LADDER OF LEARNING
A PATH OF KNOWLEDGE
A HOUSE
A JUG OF WINE
A POTATO
AN OUTLOOK AT A HORIZON
A TABLE A CONVERSATION
A TORTILLA

THE ACADEMY AS AN EVER-EXPANDING TABLE FOR LAUNCHING,
    LEARNING AND LUNCHING
SEATING ARRANGEMENTS WILL DETERMINE THE
    CONTINGENCIES OF LEARNING

INVESTIGATIONS INTO LAUGHING MATTERS
ENQUIRIES INTO HUMAN UNDERSTANDING.

THE ACADEMY WILL ASSEMBLE AT THE ROUND TABLE ITS
DELIBERATIONS SPIRAL ITS CONSIDERATIONS DIALECTICAL
ITS TIMETABLE CIRCULAR ITS TERMS CYCLICAL ITS
EXAMINATIONS REVOLVING ITS DEGREES THREE HUNDRED
AND SIXTY ITS NUMBERS ROUNDED ITS TERMS OF REFERENCE
SPHERICAL ITS ENQUIRIES HELICAL ITS INVESTIGATIONS
CIRCUMSPECT ITS CONTEXT CIRCUMAMBIENT ITS AMBITIONS
CIRCUMNAVIGATIONAL ITS SPACES CURVED ITS
CONVOCATIONS CIRCUMSTANTIAL

THE ACADEMY WILL BE OPEN TO ALL TALENTS OPEN TO
SUGGESTION OPEN TO OFFERS OPEN ALL HOURS OPEN TO
IDEAS
OPEN TO PERSUASION OPEN TO CRITICISM OPEN TO DISCUSSION
OPEN TO INTERPRETATION OPEN TO REPRESENTATION OPEN TO
INSPIRATION
OPEN
NO ADMINISTRATION WITHOUT SENSATION
INVISIBLE

Chair's summing up and plenary session

MARJORIE ALLTHORPE-GUYTON, UTE META-BAUER,
AND GUADALUPE ECHEVARRIA

MA-G: I think the analysis from Ute and Guadelupe of two institutions that are not from this country were particularly revealing. Ute, you saw what you were doing as a kind of virus within your own institution – a strange thing. And Guadalupe, your atelier is a kind of peripatetic art terrorist in different cities. I will now ask the audience if they wish to address the three contributions that we have heard this afternoon.

QUESTIONER: I'd like to go back to the Phyllida Barlow's paper. There was much talk afterwards about 'the alternative space' and I'd like to know what that alternative space is? Earlier I spoke to somebody who suggested that the alternative space might be the Internet, and I felt that was quite relevant incidentally to the title of Ute's paper, 'This Is Tomorrow'. Personally, I don't know whether or not the Net will give us the space, that alternative space, which we considered earlier. Does anybody have any views?

MA-G: Do you mean an alternative space as an academy, as it were, on the net?

QUESTIONER: No sorry, the way the students present their work.

MA-G: Students are already producing work on the net.

QUESTIONER: Yes, but I want to know what are the other alternative spaces? The spaces to which Phyllida was referring as alternative to the sort of ether-type space now presented in catalogues. With the exception of the net, where are these other alternatives?

UM-B: The alternative spaces are everywhere. For example, I admire the work of Bill Furlong. He uses a simple cassette, which you can take into your car to introduce artists' works, talks, etc. You can take it with you in your Walkman. A lot of artists have made simple photocopies to introduce their work and I think the net might be one of the spaces. It is clearly non-hierarchical. I think there are bigger problems and that's why I want to have this chorus of art historians, art critics and artists. The museums and the institution don't consider these other forms of production. These works are simply just disappearing. What is quite important to me, if we think about the future, is not just how we educate artists, or what we offer to them, but also that we have to force the mediators at the same time to follow that. That's the bigger problem to me; it's happening, but it's as if we're slipping through holes in the ground.

MA-G: What we're contesting here is closure: closure of minds, closure of processes, closure of ways of going on. This is a threat to many other areas. Science is threatened; the whole enterprise of science is threatened by a similar instrumentality. Science is much more closely laced and corseted by other processes like the drug industry or whatever other massive economic relationships science has. On the other hand, there is increasing interest from that community in the process of art. We've got a conference coming up hosted by the Royal Society, where artists will be talking with geneticists. I think there is common ground with other thinkers and other modes of inquiry who are also experiencing our perception of the rise of the instrumental mind. We shouldn't call it 'the politician's mind'; it's something more pervasive, to do with the late-century zeitgeist. What I'm grappling for I suppose, and I'll say this when I sum up, is that there's a very big battle here: it isn't just art wars, it's real war. It's a sort of fundamental issue to do with human culture.

QUESTIONER: I have a question for you, Marjorie, in view of what you've just said. If I were to have an impression of the Arts Council over the last twenty years, it's that it's increasingly concerned with the big and socially instrumental. Twenty years ago, I might think that if somebody got an Arts Council grant, they'd been taken seriously by some distinguished people concerned with art. Now, if I see somebody has got an Arts Council Grant, I'm a bit more inclined to think that there's something wrong with them in one form or another. It's an institution hell-bent on doing good and turning art and culture into an instrument of welfare that isn't actually in tune with, and manifest in, the institutions for which it works.

MA-G: Very briefly, I gave a paper at the Gambernight Academy in Mount Street, which will be published. I was asked to talk about the Arts Council, which I thought would be very boring to these postgraduate students. But what I found was that it got quite interesting for me to do it because I looked at the history of my own institution and who had made policy over the fifty years since 1946, and what it had achieved. One of my colleagues wrote a book called *The Politics of the Arts Council* in about 1980, which contested its elitism and the fact that the largest proportion of funds went to several professional artists, in whatever art form, and that the amateur and the practice of creativity across all peoples was not something that this state body had addressed. I found myself writing in great support of what is called the 'selective tradition', for what it had achieved. Certainly in terms of the visual arts in this country, there's a clutch of galleries that have done what they couldn't have done if they'd been under the auspices of the Local Authorities for example, although that's changing slightly now. There's no doubt that over the last ten years, the Arts Council has moved towards what one of my members of Council called a more 'stereophonic' process, where a vastly bigger range of practice and a wider social agenda has been embraced. The Lottery of course has been largely harnessed for projects that are nothing to do with art, but are to do with urban regeneration (although art has a relationship to that), social processes, often as a panacea to more fundamental problems that can be dealt with more fundamentally at the core business of Government. There's no question that all these can be contested as possibly a dangerous path for a body or bodies that exist not only for very broad cultural reasons, but to support the production of art and its understanding by as wide an audience as possible. So I take on board your point, and say that I do physically consider it all the time. The last statement I made in the paper was that the worm in the apple of this whole new direction of funding would lead to the modification of art, which is exactly what is occurring.

QUESTIONER: Could I just talk a little bit about one of the themes that has come out of the conference today? Those of us who are intimately involved in art education are so close to the issues that sometimes it's hard to stand sufficiently outside to make a black and white judgement. This is to do with the eroding factor of the increasing accountability and bureaucracy and measuring of one sort or another. We are certainly in what I call an 'accounting culture' that impacts increasingly on the sorts of activities we do. So that's to do with external constraints. But I'm very interested in the two models that Ute and Guadeloupe have mentioned, which seem to give you a wonderful freedom in which to develop those models. Ute, you said you had complete freedom to do what you wanted to do at the Academy. What are your constraints? Who measures you? Who are the auditors?

UM-B: The ignorance within the Academy has helped us to do what we wanted. Basically they didn't care what we were doing. But now we have a bigger response outside of the school and they've become a bit more aware of what we're doing, it is getting a bit problematic. I would say that this master-school system still gives freedom to the individual teachers, and that's the beneficial side of it. You really develop your own curriculum, your own set-up for the students, and I think that's a very good thing. I saw it as more like a school in America and there's a very open structure, like in Germany and Austria. So I think both models have good and bad sides, but what I think is the most important thing is to know that 2 per cent of the people we educate basically go into this classical model we've seen: art school-gallery-museum. And I know that in London there are five schools of art and I wonder what happens to all the people coming out of them? I think it definitely doesn't help to produce a big bureaucracy. You said there's a health and safety department to decide if you can install an item or not in the room, or something like that. I've never heard of such a thing ever in my life and definitely I think it doesn't help one free one's mind as an artist. I think as artists you should do whatever you want. Even, as Gavin said, burn down the school. What we have to get rid of is big bureaucracy, and now, as a full-time Professor for the first time, I've seen what that means. Before, I was always a guest Professor and had great freedom. And now, even in Austria, we have a lot of administration meetings and I think we have to get rid of all of that.

QUESTIONER: The problem we have in this country is that we are increasingly controlled in every aspect. I was recently very conscious of that fact at a tourist spot in Nîmes – the Pont du Galles. This is an extraordinary Roman bridge, which is totally murderous. If you walk along the top, which is about three-feet wide, you're in severe danger of falling off. But people walk along the top the whole time and it's several feet up in the air and there are no railings, absolutely nothing. Now here, under English Heritage, this bridge would be covered in railings three-feet high. It's just an example of how in every aspect of English life, we're administered, and this is at the heart of some of the problems.

GE: Yes, I think that administration and production of art projects in general is an extremely important thing and for me the main thing is that we happen to be in a certain culture. 'The accounting culture' is a very nice term and I'll use it. For me, the most important thing to do in the school is to change this culture. Otherwise we couldn't do anything, and that means that, for instance, you make choices and you budget. You transmit a certain behaviour in the school, and I think for an art school or an art institution it's a basic thing. So for me, it's more like a production situation in general, an accounting culture. One of the most important things is that in France we're fighting very much against the idea that all the teachers have to be functionaries. We have this law that was brought in without advice a few years ago and now we're having a big fight to change it because we also think that the teaching staff have to be mobile. So that's one of the parts of this culture that is extremely important, and I cannot see how we can make a school project without a certain open culture in the administration.

QUESTIONER: I identified a lot with what Mel was saying, and having worked in both secondary education and in art education, I've discovered the difference between the two. In secondary education there's a culture of discipline and fear, so that children in our schools are taught with discipline followed by fear. In art schools, we're teaching a culture of self-discipline rather than discipline from above and this is not generally understood by our culture. My question is, if we're in the business of being artists and connecting and communicating, why do people not understand us? So then I think in this climate the discussion we've had today is all about taking responsibility for how people see the art world, art education, etc. so that we can have some effect on the children in schools and the way they're taught and the way art is seen in its context in the general education. As an artist, I take that responsibility on board, and I think it has to be said the image of where artists are coming from maybe comes from the artists themselves, so we should take responsibility for how we're seen.

QUESTIONER: Following on from that, I felt a challenge earlier on; did anyone else here feel really worked up enough to do something about Government policy? Just recently, there have been people from the theatre and from music who've been prepared to stand up and criticise government policy – freezing, cutbacks, etc. Peter Hall was very eloquent a few days ago about the importance of theatre and that kind of experience in culture; exactly the kind of things we've been talking about today. One thing that worries me slightly is that we've all got our own fights going on in universities and colleges, but what about outside? Do you feel that you have access to any open ear in government that you might actually be able to persuade or to educate towards an understanding of what we've been discussing here? There's a general agreement about what we're talking about and what we're trying to deal with and how we're trying to operate. And this is also true in Vienna and Bordeaux. It's not as though we had to go through a big educational experience today. We know what we have to offer and how we can operate and the ignorance seems to be outside of this institution and the academy structure. But that's where the funding is coming from and to a large extent that's where the restraint is coming from too. Is there a way of actually being able to mobilise the kind of power that we've had in thought here today?

MA-G: I think, politically, the most effective speakers are those who are practitioners in every field. I don't think institutional heads have the same impact in terms of a wider public. The reason why Simon Rattle immediately gets consumed into the creative National Curriculum Working Party is because it's realised that he's a figure whom the public will respect. Administrators and officials in education will not have as much of an image with the public. When practising artists, musicians, writers speak out, they're heard, and they're heard by the politicians. What we don't have is enough official artists who are prepared to do that. There is a different culture in art, and artists are not so declamatory on the whole.

GE: I don't know how it is in England, but in France there's an enormous industry and many working people around the theatre industry, and in art that doesn't exist or is not recognised or we've never defined it properly.

MA-G: I'm sure your heads are very full now, I know mine is, with all these extraordinary contributions. We started off with our first speaker Brian Sedgemore, who will have made a certain amount of a stir, when we watch the ten o'clock news tonight, on accountability and how this is swamping all the intelligent thought in the way education is dealt with in this country. One could say that throughout the whole of the day the consensus has been that to contest bureaucracy is an essential and urgent need in order to maintain the kind of subversiveness, the critical edge and suppleness of the fellowship and collaboration in how art schools work when they're allowed to. It's also essential to contest narrowness – narrowness of discipline, narrowness of approach – and I think it was summed up humorously and brilliantly with the Knife Edge Academy. We need to maintain that kind of totally open attitude and thinking, which contests closure of all kinds. Ultimately, the enemy is the instrumental and utilitarian. I'm privileged to have been here today with ten extraordinary speakers and a very receptive audience and I thank you all for coming.